Marketing Research in the Developing Countries

**PRAEGER SPECIAL STUDIES IN
INTERNATIONAL ECONOMICS AND DEVELOPMENT**

Marketing Research in the Developing Countries

A HANDBOOK

John Z. Kracmar

**Foreword by
Jan Tinbergen**

PRAEGER PUBLISHERS
New York • Washington • London

The purpose of Praeger Special Studies is to make specialized research in U.S. and international economics and politics available to the academic, business, and government communities. For further information, write to the Special Projects Division, Praeger Publishers, Inc., 111 Fourth Avenue, New York, N.Y. 10003.

PRAEGER PUBLISHERS
111 Fourth Avenue, New York, N.Y. 10003, U.S.A.
5, Cromwell Place, London S.W.7, England

Published in the United States of America in 1971
by Praeger Publishers, Inc.

Library of Congress Catalog Card Number: 76-136144

Printed in the United States of America

FOREWORD

The link between development planning for low-income countries and the related problem of marketing research is sufficiently close to enable me to see the interesting contribution this study makes, although the latter subject is not entirely my field. Market analysis is a necessary base for any business activity and must always be geared to the particular circumstances of the market concerned, as well as to the habits of the prospective buyers.

Dr. Kracmar's book makes many interesting contributions to these subjects and I am sure the book will find a wide circle of readers. It deserves it.

Jan Tinbergen
The Hague

PREFACE

Marketing research is an important and exciting subject. In the developing countries it is also a controversial subject, for doubts exist among some practitioners and writers as to the feasibility of applying research techniques in the often primitive environment of the markets in these countries.

The object in writing this book has been to help bridge the gulf in the literature by contributing an affirmative opinion to the general discussion of the obstacles and possibilities of marketing research in the developing areas. Further, an easy, understandable description of various techniques that have been found to be successful in the developing countries has been provided, with case histories giving evidence of a number of thorough surveys made recently in some of the poorest countries on each continent. Finally, the statistical tables, addresses, glossary of terms used in marketing research, and dictionary of selected technical terms in the principal languages of the developing countries should be helpful tools for those interested in undertaking marketing research in these areas.

Some of the chapters on research procedures may seem too rudimentary. Indeed they are, but this is the end result of checking and rewriting the material in order to make the book easily understandable at the first reading by a practical businessman, student, or anyone in the developing countries interested in marketing research. The author believes simplicity and clarity to be chief merits of this book. Attention has also been paid to making the material easily teachable.

The reader can feel confident, though, that this book embodies the basic methods of marketing research and that the suggested methods and particular techniques have been tested in the developing countries. Anyone interested in, engaged in, or intending to associate himself with the area of marketing research will find in this book the equipment that can immediately start him on research projects and report-writing, for he will be guided by the accumulated experiences of others as they are described here.

This book does not, however, pretend to be a conclusive description of all marketing research practices. References to consumer markets predominate, as these have been the author's major interest. Readers who intend to progress further, or who are more interested in industrial or agricultural marketing research, for example, will find help in the annotated bibliography.

Besides the hope of encouraging more market research in the developing countries, the purpose of this book is also to convince the merchant, industrialist, and manager who have been served by sophisticated marketing research in the advanced countries that research suited to the area can assist them in their undertakings in the developing world as well. The ultimate purpose is thus to stimulate investment for the improvement of the economy and prosperity of the developing countries by giving the reader confidence that such investments and efforts to solve the classical questions of "what shall be produced, how, and for whom?" can be encouraged and controlled in the developing countries by research methods based on those used in the advanced countries.

The author's thanks for help received must be extended to the Singer Sewing Machine Company, with which he has the good fortune of being associated. Because of its long history of outstanding producing and retailing methods, applied with the same intensity on every continent of the world no matter what the stage of economic development, the company has a firm foothold today (1970) in almost every village of the developing world. The author has thus been exposed to the endless variety of marketing problems that demand solution.

The author is also grateful to L. Leo Taub of Hunter College, New York City, for helpful suggestions relating to matters of language and style.

Praeger Publishers has cooperated magnificently, especially Mary C. Mone, editor, Praeger Special Studies, from whom the author has learned a great deal about the craft of book-writing.

CONTENTS

	Page
FOREWORD, by Jan Tinbergen	v
PREFACE	vii
LIST OF TABLES	xiv
LIST OF EXHIBITS	xvi

Chapter

1 GENERAL CONSIDERATIONS 3

World Economy and Role of Marketing Research 3
Possibilities and Obstacles of Marketing Research in
    Developing Countries 6
        Illiteracy 7
        Research Skills and Scientific Approach 10
        Availability of Statistics 14
        Prejudices and Opportunities 17
Modification of Research Methods 23
Plan of Book 27

2 INTERVIEW 29

Personal Interview 29
        Ultimate Objective 30
        Informal Interviewing 30
        Questionnaire Characteristics 31
        Interviewers 42
        Supervision 48

Chapter   Page

    Depth Interview   51
    Group Interview   52
    Mail Surveys   53
    Telephone Interview   54
        Setting Up Telephone Survey   55

3 SAMPLING   59

    Basic Sampling Methods   59
    Sample Size   61
        Calculation of Probability Sample   61
    Sample Validating   63

4 QUANTITATIVE RESEARCH   67

    Market Potential   68
        Area Market Potential   68
        Market Saturation and Market Potential   77
    Forecasting   81
        Mechanical Forecast   83
        Lead Series   83
        Opinions and Expectations   83
        Causal Forecast   84
        Business Cycle   85
    Source of Statistics   85

5 PRODUCT RESEARCH   90

    Adapting Existing Product   90
    New Product   92
    Product-Line Analysis   95
    Package Research   97
        Rules of Good Package Design   97
        Mechanical Test Equipment   98
    Panel Research   99
    Test Marketing   101
    Conclusion   101

6 PRICE RESEARCH   103

    Competition-Price Survey   104

Chapter		Page
	Price-Acceptance Test	105
	Price-Sales Volume Relation	109
	Measuring Elasticity of Demand	111
7	ADVERTISING RESEARCH	113
	Copy-Testing	114
	Checking of Advertising Message	114
	Copy-Testing Methods	116
	Media Research	119
	Circulation Analysis	119
	Broadcast Media	121
	Broadcast Media Research Methods	122
	Advertisement Timing	124
	Budgeting	127
	Methods of Advertising Research	129
	Cooperative Advertising	134
8	RETAILING RESEARCH	135
	Store Location	135
	History of Site	135
	Vicinity of Site	136
	Business District	137
	Pedestrian-Traffic Measurement	137
	Sales-Efficiency Measurement	139
	Space-Productivity Ratio	139
	Rent-Paying Capacity	141
	Retail Shop Inventory Audit	142
	Retailers' Market Share	144
	Personnel Efficiency	144
	Display Efficiency	145
	Testing Power of Display	146
	Display Viewpoint	146
	Display Design	147
	Optimum-Location Measurement	151
	Laboratory Shop	151
	Mail-Order Catalogue Research	154

Chapter		Page
9	FINANCIAL MARKETING RESEARCH	157
	Ratios	157
	Asset Ratios and Gross Margin	158
	Cost Ratios	160
	Break-Even Point	161
	Procedure	162
	Illustrative Application	163
	Questions Answered by Break-Even Analysis	166
10	THE REPORT	168
	Preparing Report	168
	Tabulation	168
	Interpretation	170
	Writing Report	172
	Sorbonne Method of Reporting	172
	Popular Report	173
	Graphic Presentation	175
	Construction of Graphs	175
	Graph Types	176
	Plotting Trend	179
	Correlation Graph	181
11	ESTABLISHING MARKETING RESEARCH IN A FIRM	183
	Research Personnel	183
	Objectives	185
	Efficiency Control	186
	Work Load	187
	Intellectual Climate	190
	Budget	191
12	CONCLUSION	192
	APPENDIXES	
A	CASE HISTORIES OF SELECTED ASPECTS OF MARKETING RESEARCH IN THE DEVELOPING COUNTRIES	197

Appendix		Page
1.	Using Mail Questionnaires: Colombia	199
2.	Conducting a Telephone Survey: Kenya	202
3.	Collecting Statistics: Congo and Somalia	203
4.	The Importance of Statistics on the National Economy: Ethiopia	204
5.	Gathering Worldwide Statistics: The Example of Sewing Machines	205
6.	Using Marketing Research Techniques for Supply and Demand Analysis: India	206
7.	Measuring Marketing Potential for Supermarkets: Argentina	209
8.	Handling the Shoplifting Problem in a Large Store: Venezuela	210
9.	Market Survey for the Establishment of Machine-Tool Manufacturing: East Pakistan	212
10.	Advertising Media Research: Ceylon	213
11.	Sampling Field Techniques: Peru	216
12.	Instructing Interviewers: Brazil	225
13.	Export Market Research on Developing Countries	232
14.	Rush Research on Exports to Developing Countries	233
B	GLOSSARY OF TERMS USED IN MARKETING RESEARCH	235
C	MULTILINGUAL DICTIONARY OF SELECTED TECHNICAL TERMS USED IN MARKETING RESEARCH	271
D	INDICATORS OF MARKET SIZE OF COUNTRIES HAVING LESS THAN $700 PER CAPITA INCOME ANNUALLY	293
E	MARKETING RESEARCH FIRMS IN DEVELOPING COUNTRIES	301
BIBLIOGRAPHY		315
ABOUT THE AUTHOR		323

LIST OF TABLES

Table   Page

1. Illiteracy in Developing Countries   8

2. Earnings on U.S. Investments in Manufacturing Abroad, 1960-68   20

3. Annual Rates of Currency Depreciation in Selected Countries, 1958-68   21

4. Market Potential Derived from Purchasing-Power Index in Portugal   75

5. Market-Saturation Computation from Sales History and Survival Rate for Sewing Machines in Portugal up to 1969   78

6. Monthly Percentages of Year's Sales for Selected Types of U.S. Stores   128

7. Average Advertising Budgets in Percentage of Annual Sales for Selected Types of U.S. Stores   130

8. Sales Per Square Foot of Selling Area for Selected Store Departments in United States, 1968   140

9. Rental Rates in Percentage of Retail Sales for Selected Types of U.S. Stores   141

TABLES IN THE APPENDIX

Appendix Table   Page

1. Consumer Response to Mail Questionnaires in Bogota, Colombia   201

2. Urban Stratification for Consumer Survey in Peru   219

Appendix Table   Page

3. Urban and Rural Stratification for Consumer Survey in
    Peru   223

4. U.S. Gross National Product and Private Domestic
    Investments, 1919-28   264

LIST OF EXHIBITS

Exhibit   Page

1. Example of Textless Instruction   9

2. Interview Show-Card Used in Consumer Survey in South Africa   38

3. Interview Show-Card Used in Consumer Survey in French Africa   39

4. Sample Questionnaire in Final Form   41

5. Punched Card for Questionnaire in Exhibit 4   43

6. Example of Influence of Four Interviewers on Survey Results   50

7. Sample Telephone Call Sheet   57

8. Example of Validating Sample by Frequency of Answers   65

9. Method of Estimating Potential Market in Group of Countries   69

10. Marketing Map of Portugal   71

11. Market Potential Derived from Consumption Statistics by Principal Political Subdivisions   73

12. Market Potential Derived from Population Statistics by Principal Political Subdivisions   74

13. Graph of Market Potential Derived from Purchasing-Power Index   76

14. Graph of Market-Saturation Computation   79

Exhibit   Page

15. Example of Change in Proportion of Units Still in Use
    Against Those Retired During Service Life   80

16. Popularity of Colors for Home Appliances in Central
    America   91

17. Four-Product Paired Comparison   94

18. Product-Line Analysis Through Comparison of Price,
    Sales Share, and Gross Margin   96

19. Example of Competition-Price Survey Indicators   106

20. Optimum Acceptance-Price Test   108

21. Advertising-Efficiency Measurement   120

22. Four Steps in Advertising Timing Quick-Check   125

23. Two Examples of Advertising Expenditure and Sales
    Trends   126

24. Example of Computation of Cost Per 1,000 People
    Seeing Newspaper Ads   131

25. Example of Computation of Cost Per 1,000 People
    Watching TV Ads   132

26. Survey of Methods of Advertising Research   133

27. Example of Inventory Audit Statement of Nielsen Index   143

28. Application of Optimum-Location Measurement:
    Experiment with Nine Shelves   152

29. Example of Price-Quotation Comparison by Price
    Bracket of Three German Mail-Order Catalogues   155

30. Example of Financial Statement for Break-Even
    Analysis   164

Exhibit	Page
31. Break-Even Chart	165
32. Example of Counting Sheet	169
33. Example of Typewritten Chart	177

EXHIBITS IN THE APPENDIX

Appendix Exhibit	Page
1. Marketing Map of Peru	218
2. Block Numbering in Spiral Fashion on Hand-Drawn Map in Consumer Survey in Peru	221
3. Illustrations of Interviewer's Itinerary in Consumer Survey in Brazil	226
4. Table of Random Numbers for Selecting Floor on Which Interview Should Be Conducted	229
5. Example of Frequency Distribution	246
6. Gross National Product and Principal Components Circulation	248
7. Example of Moving Average	254
8. Population Pyramid	257
9. Normal Curve	262
10. Scatter Chart	265

Marketing Research in the Developing Countries

CHAPTER 1 GENERAL CONSIDERATIONS

WORLD ECONOMY AND ROLE OF MARKETING RESEARCH

When we look at this world of ours, we see that today, despite conflicts and threats of suicidal wars screaming at us from the headlines, mankind is united in sharing the same vision, the same objective, and the same hope. It evolves from the recognition spread throughout the world, even among the most primitive and isolated communities, that it is possible for the individual, as well as for society, to improve man's lot. It evolves from the realization by the people of all continents that we have the tools at our disposal—the technological, conceptual, and social tools—to enable man to raise himself, through his own effort, at least to a level at which society no longer has to live in a climate of extreme inequality and tension between the few rich and the many poor, as have all earlier societies of man.

Scientists believe that in the future they will be able to increase farm productivity drastically and be able to farm the sea by breeding and controlling fish in large quantities and by cultivating underwater plants. Against this forecast, however, stands the fact that whether hunger is eliminated depends upon the mechanics of distribution—a problem for economists and marketers, not for agricultural technicians.

Whether hunger is done away with also depends upon the following realities of the present developing countries, which may

3

become explosive issues throughout the world before the above expectations materialize. Roughly 25 per cent of the world's population has in its hands about 80 per cent of the world's income, whereas the remaining 75 per cent, who live in the developing countries, receive only the remaining 20 per cent. The population is forecast to double within twenty-thirty years, and most of this growth will occur in the developing world. Finally, there is the widening economic gap that exists between the developed and the developing countries.[1]

What we are engaged in today is essentially a race between the promise of economic development and the threat of worldwide class war. Thus, the tremendous vision of liberating man from his age-old bondage to starvation through economic development is, at the same time, a source of danger because a catastrophe must result if it cannot be realized at least to a modest degree. Economic development would seem to be the opportunity, and class war the danger, of our age.

Foreign aid by governments or by the World Bank is a good step and an essential one in the right direction, although such aid is needed in much larger amounts than are now being provided. It is also limited by what governments can do. More food will not appear and living standards will not rise until thousands of new factories are designed and put into operation and their output is distributed and sold from local sources in the developing countries. Improved living conditions through

---

[1] Statisticians at the United Nations have estimated the average growth rate of per capita income (at constant prices) of developing, or poorer, countries as a group. During the 1950's, their growth rate was 2.3 per cent, and it dropped to 2.2 per cent during the 1960's. The corresponding figures for the developed countries were 2.7 per cent and 3.7 per cent, respectively. (United Nations, Statistical Office, Department of Economic and Social Affairs, *Statistical Yearbook, 1967.* [New York, 1968].) The gap between the United States and Europe will also widen, as measured by the gross national product (GNP) in dollars per capita, according to figures supplied by the European Institute of Business Administration (INSEAD), [43 rue de Tocqueville, Paris 17] "European Business," No. 16 (January, 1968).

	1965	1985
U.S.A.	$3,460	$5,600
Europe	1,700	3,000
Difference	1,760	2,600

direct assistance from the outside mean erratically increasing birth rates, with the net result that, in a vicious circle, there are more and more people to be fed. Furthermore, suddenly increased activity in the richer commercial centers through outside assistance leads to frustration of the population in the peripheral and economically stagnant areas. Such assistance there often heightens the inherent political tension and leads to open conflicts, bringing both social unrest and economic setbacks.

Conversely, know-how in marketing contributes to a self-generating, permanent, and indigenous source of economic growth. Marketing is one of the potential levers for converting danger into opportunity in a peaceful way. The importance of marketing is easily demonstrated by the fact that approximately 60 per cent of the ultimate cost of the product of American industry is its marketing and distribution cost.

What is true of marketing in this respect is also true of marketing research, whether used by governments or by business in a free-enterprise system. It is not by any means a panacea; it is only one of the things that is needed, but it is central in this new situation. Marketing research can discover latent demand and indicate the ways to convert it into an effective market. It can direct the producers to produce marketable goods and provide standards of quality for local and foreign demand. It can make it possible for the product to be brought to the market without perishing on the way, and it can allow the consumer to discriminate in order to obtain the greatest value for his very limited purchasing power. In the developing countries, this means, in effect, a twofold benefit for the nation: improved living, by expanding economic activity, and the creation of small businesses, with the consequent growth of the middle class, essential for the democratization of the social system.

In every developing country, however, marketing is the most underdeveloped part of the economy, let alone marketing research. The result is that the populations of these countries are unable to make effective use of the little they have. Economic development is not a force of nature; it is the result of the purposeful, responsible, risk-taking action of men as entrepreneurs, managers, researchers, and teachers. The industrialized countries can supply monetary aid and grants, but they cannot supply entrepreneurs and managers for more than 100 developing countries, since they themselves do not have a surplus of these. Progress would take centuries if the developing countries were to depend on learning through their own experience and evolution. The danger inherent in the inequality between the few countries that have and the many countries that have not is much too great to permit a waiting period of centuries or even decades.

There is only one way that man has ever found to short-cut experience in learning something. He has had to obtain and absorb the distillate of another's experience and skill. The role of marketing and marketing research in the developing countries is to act as an effective tool in helping poor countries to help themselves, precisely because of the easily teachable and learnable nature of the set of techniques called marketing research.

During the past few years, a great deal has been learned about the potential of marketing research in expanding an enterprise and thus strengthening the nation's economy, in measuring the markets, and in understanding the consumer. What we tend to forget while we are distracted by the successful application of marketing research in the advanced countries is that we have in our hands an instrument that may largely influence and possibly decide not only the economic future of the world but also its intellectual, social, and political future.[2]

POSSIBILITIES AND OBSTACLES OF MARKETING RESEARCH IN DEVELOPING COUNTRIES

The ways and means of doing business in the developing countries are, to a degree, established and are improving, but the opinion prevails among businessmen and some writers on marketing research that, although business can be done in the developing countries, marketing research is hard to do or cannot be done at all. Numerous reasons are given to support this superficial but widespread opinion. The most frequent areas of criticism and problems of marketing research in the developing countries can be summarized as follows: (a) illiteracy, (b) research skills and scientific approach, (c) availability of statistics, and (d) prejudices and opportunities.

[2] The effort to take costly guesswork out of marketing has already blossomed into a more than $300-million-a-year industry in the United States and Europe, and there is more than ample reason for its growth to continue.

Concrete experience during the 1960's provides practical examples with which to meet these criticisms and try to reverse the negative opinions. The author believes in the feasibility of marketing research in the developing countries, though modified as to application of methods and often limited to the enclaves of small but fast-growing industrial sectors in the cities, contrasting with primitive conditions in the rural, nonindustrial sectors.

The principles and methods of marketing are inherently universal in the free markets and so is its research. Thus, marketing research in the developing countries is the same as in the developed ones; only the application of certain methods is different.

Illiteracy

Illiteracy in the emerging countries is an enormous problem. India and Pakistan show a rate of over 80 per cent; the illiteracy rate of the native population in the emerging economies averages about 60 per cent. (See Table 1 for illiteracy rates in the developing countries.) Despite this, the problem of communication in marketing and marketing research is not as impossible as it may seem. First, the remaining 40 per cent who can read and write command a much larger proportion of the market than 40 per cent, and often the scope of surveys may not go far beyond that segment of that population. Depending upon the country and the subject of research, a part of the illiterate population usually leads a primitive, agricultural, pastoral, and nomadic life and does not enter into the measurable cash economy.

One is often misled into believing that illiterate people have inferior intelligence, but anyone who has lived among them for some time may have come to realize that instinct seems to compensate, at least in part, for what is lacking in education. It is not rare to find illiterates who understand two languages, have a good imagination and a lively response in discussion, and show inventiveness in their work. They are generally good at counting their own money and have definite ideas on how to spend or not spend it. Their willingness to listen and to learn is invariably evident.

Based on such facts, the Singer Sewing Machine Company, for instance, has succeeded in dealing with the problem of communication with illiterate customers by a method of pictorial symbolism. Exhibit 1

TABLE 1

Illiteracy in Developing Countries
(Improvement During 1960's Indicated in Selected Countries.)

Country	Year	Percentage of Illiteracy	Year	Percentage of Illiteracy
Senegal			1961	94.4
Liberia			1962	91.1
Nigeria			1963	81.0
Morocco			1960	86.2
Pakistan	1951	86	1961	81.2
United Arab Republic			1960	80.5
Libya			1964	78.3
Iran			1966	77.0
India	1951	81	1961	72.2
Syria			1960	70.5
South Africa	1946	71	1960	68.5
Jordan			1961	67.6
Honduras	1950	65	1961	64.8
Guatemala	1950	70	1964	62.1
Turkey	1950	65	1960	61.9
Zambia			1963	58.6
Nicaragua	1940	63	1963	50.4
Peru			1961	39.4
Brazil	1950	51	1960	39.3
Portugal	1950	42	1960	38.1
Dominican Republic			1960	35.5
Mexico			1960	34.6
Venezuela	1950	51	1961	34.2
Thailand	1948	46	1960	32.3
Ecuador	1950	44	1962	32.2
Colombia	1951	38	1964	27.1
Panama	1950	30	1960	26.7
Paraguay	1950	32	1962	25.2
Ceylon	1946	42	1963	24.9
Greece	1951	23	1961	19.6
Jamaica			1960	18.1
Chile	1952	19	1960	16.4
Costa Rica	1950	21	1963	15.2
South-West Africa			1960	13.3
Uruguay			1963	9.2
Argentina	1947	13	1960	8.6

Source: U.S., Department of Commerce, Bureau of the Census, *Statistical Abstract of the United States: 1969* (90th ed.; Washington, D.C.: Government Printing Office, 1969).

EXHIBIT 1

Example of Textless Instruction
(Operating Sewing Machine)

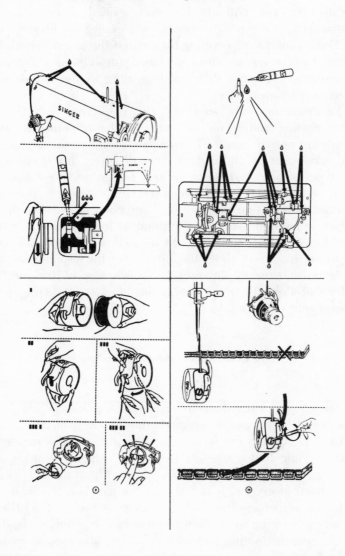

Source: Singer Sewing Machine Company (New York); reprinted by permission.

shows extracts from an instruction booklet presenting three operations in symbols and pictures: oiling of the sewing machine, insertion of the bobbin into the shuttle and then into the machine, and delicate stitch-adjusting by thread tension. Note the numbering of the steps in groups of three blocks. In fact, the textless instruction booklet designed originally for the illiterate has even gained acceptance in some industrialized countries; its simplicity appealed to literate people as well. Thus, a company operating throughout the world has substantially reduced two communications problems (dealing with illiterates and with customers speaking different languages) by the introduction of a textless instruction booklet.

Furthermore, only some of the marketing research methods require reading ability on the part of the respondents, and such methods are not the most effective. Here, for instance, belong the mail questionnaire survey and certain kinds of advertising research, such as some types of copy-testing. In general, better results are obtained and the respondent reacts best if he can state his preferences, buying habits, and other information in a personal interview. Moreover, the reliable observation method, where the respondent is not even aware that he is the subject of a test, can no doubt be used in the developing countries without much concern about the illiteracy of the respondent.

Thus, in general, illiteracy, although one of the most serious problems of a society, is not a stumbling block to marketing research in the developing countries.

Research Skills and Scientific Approach

The objection that there is a lack of research skills and a failure to use a scientific approach in marketing research in the developing countries is apparently based on the widespread opinion among business people that marketing research is a highly sophisticated and sometimes obscure activity, very far removed from the daily task of the businessman. Moreover, it is felt that the merchant in the developing countries is accustomed to dealing in tangible commodities that can be counted and with business situations that can be plainly understood. He tends to view marketing largely as a mechanistic process, involving at best such functions as transportation, storage, and somewhat more complicated matters of exchange. In point of fact, the statement is often made by traders in the developing countries that there are no marketing problems except, of course, in connection with exports. It is no wonder that these attitudes toward marketing result in a lack of appreciation for marketing research skills in the developing countries.

It is true that marketing research is not, in itself, an innovation. One may say that it has been practiced, though unconciously and in a primitive form, ever since men first began to buy and sell. What is new about marketing research is that it has now been developed along methodological lines. Marketing and marketing research have become largely systematized so that they have become both learnable and teachable. The principles can be expressed in easily understood, general concepts and, to a substantial degree, quantified. Marketing research should be one of the easiest areas to export, if only because it consists of a collection of techniques that supposedly can be applied in any free economy, regardless of the state of economic development, and because one may assume that the governments, companies, and schools in the emerging nations would eagerly seek to develop and import marketing research know-how.

The young people in the developing countries who may be interested in marketing research, the students, or those employed in the banks, trading companies, and industry, not to mention accountants, inventory controllers, planners, or sales people, must be encouraged and told that marketing research is nothing more than the systematic uncovering and orderly presentation of marketing facts, that marketing facts are usually simple facts, that a successful marketing researcher need be neither an advanced mathematician nor an advanced statistician, and that the dominant rule is just plain common sense.

Availability of Marketing Research Skills

The author has examined thirty marketing research studies to determine the amount of mathematics and statistics actually used. These studies were purchased from top-flight management consultants and marketing research agencies in Europe and the United States during 1964-68; they concern consumer surveys, distribution, diversification, company image, and product research for various client companies. It was ascertained that nothing more than basic arithmetic, algebra, and elementary statistical tabulation were used to develop conclusions.

It is hard to believe that this kind of skill does not exist among the students and teachers of business schools, colleges, and universities of the developing countries, no matter what the scholastic level of these schools may be. Traditional prejudice in the developing countries may hinder an approach to these sources; namely, that firms typically do not look upon the academic community as a source of expert advice, and often otherwise qualified academicians feel that work with a business firm is incompatible with their role as educators. The difficulty of breaking through this attitude depends upon the country and the administration of the schools. In no case should one hesitate to contact academic circles directly. The situation has changed in recent years, and one may encounter welcome and helpful cooperation in the larger schools.

A surprising number of business schools in the developing countries include marketing research courses in their curriculum. For example, forty teachers of marketing from seventeen different developing countries met at the International Center for the Advancement of Management Education (ICAME) at the Graduate School of Business, Stanford University, in the United States, to study and pursue for a year (1963-64) the purpose of marketing education in the developing countries. The countries represented were Argentina, Brazil, Ceylon, Chile, Colombia, Ghana, Indonesia, Israel, Mexico, Nicaragua, Peru, Phillipines, Republic of China, South Korea, Thailand, Turkey, and United Arab Republic.

Another example of a direct source of know-how and advancement of management and administration for the developing countries is the United Nations' International Center for Advanced Technicians and Vocational Training, in Turin, Italy (140 Corso Unito d'Italio). Permanent seminars on marketing are maintained in the curriculum for students, who are mostly members of National Vocational Centers or members of business management firms in the developing countries.

The most important sources of research skill are the marketing research firms, management consultants, and advertising agencies in the developing countries. During recent years, many Americans and Europeans, particularly the British, who have lived in the developing countries for some time and have had some experience in government or a background in economics have established themselves successfully in the management-consulting and marketing research fields. Many of these firms have grown into large organizations employing several hundred people. They are usually able to undertake research in their own and neighboring countries as well. In some countries, such as

Kenya, Tanzania, Ghana, Nigeria, Mexico, and Panama, there is noticeable competition, so that excess research skill is often available. Sponsors and clients are hesitant in coming forward, however, evidently for reasons other than lack of research skill in the country.

A partial list of firms, some of which are affiliates of American and European research firms, is provided in Appendix E. Lists of research companies can also be obtained not only from the Ministry of Commerce in the developing country itself, but also from the competent ministry in the metropolitan country for those developing countries that were in the past connected and still maintain relations with former "mother" lands.

One may succeed in obtaining the largest selections by consulting the telephone directories of the developing countries. The telephone directories are accessible at the embassies and consulates in all capital cities. In the telephone directory of Kenya, for instance, under various headings, such as "Advertising Agents," "Management Consultants," and "Marketing Consultants," several additional marketing research companies can be found that are not found elsewhere. The telephone directories of Panama City, Rio de Janeiro, Caracas, Leopoldville, Nairobi, Dar es Salaam, Abidjan, Aden, Colombo, and Singapore were examined to test the validity of this statement.

There are other sources providing lists of names and addresses with descriptions of the principal activities in research for each of the firms, such as the U.S. Department of Commerce, Bureau of Foreign Commerce, *Directory of Foreign Advertising Agencies and Marketing Research Organizations*, which can be gotten from the Superintendent of Documents, U.S. Government Printing Office, Washington, D.C., 20402.

Scientific Approach to Marketing Research

Any problem may be approached in many ways, some of which are clearly unscientific and some of which are clearly scientific. At the extremes, the difference between scientific and unscientific methods is clear. The solution of a problem by hunch, guesswork, opinion, and on the evidence of isolated examples is clearly unscientific. But the solution of a problem by laboratory experiments that eliminate or control all outside circumstances influencing the results, that employ exact measurements, and that reduce human error to a minimum is clearly scientific. Between the extremes there are many efforts at the solution of a problem that may be said to be scientific only in part. These human efforts are what really count, rather than the geographic location or the standard of living of a country. This applies to the developed as well as the developing countries.

Scientific method is most clearly applied in the procedures of the physical sciences. In the physical and chemical laboratory, one finds conditions enabling exact measurements and objective experimentation. As one passes from the physical sciences to the social sciences, it becomes more and more difficult to use scientific procedures.

In marketing, as in all fields of human activity, one constantly looks for basic laws or general principles. Just as the engineer employs fundamental scientific principles in his daily work, so the marketing man seeks to use basic generalizations in trying to solve the problems in his work. In marketing, however, the solid foundations of physical phenomena that give permanence and universality to the principles of the older sciences are lacking. Markets are in a state of constant flux. Markets are composed of human beings whose habits, attitudes, and desires are subject to constant change. Furthermore, one of the prime purposes of many marketing activities is to keep the public constantly dissatisfied with its habitual method of living and to develop new desires. This all applies to the developed as well as the developing countries.

It is a matter of controversy among writers on marketing research whether or not it should be claimed that marketing research is a science. Some writers maintain that it is not, and that it would be wrong to claim for it a greater accuracy than it is capable of producing, quite apart from the fact that by so doing it would gradually fall into disrepute. What can be claimed, however, is that the techniques of marketing research are based on scientific methods of collecting, analyzing, and interpreting facts. These methods are borrowed from various fields, such as mathematics, statistics, psychology, sociology, history, and engineering. Other writers, however, maintain that marketing research has become a science by virtue of such borrowing.

Availability of Statistics

Hardly any other criticism has done so much damage to the developing countries in discouraging industrial and business investment than the stereotyped repetition of complaints about the lack of statistics and information on the national economies. It is the nature of research in any field that the researcher obtains only a small fraction of the facts. The larger part must be produced by the researchers themselves, and it all depends on their abilities and research facilities. Endurance in systematic searching, accurate observation, a willingness to experiment, and sound procedures are among the principal tools. A successful archaeologist does not have to find the whole town and its temple to establish the period and its civilization. As Heinrich Schliemann has said, "One single button is enough to ascertain the period, civilization, and even the religion." In anthropology one single bone should be enough to ascertain the whole stature, age, diet, climate, and even habits of a prehistoric man. So it must be in any field that claims to be or hopes to become a science.

Granted, marketing deals with the interplay of the ever-changing emotional desires and whims of inherently unstable humans. It cannot ever achieve the axiomatic stability of findings of the exact sciences, such as mathematics, physics, or astronomy. Marketing research is concerned with the study of human behavior, and in human behavior it is quite impossible to achieve absolute accuracy. But in business absolute accuracy is seldom necessary. What is important, and feasible even in the developing countries, is that reasonably reliable data be forthcoming on which plans can be formulated with the assurance that they will not be entirely wrong. In any case, where facts can be obtained, it is better to be 50 per cent certain than to rely on mere guesses.

Besides, as to the lack of statistics, what was true in the developing countries twenty years ago, or even five years ago, is no longer true today. In recent years the availability of statistics from developing countries has improved remarkably. Now one is usually surprised at how many statistics are available on the developing countries if one really tries to obtain them. (See section in Chapter 4, below, on sources of statistics; Appendix A, Case Histories 3, 4, and 5, which deal with various aspects of collecting statistics; and Appendix D, which gives indicators of market size of many developing countries.)

One of the activities of the United Nations since 1958 has been to provide free expert statistical assistance to any member country that asks for such help. A statistical expert would stay in the country as long as it was necessary to organize a population census and collect basic statistics on the structure of the economy and the dominant commodities of that country. He would also train native personnel or provide the personnel from abroad to carry on permanently in that activity. (See Case History 4, on the importance of such statistics.)

Assistance in Statistics and Marketing Research

Government agencies in almost every industrial country offer marketing research assistance in one form or another. Several examples follow.

The U.S. Agency for International Development (AID), Washington, D.C., provides statistics and economic studies and helps investors in developing countries in a number of ways.[3] It serves as a source of information concerning investment opportunity in the developing countries in general. AID administration has been aware for some time of the existence in many parts of the world of a large number of practical projects covered by marketing research studies and surveys that deal with particular investment opportunities in developing countries. Some of these studies were financed by AID, but others were financed by, or under the auspices of, international banks, foreign governments (in both developed and developing countries), foundations, universities, and private firms.

AID has brought together a single listing of such studies made during 1966-70 and has abstracted the investment information that they contain. Abstracts of more than 1,000 such studies have been prepared on report cards so that investors may easily obtain relevant information on specific investment opportunities. In some cases, the cards are available in French, Spanish, or Portuguese, as well as in English, to encourage joint ventures. The index is published periodically and supplemental sheets are issued every few weeks.

Another tool at AID's disposal is the so-called Investment Survey Participation Grant. The Investment Survey Program is designed to encourage American firms to explore and study opportunities and to conduct marketing research studies in developing, friendly countries. If

---

[3] Other potential AID systems of assistance are (a) the Guarantee Program, with the Specific Risk Guarantee, through which AID guarantees the investor against inconvertibility of currency, expropriation, and the risks of war, revolution, and insurrection; (b) AID's Extended Risk Guarantee, which can cover 75 per cent of the loan capital for a given project against credit risks, as well as political risks; and (c) dollar and local currency loans.

a firm does not make an investment as a result of the survey, AID pays up to 50 per cent of the cost, and the survey then becomes U.S. property. If the firm does invest, AID pays none of the cost of the survey.

The British National Export Council (BNEC) provides collective marketing research assistance for exports from the United Kingdom. The assistance may be given to trade associations, to a chamber of commerce, or to similar nontrading bodies that organize research projects on a collective basis. Applications from individual companies are not, therefore, admissible, but applications of trade associations are considered.

Where a marketing research project is undertaken by the sponsoring organization, 50 per cent refunds for travel and accommodations are made available. Refunds are not available for desk surveys in the United Kingdom. Where a professional consultant or outside agency is employed by the sponsoring organization, 50 per cent of the fee for professional services may also be refunded. Consultants need not be British.

Statistics and other desk studies of a large number of foreign markets (over sixty developing markets so far) have been made available by various government-sponsored bodies in Italy, with a view to helping trade with these countries. The Instituto Nazionale del Commercercio Estero, in Rome, has published some 100 reports, each dealing with the study of a particular group of products in a given foreign market. Products considered range from gloves to tractors.

Spain's Finance Ministry, through the Consorcio de Compensación de Seguros (CCS), is establishing a marketing research insurance system designed to compensate companies entering export markets on the basis of research findings that prove faulty. Companies may apply to the CCS or the Finance Ministry's export division for coverage of up to 50 per cent of marketing research expenses (more in special cases) not recovered by export sales. Premiums and terms vary by industry, foreign market, and volume expected.

Prejudices and Opportunities

The economies of the emerging countries can be characterized as predominantly production oriented and, as such, concerned primarily with an efficient production system rather than with distribution. This fact, coupled with the fact that demand typically exceeds supply, leads to the opinion that little attention is given to the consumer and how his wants and needs affect the decisions of the business manager.

Further, the resources are very scarce for most commodities. Therefore, the governments of these countries follow the policy of deliberately not encouraging competition. Under such conditions, there is little if any competition within a given industry. Moreover, most companies are family controlled and do not want to expand or change. Their major objective is to maintain the status quo. The justification for this is that, in most of these countries, markets are of necessity very small and are limited by so many multiple cultural norms that the economies that could be gained from mass production and mass distribution are lost. They are too small and dispersed to make it possible to organize profitably large-scale distribution for a single-product line in an effective manner. As a result, many products for which there may be an adequate demand at a reasonable price are produced and distributed under monopoly conditions.

A strong argument can be made in favor of the use of marketing research by these governments, but there again the objection is that civil servants in developing countries have little desire to make decisions and that the whole reward system in these countries is such that one can only lose by doing so. Marketing research is feared by governments, business companies, and institutions because it might be used as a means of pointing out certain deficiencies. The less information is available, the better.

Because monetary inflation and devaluation are the major deterrents to good business results in the developing countries, success in speculation rather than in selling is regarded as the height of business efficiency. Therefore, what is really sought is advice on how to protect against losses from inflation and devaluation rather than advice on marketing. In addition, the consultants in these matters are usually foreigners, people who have somewhat limited confidence in the developing countries.

It must be granted that marketing research is a waste of money and time when used where there are no problems to be solved. A recent meeting of marketing researchers in New York was conducted under the slogan "Problems Are Our Business." Ambitious as this slogan may be, it sets the sky as the limit of the field and suggests that the companies that are in the fortunate and, indeed, exceptional position of operating without problems and that sell whatever they produce, while protected by the government, have no reason to be interested in marketing research.

But one does not need much industrial statesmanship to see that government policies that try to exclude competition and preserve family-owned companies, thus maintaining the status quo, belong more and more to the past. Earnings on capital investment in the developing world are on the rise. (See Table 2 for earnings on U.S. investments abroad.) The capital of the industrialized countries is seeking better profit than can be realized at home and the benefit of getting in early in the industrialization of the developing countries. The profits are higher in the developing countries, even when additional risks, or the cost of insurance against these risks—in particular, inflation and devaluation, expropriation, war, revolution, and the like—are counted.

The nature of marketing research is such that it reveals facts that may be favorable for some and unfavorable for other members of management or administration. This is both the good and the evil of marketing research seen from the point of view of the persons involved. It is by no means an aspect particular to the developing countries. It applies to any part of the world and is common in the industrialized countries as well. There are ample cases of postponed studies and those never made, or made secretly, because of the risk for the persons involved and because they afford too intimate an insight into the enterprise. In fact, this is one of the obstacles to marketing research in general. The stamp "Confidential" is gaining great favor in company administrations, sometimes to the extent that the management even keeps secrets from itself.

The risk of losses from currency inflation and devaluation is one of the most devastating deterrents for results in business. It is present throughout the world and varies in degree from country to country, whether developed or not. In fact, six developing countries show the stablest currency in a recent survey. (See Table 3 for annual rates of currency depreciation in selected countries.) Indeed, it is the province of the skill of the merchant in the developing country and the principal aim of management in general to prevent such losses.

The dictionary describes speculation as taking advantage of an expected rise or fall of price or taking part in any risky business venture on the chance of making huge profits. There is no basic conflict between the above definition and the normal striving of business people for success. Marketing research is an activity based on business education and knowledge, with particular stress on seeking new business horizons. Thus, it aims toward helping business people in general to seek a better return on capital from less- to more-profitable

TABLE 2

Earnings on U.S. Investments in Manufacturing Abroad, 1960-68
(In Millions of Dollars)

Year	All Areas	Europe	Latin America	Other Areas, Except Canada
1960	1,176	487	147	144
1961	1,203	530	172	141
1962	1,307	496	173	178
1963	1,541	627	171	218
1964	1,852	782	243	262
1965	2,022	859	289	268
1966	2,104	860	342	274
1967	2,055	847	269	327
1968	2,514	1,038	408	395
1960-68 *(in per cent)*[a]	*113.7*	*113.3*	*177.5*	*174.3*

[a]Note increase in "Latin America" and "Other Areas" of approximately 178 per cent and 174 per cent, respectively, whereas "All Areas" and "Europe" show only around 113 per cent. "Other Areas" includes mostly developing countries.

Source: Table supplied by National Foreign Trade Council, New York, and taken from U.S., Department of Commerce, *Survey of Current Business* (October, 1969), p. 30.

TABLE 3

Annual Rates of Currency Depreciation in Selected Countries, 1958-68[a]
(In Per Cent)

Country	Rate	Country	Rate
Guatemala	0.2	Netherlands	3.2
El Salvador	0.3	Ecuador	3.3
Venezuela	0.9	Norway	3.3
Thailand	1.2	Portugal	3.3
Greece	1.9	Sweden	3.5
Honduras	1.9	France	3.8
United States	1.9	Philippines	3.8
Luxembourg	2.0	Finland	4.7
Australia	2.2	Denmark	4.9
Germany		Israel	4.9
(Federal Republic)	2.2	China (Taiwan)	5.0
South Africa	2.2	India	5.9
Belgium	2.3	Spain	5.9
Morocco	2.3	Bolivia	7.1
Mexico	2.5	Turkey	7.3
Switzerland	2.7	Iceland	7.8
Jamaica	2.8	Colombia	9.6
Pakistan	2.9	Peru	9.6
United Kingdom	2.9	South Korea	10.8
Austria	3.0	South Vietnam	13.5
New Zealand	3.0	Chile	20.1
Iran	3.1	Argentina	23.8
Ireland	3.1	Brazil	32.1
Italy	3.2	Indonesia	58.9

[a]The first six countries are developing nations and show the most stable currencies in the world.

Source: First National City Bank, New York, *Monthly Economic Letter* (September, 1969).

business areas. In the developing countries it may be real estate, transportation, hotels, banking, building, elevators, or public utilities, such as roads, tunnels, and bridges. This holds for investments both at home and abroad. It is a legitimate research effort and activity to help seek the most profitable areas, to prevent undeserved losses, and to put capital to the best use, possibly for a huge return.

The words "speculation" and "profit" have been subjected to much derogatory propaganda for many years, but there is nothing to worry about except one's own doubts. If the businessman in a developing country seeks, above all, success in speculation, then marketing research can, indeed, serve speculation in the above-described sense.

An opportunity illustrating how people in the developing countries are becoming part of the prosperity of the advanced countries is reflected in the impact that Sears Roebuck[4] has had on several countries of Latin America. The countries of Latin America in which Sears operates—Mexico, Brazil, Venezuela, Colombia, and Peru—are not "underdeveloped" in the same sense as are Indonesia or Somalia. Still, in every respect except income level, these Latin American countries are at best "developing," and they have all the problems of economic development, perhaps in even more acute form than the countries of Asia and Africa have, precisely because their development has been so fast during the 1960's.

In these countries, Sears is not a "low-price" merchandiser. It caters to the middle class in the richer of these countries and to the upper middle class in the poorest of these countries. Sears is a mass-marketer even in Colombia or Peru. What is perhaps even more important, it is applying in these "underdeveloped" countries exactly the same policies and principles that it applies in the United States, carries substantially the same merchandise (although most of it is produced in the countries themselves), and uses the same concepts of marketing. Its impact and experience are, therefore, a fair test of what marketing principles, marketing knowledge, and marketing research can achieve.

The impact of this one American concern, which has no more than a mere handful of stores in these countries and handles no more than a

---

[4] Sears Roebuck Co., Inc., is the world's largest retail company (stores and mail order). Its 1968 net sales amounted to U.S. $7,330,089,582, according to the company's 1968 financial statement.

small fraction of the total retail business of these countries, is truly amazing. In the first place, the latent purchasing power has fast become actual purchasing power; or, to put it less theoretically, the people there have begun to organize their buying and to go out for real value in what they buy. Second, by building just one store in any city, Sears forces a revolution in retailing throughout the whole surrounding area. It forces store modernization. It forces consumer credit. It forces a different attitude toward the customer, toward the store clerk, toward the supplier, and toward the merchandise itself. It forces other retailers to adopt modern methods of pricing, of inventory control, of training, and of window display.

The greatest impact that Sears has had, however, is in the multiplication of new industrial business for which Sears creates a marketing channel. Because it has had to sell goods manufactured in these countries rather than import them (if only because of foreign exchange restrictions), Sears has been instrumental in getting literally hundreds of new manufacturers established, making goods that, a few years ago, could not be made in the country, let alone be sold in adequate quantity. Simply to satisfy its own marketing needs, Sears has had to insist on standards of workmanship, quality, management, and, above all, management of people—which, in a few short years, have advanced the art and rules of management in these countries by at least a generation.

It is hardly necessary to add that Sears is not in Latin America for reasons of philanthropy, but because to be there is good and profitable business with extraordinary growth potential. In other words, Sears is in Latin America because marketing and its research are the major opportunity in the emerging countries.

MODIFICATION OF RESEARCH METHODS

Ideally, the three basic marketing research methods—the survey method, the observational method, and the experimental method—whether applied in the industrialized countries or modified for the emerging countries, should show the same typical characteristics of good research. Thus, they should be objective, reliable, sensitive, valid, and inexpensive.

These characteristics usually take the form of affirmative answers to the following questions:

Objective: Can results be classified or scored in the same way by two or more persons or machines?

Reliable: Are results the same when the same technique is used repeatedly? Are the results the same when other research methods are used?

Sensitive: Does the technique measure something under the control of the decision-maker? Does it obtain different scores for different levels of the controllable factor?

Valid: Does the technique measure what it is supposed to measure? Does it apply when factors measured are linked and explained by other and multiple factors?

Cost: Does the technique provide the ultimate of precision and the greatest amount of information per unit cost?

It would be a mistake to assume that modification of research methods for their application in the emerging countries means the reduction of these methods to rudimentary steps in the procedure. Simplification, necessary and feasible as it may be in the developing countries, if applied at the expense of the above requirements, would produce a distorted picture of the market and of the consumer, and it would bring disrepute to the concept of marketing research even before it really becomes accepted in these countries.

The reader will now be shown how modifications of the methods are embodied in this book. They follow from the text without pointing specifically in each case to the difference between the method of application in the advanced countries and that in the developing countries. Nor are there any extensive comments on the reasons for such modifications. In this way, no one is offended by the stereotyped repetition of the various underprivileged aspects of these nations in matters of cultural and technological development.

The modifications are given in various ways, as will be evident from a number of the following examples. All the examples of modification are taken from Chapter 2. There, the modifications on research for the developing countries are numerous and mandatory, because full communication in the interview is the cornerstone of a good survey.

Most often, the modification takes the form of a suggestion that something be done as part of the procedure that, in the advanced countries, would be out of the question. Also, the procedure often suggested, though once routine, is less and less practiced in the advanced countries today. Modification may also take the form of simplification and restriction, or omission of the description of some procedures that would probably be hard to carry out in the developing countries.

As to the suggestion to do something that would be out of the question in the advanced countries, two examples follow. It is common practice in the advanced countries to use female interviewers almost exclusively in consumer surveys. In this book, however, men are mentioned in all references to interviewers. The reason must be self-evident to any reader. The use of female field workers would preclude the application of a geographically dispersed sample and the possibility of evening recalls, both of which are essentials of a rigid random sampling application. Because of poor transportation, women in the developing countries refuse to travel alone and to enter poor areas with inadequate lighting and a high crime rate. Thus, the use of male field workers is a substantial modification of research in the developing countries. There is not much point in belaboring these reasons, however.

The second example concerns the number of members to be included in a consumer group interview. In the advanced countries, it is customary to invite from eight to twelve respondents to a group interview; even fifteen members may produce useful results in a well-organized discussion group. In the description of group interviews in this book, however, only four to six consumers are suggested for groups in the developing countries. The reason is that experience shows that in developing countries it is difficult to get a larger group together. Moreover, in large groups, it is likely that one or two participants will dominate the group's thinking, and also, in general, it is extremely difficult to control large groups and to obtain and record the necessary amount of classifiable consumers' opinions in an orderly fashion. Lack of discipline and willingness to obey the rules of conducting such a meeting is the usual cause of such difficulties—and, again, there is not much point in stressing the somewhat derogatory reasons when a straightforward suggestion about the number of group members can suffice.

Examples of steps recommended for the developing countries that are practiced less and less in marketing research in the advanced countries today can be seen in the following. Display cards, illustrations, samples, and all possible visual material shown by the interviewer to ensure good communcation with the respondents are invariably of great value in the developing countries but are little used in the advanced countries. The same applies to the detailed description of "How to assist the respondent's thinking and aiding his memory," or "Helping the respondent to express himself." Also, the suggestion of improvising experimental interviews within the group of interviewers in the instruction meeting between the supervisor and the field staff proved to be the surest way of making the questionnaire clear in the countries where marketing research is in its infancy. Here the reason for modification is also obvious. All this improves communication with illiterate respondents or with people who have little education, sometimes resulting in limited appreciation of new things or abstract ideas.

Another example of modification is simplifying the methods of research that are very successful in the advanced countries but are out of the question in the developing countries, such as the telephone survey. In the majority of the developing countries the postal service is very poor, let alone the telephone service. The number of registered telephones is small, and there are varying attitudes toward the use of a telephone. Generally speaking, telephone users, particularly women, are highly suspicious of strangers on the phone. Also, because of their respect for (or even fear of) the instrument, many men and women will not spend much time using it. Nevertheless, despite all these entirely valid reasons, when a telephone survey was tried out in one developing country (Kenya), it worked (see Case History 2), and it has worked in other developing countries. But it worked only in a restricted area and on the improvised "do-it-yourself" scale described in this book. (See the appropriate section of Chapter 2.).

Sometimes the modification is arrived at by failing to describe certain procedures that are not feasible in the developing countries but are commonly used in the advanced countries. For instance, in the developing countries, dwellings are often inhabited by many individuals and several primary families. It is thus usually difficult to find out who the housewife is. Given the existence of poor living conditions, this book refrains from describing the procedure used in selecting the particular individual within a family who is supposed to be interviewed.

Trying to succeed in this has generally proved a waste of time in the developing countries, although it is a rather important step in order to get a perfect random sample in the advanced countries.

Then, too, as regards the mail survey, there are apparently those who do not believe in writing answers that will be read by a stranger. Therefore, if the questionnaire is answered at all, it is the male head of the family who answers it, regardless of the actual addressee. For this reason, in the section of Chapter 2 that describes the procedures used in a mail survey, a description of how to collect the full names and addresses of particular individuals whose opinions it would be desirable to obtain within a family is omitted.

Similar examples of modifications in research procedure could be given *ad infinitum* and could be applied to most of the contents of this book. The necessary modifications of research methods in the developing countries cannot be objectively ascertained in all cases, however. It must be remembered that marketing problems are not solved in terms of absolute certainty but in terms of probability. Nor are the methods used in solving problems final; rather, they are in the process of constant revision to suit changing environments.

PLAN OF BOOK

In the following chapters, careful attention is given to describing the various techniques that have proved to be most successful in the developing countries. The greatest stress has been put on the description of the interview in Chapter 2, because, when the investigator and respondent are face-to-face, they are engaged in the most successful way of communicating in the emerging countries. This, coupled with Case Histories 11 on sampling field techniques and 12 on instructing interviewers, is crucial to the understanding of the message of this book when it comes to stimulating self-starting surveys in the developing countries.

In the more complex chapters—such as Chapter 3, "Sampling," and Chapter 4, "Quantitative Research"—no previous knowledge of the subject is assumed, and the key terms are fully covered in the glossary in Appendix B by means of detailed definitions. The glossary is an integral part of this book; it should be read and understood term for term, as definitions may often replace lengthy descriptions of essential marketing research terms in the text. Knowledge of these two basic chapters enables the reader to understand other chapters. They contain the minimum but mandatory information needed by students of any business subject, professionals in marketing research, or management consultants in the developing countries. For the latter, there is also Chapter 10, "The Report," which deals with the presentation of marketing research findings, and Chapter 11, "Establishing Marketing Research in a Firm," which, it is hoped, will be amply used by managers and directors of various enterprises in the developing countries.

Chapters on the traditional marketing research subjects—such as Chapter 5, "Product Research," Chapter 6, "Price Research," and Chapter 7, "Advertising Research"—will, obviously, be used as the situation requires. In some of these situations, the product is the most important single problem calling for marketing research. In others, price or advertising will be the problem. The process is described for each in a basic manner that draws on extensive experience. Reference to pertinent case histories is made in each chapter.

Highly sophisticated marketing research in some advanced countries—such as the United States, France, and Germany—concentrates mostly on the subject of the imponderables in advertising. The basic description of advertising in this book makes this sophistication evident, and it sometimes suggests even further refinements through the use of mathematics, psychology, and sociology that, undoubtedly, will have to be applied in some of the developing countries too from time to time.

Conversely, Chapter 8, "Retailing Research," and Chapter 9, "Financial Marketing Research," are simple presentations that cover research on general business practice and may be used independently by anyone engaged in such activities or in research projects.

2

PERSONAL INTERVIEW

Whether in an industrialized or in a developing country, the respondents are only human. Any reply is subject to error due to inadequate knowledge, faulty memory, or untruthful replies evoked by considerations of pride or suspicion. It is such errors that a good interviewer and a good questionnaire try to avoid. It is important to bear in mind that a questionnaire is not just a carefully compiled logical sequence of questions, but a means of gaining communication. It is a truism generally accepted by marketing researchers that verbal communication (that is, hearing alone) cannot produce good results. Other senses and, ideally, all senses—sight, smell, taste, and touch—come into play when human beings communicate effectively. Introduction of samples, illustrations, and demonstrations are practical methods of maintaining the respondent's interest throughout the interview.

Although the accuracy and quality of the information obtained will depend very largely on the skill and personality of the interviewer, the questionnaire can be of the utmost value in helping the interview to run smoothly and in ensuring the cooperation of the respondent, as well as guiding the interviewer. Basically a successful interview depends on the following: (a) determination of the ultimate objective, (b) informal interviewing, (c) a good questionnaire, (d) the skill and personality of the interviewer, and (e) experienced supervision.

Ultimate Objective

The marketing research man must, with the guidance of the manufacturer or others sponsoring the survey, define the ultimate objective, so that he knows exactly what the survey is expected to achieve. Suppose that a survey for the purpose of investigating the market for a new refrigerator is designed to discover consumer habits. The investigator might list the following as questions relevant to the survey:

Who are the owners of refrigerators?
What are the characteristics of these users?
What brands do they have?
What are the most popular sizes?
What are the prices?
What features do people want?
Why did they select the brands they have?
Would any features make present brands more attractive?
How long do they expect refrigerators to last?
Through what channels did they acquire them?
What do they think about service?
What is the size of the market for used refrigerators?

When this sort of preliminary list has been compiled, it will again be necessary to consult the sponsor of the survey in order to obtain the benefit of his experience on individual points of special importance or of a technical nature, in order to ensure that there is agreement on the ultimate objective.

Informal Interviewing

It is necessary to select a dozen or so respondents, as varied as possible, for the purpose of informal interviewing in order to test out the points listed. The interviews are entirely informal and are not controlled by a questionnaire or in any other way. They amount, in fact, to a friendly chat or conversation about the subject matter.

Informal interviewing is not concerned with discovering *what* people think about the various issues involved; that is what the survey itself will discover. What informal interviewing sets out to do is to find out *how* people think about these issues and how they react to them, so that the questionnaire can be framed along the lines of thought that will be most natural to the respondents. Informal interviewing will often bring out points that did not occur to the person in charge of the work. In the case of the survey for refrigerators, such a point might be the question of how to clean underneath it.

The method used in informal interviewing generally is to allow the respondent to talk naturally about the subject, but to keep him to the point and not let him go off on a tangent that has no bearing on the subject. He must be made to reveal everything that he feels and thinks about these points. The interviewer must note all remarks that may be relevant and pursue them until he is satisfied that there is no more to be gained by further probing. Properly conducted, this kind of informal interviewing will give the researcher an intimate feel for the subject and is particularly important where technical products are concerned.

The importance of the informal interview can also be seen in the development of the researcher's hypothesis, which gives the research its entire direction. The hypothesis may be called the tentative idea for the probable solution of the problem. The hypothesis plays as important a role in the research work as medical diagnosis does in the work of a physician.

Questionnaire Characteristics

The questionnaire is the most important single aspect of the personal interview. If the questionnaire is faulty and leads to incorrect information, then no amount of analysis and interpretation will put it right. There are several fundamental characteristics of all good questionnaires:

(1) It must be as simple as the subject matter will allow.

(2) It should make it easy for respondents to give the necessary information and for the interviewer to record the answer.

(3) It should keep the interview to the point while enabling it to be handled tactfully.

(4) It should be so arranged that sound analysis and interpretation are possible and the respondent remains interested throughout the interview.

To achieve this, there are certain principles to be borne in mind.

Classification Data

The term "classification data" means information regarding the respondent himself, or the respondent's family, if that happens to be the unit under study. Information, such as name, address, age, sex, size of family, and economic status, is used to make the analysis of the answers obtained in the field meaningful. Direct questions concerning age and income should be avoided. Most of the time, the answers are evident or can be estimated. The names of the respondents enable a proper checking by the supervisor.

Such data help in tabulating answers. Correct sorting, listing, interpretation, and counting of the answers depend upon the clarity of the classification data. Which classification data are needed must be decided when determining the ultimate objective of the survey.

Importance of Single-Element Questions

An apparently simple question may turn out to be a very involved one, particularly where questions are designed to elicit reasons for a particular action. For example, in the survey for refrigerators, it would be possible to ask "Why did you purchase this particular brand?" On the face of it this is a simple question, but, if one looks at the possible answers and combinations of answers, it will be realized that it can become extremely involved.

Suppose that the respondent had the choice of four brands, A, B, C, and D, and that all these models were of the cubic capacity he wanted. The features of brands A and B were more in keeping with what he wanted than were those of C and D. He was told, however, that brand A was liable to break down frequently, while brand C had a good name for reliability. Brand B, which he particularly liked, was out of the question because it could not be adapted to his type of electric power. He finally chose brand D because the arrangements for the payment of installments were favorable and the model represented a compromise regarding most of the features he wanted. How would he then have answered the apparently simple question? It is essential, therefore, that all questions be broken down into their component parts, each of which should be considered separately, so that each question is concerned with a single idea.

When several alternative replies can be expected, e.g., in so-called multichoice questions or ranking questions, the order of the prelisted replies should be rotated, because respondents tend to choose the one that appears first. The replies may be prelisted on the questionnaire or on show-cards. Not more than five alternatives should be prelisted or put on a show-card. Graduation of replies is obtained by suggesting categories such as very important, quite important, neither important nor unimportant, of no importance. For frequency of use, one can employ such terms as often, occasionally, never.

Ambiguity in Questions

Ambiguity will often be the result of carelessly worded questions. For example, if a respondent were asked "Do you drive a car?" he might interpret this question to mean did he own a car and consequently drive one, or could he drive a car whether he owned one or not.

Another source of ambiguity is the inclusion of two items in one question. In the question "Do you like the quality and style of X brand of overcoat?" the respondent is given the opportunity to answer only "Yes" or "No," whereas he may like the quality but not the style, or vice versa. To make his point he would have to enter into a long explanation, and the interviewer would have difficulty in noting his answer correctly.

Words that are unlikely to be universally understood by the respondents in a particular survey must be avoided. Questions must be worded so that the least educated of the respondents will understand their meaning.

Leading and Misleading Questions

A leading question is one that suggests the answer to the respondent. To say "Don't you think that the capacity of X brand of refrigerator is rather small?" is to imply that it is and that the answer should be "Yes." Misleading questions usually arise out of biased thinking. For example, "Would you not prefer to buy X brand of cigarettes because of its better quality tobacco?" might be all right in an advertisement, but it has no place in an objective questionnaire.

Personal and Embarrassing Questions

The researcher must be clearly aware of the various customs, mores, and traditions in the country or community and how they may affect the answers. Questions relating to racial or religious prejudices should always be avoided. This difficulty is encountered where pride and social position are involved. For example, a middle-class housewife, when asked what magazines she reads, would probably name a number of high-class magazines but would fail to mention those she considered lowbrow. The usual method of overcoming this difficulty is by observation or by asking specific questions that would check on the respondent's knowledge of the magazines in question.

There is a great reluctance in the developing countries, among both men and women, to discuss certain subjects with strangers. Although the degree to which certain topics are taboo varies from country to country, such subjects as ownership of various furnishings, installment purchase arrangements, education, details on occupation, health, hygiene, sex, and other personal details are difficult to discuss. It is good practice to include these questions at the end of the questionnaire so that, should the respondent take offense at a series of highly personal questions, the other information will already have been collected.

Helping Respondent's Thinking and Aiding His Memory

The respondent should be asked only for such data as he can clearly remember. One has to bear in mind that people will not admit that they cannot remember. They would rather make guesses. But questions that elicit guesses as answers should always be eliminated.

To help a respondent answer a specific question it may often be necessary to ask two or three preliminary questions. This will condition his mind for the important question or will stimulate his memory. If a man is asked what he did at 9:00 p.m. the day before yesterday, he will have a certain amount of difficulty in remembering. But if he is first informed that the day before yesterday was Monday and is then asked at what time he left his work, he will associate his actions with the day, he will picture himself leaving work, and he will then generally remember what he did subsequently. This conditioning of a respondent's mind may also be achieved if the question is introduced by saying slowly, "Thinking back to the time when you. . ."

Thus, the order of the questions should follow the respondent's own train of thought. Once a train of thought has been started, it is important that it should not be broken by any sudden or extraneous question. To achieve the best results, a respondent should be led gradually from one subject to another related subject.

Helping Respondent Express Himself

Many people who have good memories and are willing to cooperate lack the capacity to express themselves clearly. This is particularly true when it is a question of attitudes, which must be indicated precisely. In such cases, it may be necessary for the interviewer to introduce a series of short simple questions that will help the respondent to express himself. For example, asked why he uses a product, a respondent may answer "Because I like it." This answer does not contribute much to the results of the survey. It is necessary to ask "specifying questions" that will elicit the required information. Thus, the respondent may be asked "What do you particularly like about it?"

Similarly, to ask how many bags of flour a housewife uses per year will be futile as a housewife does not think in terms of yearly consumption. The question "How many days does one package of flour last?" may be more satisfactorily answered. Also, the question "How often do you use your sewing machine?" will probably be answered in a way suggesting that the housewife is a diligent and rational person rather than a lazy one. The real frequency of use will be obtained more reliably when two questions are asked: "When did you last use your sewing machine?" and "When before that?"

Sequence of Questions

To build up the necessary rapport between interviewer and respondent, the opening questions should be simple and likely to arouse confidence and interest. Difficult questions that the respondent may not be able to answer and that he may construe as casting reflections on his intelligence or education must be avoided at the beginning of the interview if the interview is not to be cut short.

The influence of one question on a subsequent question is of particular importance. For example, if a questionnaire begins by asking the respondent about brands, he may not mention a particular brand because it is unimportant to him or because he knows little about it. If, however, that brand had been mentioned in a previous question, the respondent would remember it and mention it when answering the subsequent question, thus introducing a bias.

It is natural for a respondent to become more indifferent to the questionnaire as it nears its end. Because of impatience or fatigue, he may give careless answers to the later questions. Those questions, therefore, that are of special importance should, if possible, be included in the earlier part of the questionnaire.

Length of Questionnaire and How to Hold Attention

It is reasonable to assume that an enthusiastic photographer is more willing to answer a long questionnaire about his hobby than is a housewife about household commodities. Again, a prosperous housewife may not be willing to give as much time to an interview as a less prosperous one. On the whole, it is best for questionnaires to be as short as possible. A long questionnaire is open to the danger of causing boredom before it is completed or of being discontinued in the middle for some reason as an appointment or an engagement. An interview should last not more than ten minutes when conducted in a city street and fifteen minutes in a dwelling. But in a rural home the interviewer may find cooperation for, on the average, thirty minutes.

Brevity for its own sake is not a virtue in a questionnaire, however; nor is a questionnaire good just because it is short. Some questionnaires containing two or three questions may fail, whereas a questionnaire of fifty questions may be be highly successful. Maintaining cooperation throughout a long questionnaire depends upon the interest that the respondents have in the subject, the skill of the interviewer, and, only then, upon the design of the questionnaire. Illustrations, samples, demonstrations, show-cards listing or picturing alternatives discussed in the particular questions, and statements that relax the respondents are known to be among the means used to maintain the respondents' interest. The only way to decide whether or not a questionnaire is too long is to test it in the field by comparing the results when alternative means of stimulating interest in the subject are used.

As to the show-cards and illustrations, the childlike nature of the drawings of objects discussed in the interview has proved to have had good appeal to the respondents in the developing countries and solves the problem and reduces the cost of having printed cards made. One interviewer in South Africa reported that cards, as shown in Exhibit 2, proved to be a direct door-opener for him when he declared that his eight-year-old daughter had drawn the pictures. Exhibit 3 shows a similar freehand drawing of a show-card used for helping to answer a somewhat complex technical question: namely, what kind of zigzag stitch was preferable of three varieties available on the market? (The latter was used in Abidjan in French West Africa.)

Piloting and Final Form

Even after the research worker has proceeded along the lines suggested, his draft questionnaire is a product evolved by one mind, possibly two or three. Until it has actually been used in interviews and with respondents in whom the survey is interested, it is impossible to say whether it is going to achieve the desired results and avoid misunderstandings. For this reason, it is necessary to pretest the questionnaire before it is used in the survey proper, to make sure that it meets all the requirements of the survey and contains no flaws. If it does, then the pretest will show up the flaws, and they will have to be corrected. This procedure is called "piloting the questionnaire." In other words, a pilot test is carred out as a guide to the survey itself.

In concrete terms, the purpose of piloting a questionnaire is to discover—

(1) Whether the questions as they are framed will achieve the desired result.

(2) Whether the questions have been placed in the best order.

(3) Whether the questions are understood by all classes of respondents.

(4) Whether any bias is being introduced by the questions themselves or by the way they are put.

(5) Whether additional or specifying questions are needed or whether some questions should be eliminated.

(6) Whether the instructions to interviewers are adequate.

EXHIBIT 2

Interview Show-Card Used in Consumer Survey in South Africa[a] (Assist to Answer Question "What Is Your Sewing Machine Used For?")

[a]This freehand style of drawing proved to have good appeal in interviews conducted in the developing countries.

Source: Singer Sewing Machine Company (New York); reprinted by permission.

EXHIBIT 3

Interview Show-Card Used in Consumer Survey in French West Africa[a]
(Assist to Identify Three Different Kinds of Zigzag Stitch)

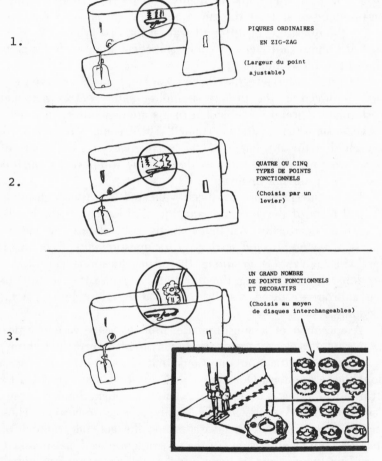

1. PIQURES ORDINAIRES EN ZIG-ZAG

(Largeur du point ajustable)

2. QUATRE OU CINQ TYPES DE POINTS FONCTIONNELS

(Choisis par un levier)

3. UN GRAND NOMBRE DE POINTS FONCTIONNELS ET DECORATIFS

(Choisis au moyen de disques interchangeables)

[a]This freehand style of drawing proved to have good appeal in interviews conducted in the developing countries.

Source: Singer Sewing Machine Company (New York); reprinted by permission.

39

Whether the questions are understood by all classes of respondents is, of course, vitally important in surveys concerned with all classes of respondents, from the university graduate to the illiterate. Obviously, questions must be simple enough for the latter to understand, but not so worded that the former will take offense.

The procedure for piloting a questionnaire follows. A small number of respondents is selected. They are representative of the types of respondents to be interviewed in the actual survey. Interviewers engaged in pretesting must be highly skilled. They should employ the questionnaire as it is at the time, but they are allowed discretion in putting the questions in different ways if the first attempt fails. At this stage, the important element is not statistical analysis, but merely the form of the questionnaire.

After the interviews have been completed, all the interviewers who were employed in the pretest should be gathered together, and the questionnaire should be subjected to a searching inquiry in which their views and impressions are ascertained. There is much to be said for the research director in charge of the survey carrying out some of the interviewing personally, since by doing so he will obtain a much better grasp of the problems involved.

If the questionnaire has been subjected to a thorough pilot test, the final form of the questions and the questionnaire as such will have emerged automatically. All that remains to be done is the mechanical process of laying out and setting up the questionnaire in its final form. This will involve (a) grouping the main questions and dependent questions; (b) numbering the questions; (c) inserting instructions in their appropriate place, usually in capital letters or in italics; and (d) precoding.

A specimen of a questionnaire, used to assess various aspects of the market for electric irons, is shown in final form in Exhibit 4. It begins with classification questions that give descriptive information about the respondent. Question 1 and Question 2 are designed to find out if any washing is done at home and how much. Similarly, Question 3 and Question 4 deal with the supply of electric current. These are general "opener" or "filter" questions; the general conduct of the interview, and whether some of the subsequent questions are asked, will depend on the answers to them. Incidentally, Question 3 would almost certainly be answered by observation.

The questionnaire is coded for punched-card classification of replies. The first number (the one preceding the diagonal) indicates the

EXHIBIT 4

Sample Questionnaire in Final Form

SPECIMEN QUESTIONNAIRE

Job No. ....

Name ....
Address ....
Town 2/
Investigator 3/
Checked by ....

		No. in Family:	M.	F.
Class A	4/1	Under 5 yrs.	5/‖ 8/	
„ B	2	5–15 yrs.	6/‖ 9/	
„ C	3	15 yrs. and over	7/‖ 10/	

Income Group:

Occupation of Chief Wage Earner................ 11/
Aids to Classification ....
Date of Interview........ Age of Housewife... 12/

1. Do you do any washing at home for your family?
   Yes, all 13/1
   Yes, some 2
   No, nothing 3

2. If "*yes, some*". What articles do you usually wash at home, and what do you send to the laundry?

	Wash at Home	*Send to Laundry*
Small articles	14/1	2
Heavy articles	3	4

3. Have you electric lighting in your home?
   Yes 15/1
   No 2

4. Have you any other electric points besides lighting?
   Yes 16/1
   No 2

   (a) *If Yes.* Where are they (rooms)? 17/

5. Do you use any of the following electrical equipment?
   Electric Washer .... 18/1 Make 19/
   Electric Iron .... 2 Make 20/
   Electric Clothes Drier ... 3 Make 21/

For those who have NO ELECTRIC IRON:

6. What kind of iron do you use?
   Gas 22/1
   Flat 2
   Never use an iron 3

7. Why do you not use an electric iron? 23/

For those who DO USE AN ELECTRIC IRON:

8. How long have you had this iron? 24/

9. Where was it bought? Not bought—gift 25/1
   Not bought—hired 2
   Bought at (type of store) ....

10. What price did you pay? 26/

11. What is its weight? 27/
    (a) Is this the right weight for you? Yes 28/1
    Too heavy ... 2
    Too light ... 3

12. Has it controlled heat? (e.g. Low, medium, high, wool, silk, cotton, linen, rayon, etc.) Yes 29/1
    No. 2

    (a) *If Yes.* Do you find these give the right sort of heat for the job, or don't you use them?
    Right heat 29/1
    Not the right heat ... 2
    Never bother to use .. 3

13. Has your iron an indicator light?
    Yes 30/1
    No 2

14. Have you any criticisms or suggestions which you feel would improve your electric iron? If so, what are they? 31/

15. If you were buying an electric iron tomorrow, what particular features would you look for? 32/

    (a) Why? 33/

16. Where would you go to buy it? (*Type of store*) 34/

17. What women's magazines did you read during the last month? 35/

18. What daily newspaper/s did you read yesterday? 36/

19. What Sunday newspaper/s did you read last Sunday? 37/

20. About how often do you go to a cinema? 38/

Source: Sales Research Services Limited (London); reprinted by permission.

41

column number, and the following number (the one after the diagonal) indicates the various possible replies. Although the questionnaire is coded, it is not completely so for every question, since there are some questions for which the number of possible replies that may be forthcoming is not known in advance. (See Exhibit 5 for a punched card of a reply to this questionnaire.)

All the questions would not be asked at every interview. For example, Question 5 would not be asked if the answer to Question 3 were "No." If Question 5 showed that an electric iron was in use, then Question 6 and Question 7 would not be asked. Similarly, Question 10 would not be asked unless the answer to Question 9 indicated that the respondent had herself bought her iron.

Question 17 through Question 20 are designed to discover the reading and cinema-going habits of the housewife. They are not essential to the main purpose of the survey, and it should be observed that they have been placed at the end of the questionnaire.

Interviewers

Interviewers, like salesmen, must be selected for the job. A poorly educated person cannot be used for interviewing among intellectual and cultured people; nor should the interviewer be so far above the respondent in intellect and culture as to render natural communication of ideas impossible. The social position of respondents is one of the most difficult problems in interviewing, and, although interviewers are versatile by nature, some will be better than others in dealing with certain social groups.

The main consideration must, of course, always be whether or not the interviewer is a good one. The question of whether male or female interviewers are employed should be carefully considered in the developing countries, however. It is interesting to note the substantial use of male interviewers in most developing countries, for men field staff produce markedly better results. Because women are by tradition quite modest, and because their role is not seen by the male head of the family as that of a worker outside the family unit, it is difficult to recruit female workers in the developing countries. Also, although this situation is changing, the number of educated women is quite small in most of these countries. In several countries, interviewing is classified as

EXHIBIT 5

Punched Card for Questionnaire in Exhibit 4[a]

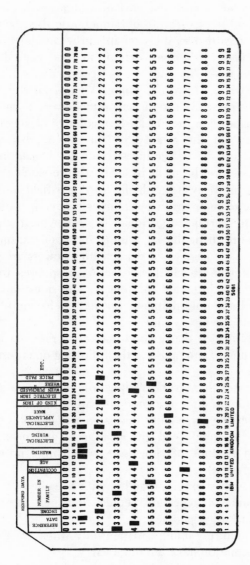

[a]Explanation of machine tabulation card: Columns 1-12 are for punching classification data. The balance, 13-80, are for sought data. The rectangles represent holes punched in the card, which are counted by a card sorter. The punching of numbers 1 and 2 in column 18 indicates that the respondent owns an electric washer and an electric iron. The punching of number 6 in column 20 indicates that the brand of the iron has been given the code number 6.

Source: Sales Research Services Limited (London); reprinted by permission.

door-to-door selling and is, therefore, not considered fit for women. Poor transportation and difficulties in evening recalls are additional factors.

Since most women have some sort of a domestic background and it is generally easier for a woman to obtain a housewife's confidence on questions that are regarded as the woman's province, however, women interviewers are used to some extent in the capital cities for interviewing housewives. This may be noticed in the capital cities of Portugal, South Africa, Argentina, Japan, Venezuela, and the United Arab Republic. The excessive use of male interviewers in the developing countries, as for instance in the Far Eastern countries, except for Japan, imposes limitations on the quality of the survey, because certain subjects can obviously be better investigated by female interviewers. Efforts should, therefore, be made by marketing research companies to incorporate female interviewers gradually into their field staff.

Thus, the use of male interviewers does bias cooperation and the responses given to certain questions. It seems clear that a male interviewer has more difficulty in gaining the cooperation of female respondents than is the case when women interviewers are used. Also, males are often unable to elicit satisfactory responses to questions dealing with products intended for females and questions about the attitudes of other household members on matters having to do with a woman's role within the family unit.

It is generally agreed that a good marketing research interviewer, whether man or woman, must possess the following qualities:

(1) A better than average education and a versatility of mind that is the product of a good education

(2) A pleasing personality that is open and makes people want to please, reinforced by cleanliness and neat attire (including an absence of sunglasses, which have proved to reduce cooperation)

(3) The ability to mix, together with a readiness to meet all classes and all types of people; thus, an extrovert's attitude toward other people

(4) An inquiring mind, satisfied only when every bit of available information has been obtained

(5) Precision, i.e., the ability to record precisely and to think precisely

(6) Being observant, i.e., the ability to obtain much of the data by observation

(7) The ability to be a "lone wolf" who is both reliable and honest

(8) A good memory (Obviously, a good memory is essential if an interviewer's reports are to be accurate. This can, however, be considerably assisted by completing reports as soon as possible after interviews.)

(9) Some knowledge of the commercial world. (Experience in the problems of business, sales, advertising, marketing, and the like is, of course, extremely useful, enabling the interviewer really to understand the purpose of everything he is required to do.)

Gaining Cooperation

The first impression made by the interviewer is, of course, of the utmost importance, and the ultimate success of the interview will often depend on a good beginning. If necessary, suitable introductions should be prepared in advance so that no time is lost in lengthy explanations and so that a good impression is created at the start. In every interview, it is essential to begin in such a way as to arouse the interest of the respondent and to ensure his cooperation. This can be done by giving the respondent a brief account of the study. This makes him feel that he is in the interviewer's confidence, which makes cooperation more likely. The name of the product or the manufacturer or other sponsor must not be mentioned, as this would tend to create a bias in favor of the sponsor.

There are various common methods of gaining the cooperation of the respondent. One may offer a premium or cash reward. Premiums are especially effective where children may be used as an entree, or where women or groups are involved. They are less expensive than cash rewards are, for it is possible to offer items that appear to have high value at relatively low cost. The chief weakness of using premiums is their tendency to increase returns from among certain groups, such as the "souvenir hunters."

One may also appeal to the instincts, pride, and vanity of the person being questioned. One may appeal to pride by saying that the opinions of leading personalities are wanted, by appointing people to "committees," and by other forms of flattery. Telling a woman that she has been singled out of her block or street for an interview is to play on her vanity.

One may use a "begging" approach. This means of securing cooperation was employed when a researcher said in a letter that he was starting in business and needed help to avoid failure. The most cold-hearted executive will usually give in to the young chap who tells him that his job depends on getting the interview or to a student who tells him that he needs the interview for his thesis.

People at times pose as having some sort of authority. By saying "We are taking a census of . . ." at the opening of an interview, one can often obtain high returns. Impressive titles on questionnaires, such as "Survey Council" or "Research Institute" or even "Academy of Marketing Sciences," hint at an authority that some people will respect. The ethics of this method are open to question, but it is used because it gets results.

One may also appeal to interest in the study itself, promising copies of the results. This appeal is especially useful with traders. So many promises to send a copy of the report have been forgotten, however, that this method is less effective than it used to be.

One should not produce a lengthy, labored approach. It is best to select the one wedge that will be most productive in the specific case, to state it succinctly, clearly, and directly, and do no more.

In the developing countries, many respondents refuse to cooperate (either in whole or in part) or distort their answers because they fear the interviewer may be a tax inspector or some other government official. The director of a household budget study for a Middle Eastern government expected that less than 50 per cent of the households contacted would be willing to cooperate, due primarily to mistrust of strangers. Many are suspicious because they believe the interviewer to be a house-to-house salesman. One can understand why those young male interviewers who either are or look like college students obtain relatively high rates of cooperation.

Refusals to cooperate in developing countries are considerably higher than those in the United States or Europe. Although the cooperation rate varies by country, the general mistrust of strangers tends to produce considerable difficulty in obtaining satisfactory interviews. Thus, for example, Thai and Indonesian women will not talk unless an acquaintance accompanies the field worker. In many villages in these and other countries, literally no one will cooperate unless the village elders have sanctioned the study. In many cases, the permission of the family head is required, and frequently he will grant the interview only if he himself is permitted to answer the questions. Interviews among the well-to-do are difficult because they are protected by servants. The approval of the local church is required in certain communities, so that nuns will accompany the interviewer, as in Ecuador.

Several countries have reported on the use of samples or premiums as a device to gain cooperation. For example, free product samples were distributed in the Philippines and Nicaragua, small gifts were given out in the United Arab Republic and Morocco, and free lottery tickets were offered in Indonesia. Appointments are used in some countries to facilitate interviewing the wealthy, whereas, in others, college students are used to "get by the servants," such as in South Africa and Ceylon.

The problem of "not-at-home" in most of the cities of the developing countries is not as great as it is in the United States and Europe. But this is not true in the villages, where in some countries the younger wife's role is at her husband's side in the fields, such as in Malawi, Mauritius, and Mozambique. Under these conditions, the not-at-home rate may reach as high as 50 per cent or more. In contrast, in some of the Middle Eastern countries, such as in Lebanon, where the wife's traditional role requires her presence in the home most of the time, the rate is much lower.

Instructions

Besides the instructions noted on the questionnaire in capital letters or in italics, instructions to interviewers should be given verbally during a meeting of supervisors and investigators. The interviewers should be told in the beginning that their work will be checked. They should be tested to make certain that they understand the questionnaire. It is usually desirable to have each interviewer go through a complete interview, from arrival to departure, with the supervisor at this time. It is essential the the investigators be given an opportunity to try the questionnaire on each other in an improvised experimental interview within the group.

Further, each interviewer should also be given a printed sheet of instructions to which he can refer in the field as and when the occasion arises. In other words, he should be told whom to interview, when to interview, and, in the case of quota sampling, how to select his respondents. In the developing countries, the instructions to the interviewers may involve quite detailed explanation, because a difficult situation may exist due, for instance, to the lack of maps for most of the middle-sized towns of these countries. (See Case Histories 11 and 12 on sampling field techniques and instructing interviewers, respectively, for illustrations of how to proceed in such situations.)

Generally, the interviewers need thorough and firm guidance, and the instructions to interviewers should cover the following points:

(1) The purpose of the survey

(2) Details relating to the types of interview required (In area sampling, this will consist of lists of names, or streets and residences; in quota sampling, a description of the types of respondents and the numbers required for each type will be given.)

(3) The best times for interviewing various respondents

(4) How the interviewer should introduce himself

(5) How the interviewer should conduct the interview

(6) Special points regarding the questionnaire, what difficulties may arise, and how they should be handled

(7) When and how to call back where first calls have been abortive

(8) When and how to send in reports

(9) How reports should be made out and what editing and checking is expected from the interviewer

(10) Whom to contact in cases of difficulty

(11) Clear understanding on matters of pay per day or per interview, number of working hours daily, lunch time, coffee breaks, and the like.

Supervision

Normally, supervisors will be responsible for training and briefing interviewers for a specific study, and for this reason each supervisor knows the interviewers for whom he is responsible and knows at what points supervision is required.

Each interviewer should go over his work with the supervisor daily so that difficulties can be overcome and errors can be checked. The supervisor must also make a percentage call-back on the respondents to ascertain whether or not the interviewer did his job correctly, i.e., accurately and without bias. This will also help eliminate dishonesty on the part of the interviewers.

A well-completed questionnaire should be an accurate record of what occurred at the interview and should, preferably, be completed at the time of the interview or as soon as possible afterward. Unless this principle is followed, distortions, caused by the interviewer's failing to remember accurately or confusing two or more interviews, are likely to occur. It is necessary that the answer to every question be complete, and it is the duty of the interviewer to satisfy himself on this point before passing on to the next question.

Bias can easily be introduced during the interview by the attitude of the interviewer or by the way he puts his questions. If the interviewer tries to assist the respondent by introducing leading questions or remarks that telegraph the answers he expects, he will often get those answers whether they are right or wrong. Further, by tone of voice or by emphasis on certain words, answers to questions can be influenced. Actually, the interviewer should never have to explain a question; questions that need explanation are badly phrased questions.

Field work always depends on the thoroughness and honesty of the persons collecting the data. Some interviewers have been known to sit in a bar or at home, completing their questionnaires with the aid of nothing but their own imagination. What is even more dangerous, because it cannot be easily detected, they may fill in answers to some of the questions at actual interviews and then complete the rest from their imagination. Most of this kind of blatant dishonesty can be eliminated by supervisors who make percentage check calls. In any case, any batch of questionnaires completed in this way will not be consistent with the general trends of the inquiry, and this fact will be detected in the research office immediately, though not until much time and money have been lost. (See Exhibit 6 for an example of interviewer influence on survey results.)

Guesswork by field workers is common, particularly in price surveys. A competitive price survey should, therefore, be thoroughly supervised and concentrated in the hands of relatively few people. For purposes of check calls, the name and address of the respondent should always be noted on the questionnaire.

EXHIBIT 6

Example of Influence of Four
Interviewers on Survey Results[a]

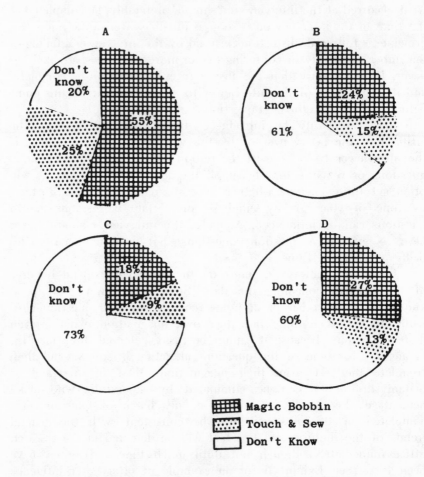

[a] Pie charts indicate responses reported by four different interviewers (A, B, C, and D) in a name-preference survey to the question "What name would you prefer for this new special feature: Magic Bobbin or Touch & Sew?" Note that reports from interviewers B, C, and D are satisfactorily consistent, thus probably reflecting genuine preference; however, the report from A shows extreme variations and may be suspect as to the honesty of the interviewer.

DEPTH INTERVIEW

Motivational research seeks, in the depth interview, to determine why people act as they do. It has received the greatest attention among all the specialized areas in marketing and distribution research. In the past, marketing research has concentrated largely on factual studies, employing quantitative statistical methods. A great deal of nose-counting work has been done to determine how many and what kind of people use a product or service, where they live, where they buy, what they prefer, how they are reached, and how they respond to marketing activities. These established tools of marketing research have revolutionized marketing practices, but they have largely failed to answer one of the most vital questions in marketing, "Why do people buy my competitor's product instead of mine?"

Sales opportunities exist, or fail to exist, in people's minds. Hence, the task is essentially psychological. The psychologist has developed many technical research procedures that are of great value in the study of market behavior. From those psychologists who have a more mechanistic point of view, techniques have been obtained for recording the facts of market behavior as they are expressed in action. From those psychologists who emphasize the motives behind behavior, special techniques have been borrowed that are particularly valuable in appraising the psychological factors that lie behind the observed facts of market behavior.

No psychologist believes that it is possible really to get at motives simply by asking people why they do something, however. The human being is so complex and so much of his behavior is governed by emotions and quirks of personality that it is impossible to discover the real underlying causes of many actions.

Personality operates on at least three different levels. First, there is the outer level, which one reveals to the world. When one speaks of a person as being blustery or calm, one speaks of this level. Second, there is the conscious inner level of personality. This level is the private world of wishful thinking, secret plans, and daydreaming. Third, there is the subconscious level. Here there are strong motivating forces that the individual himself does not recognize. Everyone has had the experience of being surprised or possibly shocked by his own unexpected reactions to many situations.

Thus, below the level of conscious motives are all the unconscious forces that sway us. One individual is different from the next because of experiences that go all the way back to infancy. For example, on the conscious level, nobody is going to admit that he ever does anything out of despicable motives. People do not broadcast the fact that they are cowards or social climbers. Some people buy an automobile as a symbol of worldly success, but they never admit this to other people. Of course, people would like to have others think that everything they do has a well-thought-out logic. Thus, people rationalize their behavior by citing all sorts of possible reasons for their acts, so that they may always look good in other people's eyes, and even in their own eyes. This is a perfectly human thing to do.

The basic problem of motivational research is to penetrate into the conscious and subconscious inner levels of personalities. A large variety of methods can be used in conducting motivational research. The procedures employed in any specific project depend upon the training and background of the individuals conducting the research, as well as the nature of the problem.

The basic methods used in motivational research are (a) depth interviewing; (b) group interviewing; and (c) projective techniques, such as word association, sentence completion, and picture responses. In the developing countries, the most practical method may be the group interview, also called "focused group discussion," described in the next section.

In a depth interview, the investigator tries to find out everything that a respondent knows or thinks about a particular subject, as well as his underlying thoughts or emotions. Although the investigator uses a list of points to guide him, the interview usually proceeds as an informal conversation, with the investigator bringing the respondent back to the subject if he wanders from the point.

GROUP INTERVIEW

In the group interviewing method, a small number of representative consumers, usually from four to six, is brought together for an informal group discussion of the matter under consideration. The discussion leader is a trained psychologist, experienced in group interviewing techniques. He has an outline of specific topics to provide him with the focus of the research; however, he allows the session to follow its natural course, bringing the discussion back to his topics as he feels the need to do so.

In addition to subjects for discussion, the group leader may also introduce various stimuli, such as products, packages, pictures, and advertisements. The entire discussion is recorded on a wire or tape recorder. Comparison of the recording of one session with that of another often shows great contrast. After a session with a group or sessions with several groups have been conducted, the discussion leader listens repeatedly to the recordings. He then analyzes their contents against the background of his psychological training and draws his conclusions with respect to the motivations uncovered. A typical group session lasts about three hours. Cash or gifts are offered to the participants.

Some similarities may be seen between the focused group interviewing procedure and the depth interviewing technique; however, there are also fundamental contrasts between the two. The principal contrast is that group interviewing depends primarily on the interaction of ideas, attitudes, emotions, and beliefs among the various members of the group. The depth interview relies on one individual for this response. In the group interview, one relies on discussion, and heated debate often ensues.

MAIL SURVEYS

In a mail survey, questionnaires are mailed to respondents with a stamped return envelope. The principal applications are studies among small, dispersed groups, for which lists of names are readily available, and also, frequently, panel operations. The advantages in developing countries are mainly that the need for skilled interviewers is eliminated, cost is much lower, and geographic coverage is wider. If replies are anonymous, frank opinions may be obtained, whereas in face-to-face interviews the respondent wants, above all, to appear as an intelligent and rational person.

In the developing countries, only a small proportion of the sample responds, however, and if follow-up efforts are made to increase the response rate, this type of survey can be very time-consuming. Returns in cities are usually 8-15 per cent, but larger returns may be expected in the countryside. When premiums in the form of cash or gifts are used, the response may be expected to reach 40 per cent. (Panels guarantee a specified percentage of return.) Reminder cards resulted in an increase in the rate of replies to 48 per cent in a premium mail survey in Oporto, Portugal.

The major disadvantage of mail surveys is that some types of people respond and others do not; therefore, bias may be involved. Furthermore, there is no control over the sequence in which questions are answered, nor over the environment, nor, indeed, over who actually answers the questionnaire. Where personal checking recalls have been made, it was found that, invariably, the male head of the family was the person who replied and was best aware of the survey. (See Case History 1 for an example of the use of mail questionnaires.)

TELEPHONE INTERVIEW

Only a small number of telephones exist in the developing countries (see Appendix D), and private telephones are registered only by the most wealthy. The buying pattern of the latter is, naturally, substantially different from that of the average local population. Nevertheless, an improvised telephone survey may provide adequate information on certain subjects at low cost and in the shortest time. (See Case History 2 on conducting a telephone survey; Case History 1, on using mail questionnaires, also contains some relevant information on telephone survey results).

A large proportion of telephones in the larger cities is registered by government, trade, and industry. These telephones are obviously suitable for trade, industrial, bank, hotel, and similar project surveys. In trade or industrial surveys, employees and merchants can be interviewed who would otherwise be hard to reach. The results of such surveys are generally quite acceptable.

Results of telephone surveys of the type described in Case History 2 are eye-openers and an incentive toward undertaking a more thorough study of such surveys; for example, for store location, product identification, opinion about a certain publicity project, checking the findings of other research methods, and the like. The telephone survey is also suitable for reaching members of the communities of Europeans living in the developing countries. Separating the foreigners from the local inhabitants on the basis of the names in the telephone directory is a relatively easy task.

Some advantages are less cost than a personal interview, no travel time or expense, closely supervised interviews, and speed in organizing and carrying it out. Disadvantages of telephone surveys in developing countries, apart from the frequent delay in obtaining connections, are the low proportion of population with telephones and the high percentage of refusal to cooperate.

The problem of high refusal to cooperate increases the size of the sample, as does the not-at-home problem in the industrialized countries. In Latin American cities, refusal may reach 50 per cent of the respondents contacted. The percentage is higher in African and Far Eastern cities. In India, Indonesia, and Thailand, very little, if any, cooperation can be expected. The people of these countries are highly suspicious of strangers on the telephone. Also, because of their telephone shyness, many women will not spend much time using it. Conversely, experience has shown that, in well-prepared telephone interviews, the refusal percentage remains between 30 per cent and 50 per cent in cities such as Buenos Aires, Rio de Janeiro, Caracas, Nairobi, Cairo, Abidjan, and Tokyo.

Setting Up Telephone Survey

Selecting Respondents

The number of calls to be placed in order to obtain an adequate sample in the developing countries is a matter of judgment. Only exceptionally does a favorable situation exist that will permit the sample size to be determined by standard procedure. A sample of 200 calls, however, will normally provide data that conform to minimum accepted research standards. This figure of 200 applies to homes.

Select the numbers to be called—a sample from the listings in the local telephone directory. First of all, determine the number of calls that have to be made during the survey, say 200. If the telephone directory has 400 pages, selecting one number on every other page will give 200 calls. Choose an arbitrary number, say 10, and go down the listing until arriving at the tenth name. Selection of numbers to be called should be done before the survey starts, and numbers should be listed on telephone "call sheets" (see below).

Selection of numbers for an industrial survey must be made with particular care. Telephone listings taken from trade publications or issued by trade associations may be preferable to the telephone directory.

Selecting Interviewers

Telephone switchboard operators can make satisfactory interviewers. The telephone interviewer should be a local person with no foreign accent. Educated women interviewers are more apt to establish contact in developing countries than are men and can therefore be used successfully as telephone interviewers.

Interviewing Techniques

The technique that should be used to ask questions depends on the object of the survey. Two basic approaches are (a) unaided recall, where no clues are given nor prompting done to obtain the answer to a question—such as "Did you see any food ads in last Monday's (name of newspaper)?"—and (b) aided recall, where key words are supplied to help the respondent answer a question—such as "Did you see the Brand X ad in last Monday's (name of newspaper)?"

Setting Up Call Sheet

Information collected during each call should be recorded on a call sheet set up in advance. (See Exhibit 7 for a sample call sheet.) To save time, the following information can be filled in on each interviewer's sheet before placing the call: (a) interviewer's name, (b) survey city (or suburb), (c) date of call, and (d) telephone numbers preselected from local directory.

The rest of the information on the sheet should be filled in when the call is made: (a) time of call; (b) disconnects, no answer (after six rings), line busy, refusal to be interviewed—indicated by check mark; (c) sex of respondent; (d) positive or negative responses—"Don't Know" (DK) or "No Answer" (NA) indicated by check in DK/NA column; and (e) other questions or additional comments.

EXHIBIT 7

Sample Telephone Call Sheet (Used for Collecting Information from Telephone Interviews)

Interviewer_____ City_____ Date of Call_____ Starting Time_____ End of Call_____

Y = Yes
N = No
DK = Don't Know
NA = No Answer

Pre-selected Numbers	Disconnects	No Answer or Not at Home	Line Busy	Refusal	Male	Female	1 Y N DK/NA	2 Y N DK/NA	3 Y N DK/NA	Other Questions or Additional Comments

Questions

Length of Interview

If connections can be obtained and lines are available, then one operator can carry out about thirty interviews on three questions in sixty minutes. This means that three interviewers are able to complete about ninety interviews in an hour, not counting busy signals, disconnections, and wrong numbers. The interview questions should be limited to a maximum of three and should avoid taboo subjects such as income, personal hygiene, and household expenditures. Any implication of trying to sell something may result in an immediate refusal to cooperate. The lack of availability of telephone lines may become a deterrent for such surveys in industrial sections of developing countries during business hours.

CHAPTER 3 SAMPLING

Sampling is one of the most important and difficult aspects of marketing research. In Chapter 1, it was stated that it is unnecessary for the marketing research man to be an advanced mathematician. Nevertheless, it is important to realize that sampling is based on mathematical theory if its principles are to be understood effectively. The branch of mathematics from which sampling derives its theoretical background is called the theory of probability, or of chance.

This chapter (and the glossary in Appendix B) will attempt to provide enough sampling knowledge for the reader to be able to recognize the pitfalls and complexities of sampling and to realize that there are situations where his sampling knowledge is inadequate to meet the situation. It is important that the marketing researcher recognizes that a little knowledge about sampling can be dangerous. He will then consult a sampling technician when necessary, just as the business executive, at the proper time, might consult a lawyer or an auditor. (The sampling techniques described below are illustrated in Case Histories 11 and 12 on sampling field techniques and instructing interviewers, respectively.)

BASIC SAMPLING METHODS

Basically the sampling methods that are now used in marketing research can be divided into two broad groups. The first of these groups can be called the random sampling approach, or probability method. The second broad group can be called the quota sampling method.

The random sampling method may be defined as follows: Probability or random sampling is a calculated method of choosing for investigation a number of units or individuals according to some mechanical or automatic principle, unconnected with the subject or purpose of the inquiry, the selection being arranged so that each unit or individual in the universe has an equal chance of being included in the sample.

The quota sampling method may be defined as follows: Quota sampling is based on the assumption that, if cases are selected from the universe according to a predetermined design that provides for specified proportions of various types of cases, based on known characteristics, the sample will be representative in terms of unknown characteristics. The quota method does not employ any sort of mechanical or automatic principle of selection, and, most importantly, the individuals are not selected in a way that gives each individual an equal chance of coming into the sample.

In practice, quota and calculated (random) sampling methods are both used frequently. The selection of any particular sampling design depends upon many factors, such as cost, experience, the problem to be solved, the need for determinable accuracy, and the time available for the research. It is not the intention of this description of sampling to imply that a random method is superior to a nonrandom method. In terms of sampling theory, however, if all other factors are equal, a random sampling method must be considered superior to a quota sampling method.

Only a random, or probability, design will produce results of assessable accuracy. This is so because cases are chosen at random and no prior assumptions are made about the nature of the population. Values based on sample results can be valid only if the sample has been drawn according to a random, or probability, rule. When quota selection is used, it is based on prior assumptions about the population, and selection of respondents is left to the discretion of the field workers. As a result, there are many potential sources of bias and error. Furthermore, there is no way to assess precisely the weight that may have decisive influence upon quota sample results.

Although the probability design will not always produce results that are sufficiently different from a quota sample design to affect any decision that might be based on the findings, the researcher will be in a position to recognize the exact sampling error if he uses a probability sample. Strictly speaking, it is impossible to obtain mathematical validation of a quota sample. This is one of the chief weaknesses of the quota sample.

SAMPLE SIZE

Strictly on the basis of intuition, one might believe that the larger the sample for any survey, the more faith could be placed in the results. Actually, the basic principle of sampling theory is that there is an adequate sample size that is large enough to represent accurately the group from which the sample is drawn (within determined limits). Increasing the sample size beyond this point reduces the chances of error more than is necessary. Further increase in accuracy as a result of an increase in the size of the sample beyond a necessary point is slight, relative to the cost of making these additions.

Calculation of Probability Sample

As to the sampling procedure, each type of sample plan has a distinct mathematical formula to relate four key characteristics (indicated A, B, C, and D in the following example) determining sample size, so that the actual size desired can be computed. Construction, substitution, and correct interpretation of these formulas fall into the province of the professional sampling statistician, who is equipped to deal with this highly technical subject. In order to demonstrate how these considerations interact to influence the necessary sample size, a simple example is given. (Those terms in quotation marks in the example are defined in detail in Appendix B.)

Suppose one wishes to obtain an up-to-date estimate of the average years of education of users of sewing machines. Assume that it is important to know this accurately because the education level is a significant factor in the sale, preparation of sewing instructions and classes, and advertising. Let us assume that the four critical sample-size characteristics are as follows:

(1) The permissible "sampling error" that can be allowed is half a year of education. If the over-all permissible error is relatively large, there will be too large an error within the subgroups (elementary school, high school, and the like), each of which makes up only part of the total sample size selected.

(2) The possibility that the sample results may fall outside the permissible error must be kept very small. One has to be more than 99 per cent sure. In a statistical sense, this means that the true value of the "universe" will be included within 3 "standard errors" on either side of the sample value in more than 99 cases out of 100. This means that there is only 1 chance in 100 that the results will be due to chance.

(3) The variation usually experienced in measuring this factor, known statistically as the "standard deviation," is estimated from previous studies to be about four years of education.

(4) With regard to cost, including expenses of probability sample design and preparing the questionnaire to be used, interviewing, tabulation, and report-writing, it can be estimated that it will cost about the equivalent of U.S. $8.60 to conduct a personal interview with a user.

The principal data are these:

(1) The permissible error limit, 0.5 years (A)
(2) The allowable confidence limit, 99 per cent, or 3.0 standard errors (B)
(3) The variation of the characteristic being measured, i.e., the standard deviation, 4.0 years (C)
(4) Cost per interview, $8.60 (D).

The appropriate calculation is as follows:

$$\text{Formula:} \quad \frac{1}{n} = \frac{d^2}{t^2 \, s^2}$$

where d = error limit   0.5 years
     t = confidence limit   3.0 (standard errors)
     s = standard deviation   4.0 years
     n = sample size   (?)

Substitute the above in the formula:

$$\frac{1}{n} = \frac{(0.5)^2}{(3.0)^2 \ (4.0)^2} = \frac{0.25}{9(16)} = \frac{0.25}{144}$$

$$\frac{1}{n} = \frac{0.25}{144}$$

$$0.25n = 144$$
$$n = 576$$

By this procedure, a sample size of 576 sewing machine users is reached. This means an estimated total cost of \$3,317 (576 x \$8.60).

This may be too much money for the management to spend on one survey at that time. If the management decides that the somewhat detailed breakdown data are not critical and that a permissible error limit of 1 year rather than 0.5 years (A) is satisfactory and a standard deviation of 5 years rather than 4 years (C) is acceptable, then the sample size necessary to get a result that conforms to the criteria set up is 225 users. The total cost of the survey will obviously decline markedly.

Suppose that the basic characteristic to be changed is, for example, the standard deviation. If this is increased from 4 years to 7.5 years, then the necessary sample size to meet the original set of criteria, including the 99 per cent confidence limit initially set, will be about 2,025 people. Where d equals 1 year and s equals 6 years, the number of people will be 324. It is apparent that a change in any of the factors involved has an important effect on the necessary size of the sample.

SAMPLE VALIDATING

After the field work is completed, it is necessary to check on the actual sample obtained so as to be certain that the information is adequate from a sampling point of view. The basic and logical rule that should be kept in mind is that all methods for testing the reliability of a sample rest upon the same assumption: namely, that the reliability of a sample is determined by the relative consistency or stability of the response from the field. The terms "consistency" and "stability" mean that the addition of more cases or interviews will not significantly increase the accuracy of the final findings.

For the developing countries, a suitable method for a short-cut reliability test may be the cumulative-frequency method. (See Exhibit 8 for a table of cumulative frequencies.) The procedure for testing a probability sample by this method may be described in four steps as follows: (a) arranging the questionnaires in chance or random order, (b) dividing the questionnaires into groups, (c) deciding the item on which the test is to be made, and (d) preparing a table of cumulative frequencies.

Chance order is important to the correct application of this short-cut test for sample reliability; therefore, shuffle the questionnaires so that they are in chance order.

The number of groups into which the questionnaires can be divided is selected to be easily manipulated. If there are 500 questionnaires, they will ordinarily be divided into 10 groups. In the determination of the number to be included within each group in large surveys, it is usually more convenient if 100 questionnaires are in each class, as this makes the calculation of percentages easy. It is not necessary for each group to contain exactly the same amount of questionnaires. Likewise, it is not necessary for all replies to be included in the groups.

Assume, for example, that there are 1,027 completed questionnaires. These might be divided into 10 groups of 100 each. The remaining 27 questionnaires may be omitted from the test or added to one of the groups. Assume that the remaining 27 have been omitted from the test and that the questionnaires have been divided into 10 groups of 100 each. The 10 groups of questionnaires would be distributed as follows:

GROUPS	INTERVIEW NUMBERS
1	1- 100
2	101- 200
3	201- 300
4	301- 400

EXHIBIT 8

Example of Validating Sample by Frequency of Answers

Group Number[a]	Frequency of Occurrence[b]	Cumulative Frequency of Occurrence[c]	Cumulative Number of Cases[d]	Cumulative Percentage of Occurrence[e]
1	63	63	100	63.0
2	72	135	200	67.5
3	78	213	300	71.0
4	75	288	400	72.0
5	71	359	500	71.4
6	65	424	600	70.7
7	67	491	700	70.1
8	81	572	800	71.5
9	59	631	900	70.1
10	61	692	1,000	69.2

[a] Numbers of groups of 100 questionnaires.

[b] Frequency with which any given answer occurs in each of these groups.

[c] Cumulative totals from Column 2.

[d] Total cumulative number of questionnaires that are included in each group.

[e] Cumulative percentage of occurrence of tested item, arrived at by dividing Column 3 by Column 4. Sample is valid, because there is reasonable stability or consistency of cumulative percentage of occurrence from first to last group.

GROUPS	INTERVIEW NUMBERS
5	401- 500
6	501- 600
7	601- 700
8	701- 800
9	801- 900
10	901-1,000

Select from a questionnaire, or from a schedule reporting observations, one or more items to be used in the test for reliability (usually a reply or replies to a specific question). If only one question is asked in a survey, the sample must obviously be tested on this basis alone.

Count the frequency with which the item being tested occurs and calculate the cumulative percentage of the occurrence.

CHAPTER 4 QUANTITATIVE RESEARCH

Quantitative market analysis primarily covers determining the economic potential and forecasting the size of national and regional markets. Procedures determining market saturation and basic techniques of forecasting are also described here. The statistical procedures used in this chapter are simplified as to computation but will still provide good orientation on the market potential in most developing countries for any given commodity. Knowledge of statistical sources is a mandatory prerequisite; and the well-established sources of statistics are listed in the last section of this chapter.

Quantitative research procedures are particularly important concepts for the developing countries in that the planning of business enterprises often starts from scratch there or new products are introduced that were unknown before. The straight statistical numbers for population and income that are used for the industrialized countries must be substantially adjusted for the developing countries due to the limited purchasing power that fluctuates erratically from region to region and to the geographical dispersion of the population. The latter adds to the limitations of buying ability.

The fact is often overlooked that in the lower-income countries many families do not live in normal registered houses or apartments; many lead self-subsisting lives in agricultural or nomadic pastoral communities. Often the primitive way of life excludes them from the measurable economy. Therefore, findings from surveys and general considerations concerning market size and potential must be applied only to the adjusted, and thus reduced, population.

MARKET POTENTIAL

According to the example shown in Exhibit 9 of a pragmatic, quantitative analysis for estimating a potential market in a group of countries, the percentage of population that may be included in the potential market demand varies with per capita income from country to country. Greece and Spain may include about 67 per cent of their population when estimating the potential market for a sewing machine or similar household item valued around $100, but countries such as Peru and Costa Rica may include only about 50 per cent of their population, and Brazil, Ecuador, Zambia, and Senegal can include only 30 per cent of their population to arrive at the potential market for such a household item. The population of the potential market may be expected to have incomes that give them the buying power of an average family in industrialized countries.

The curve shown in Exhibit 9 of evaluation of demand in the developing countries for a given commodity is the result of experience in each of the countries plotted. It indicates that failure to take into consideration the large differences in income from country to country may be costly in underestimating or overestimating the market potential, and that business people develop a market at their own peril if they do not determine fairly accurately beforehand the potential size of the market. It also indicates that the statistics of a single country, taken alone, cannot serve as an adequate yardstick of market size. Only in relation to other countries does the income of a certain country become a meaningful measure. Such measures also presuppose concrete experience in several countries, preferably at both extremes and in the middle of the income scale. Besides determining the size of the national market, the market potential by areas or provinces is equally or even more important.

Area Market Potential

It is common, well-established practice in international trade to view and analyze sales and all other business data in terms of geographic areas, generally by countries. The uniform legal and economic order of

EXHIBIT 9

Method of Estimating Potential
Market in Group of Countries
(For Sewing Machine Priced at U.S. $100)

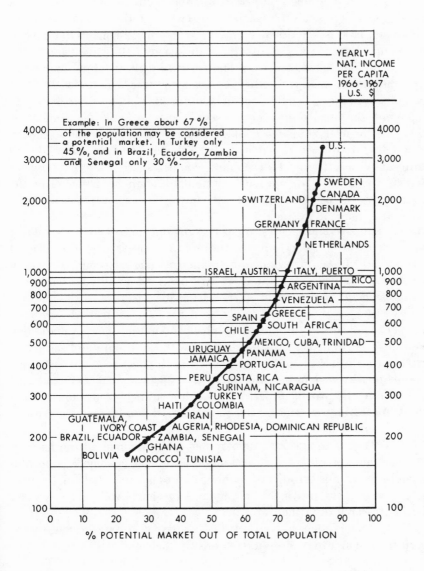

% POTENTIAL MARKET OUT OF TOTAL POPULATION

Example: In Greece about 67% of the population may be considered a potential market. In Turkey only 45%, and in Brazil, Ecuador, Zambia and Senegal only 30%.

YEARLY NAT. INCOME PER CAPITA 1966-1967 U.S. $

a national market serves as a natural background, and official statistics serve as a natural yardstick for measuring performance of any enterprise against the national market potential. Unfortunately, the analysis often stops right there, at the level of the national market, without proceeding further with the analysis of smaller geographical areas within the country in the same manner.

In the developing countries, real opportunities for marketers lie in regional and cultural market segments, rather than in broad national markets. National markets are highly fragmented in terms of income, social class, language and tribal differences, and other socio-economic characteristics. The institutional structure needed to integrate these markets either is organized very inefficiently or is completely absent. The boundaries of most regions were drawn to represent the local dominance of a particular subcultural element so that the official statistics could conform to the cultural segments. Examples of this are found in India, Pakistan, Nigeria, and states in tropical Africa. In most developing countries, there are government statistics available on provinces, similar to those issued for the country as a whole. (Exhibit 10 shows, as an example, an area marketing map of Portugal.

Progressive and successive business organizations take advantage of these data on the developing countries to measure performance and assess sales quotas in proportion to the real market potential in each territorial political subdivision, such as province, county, department, *arrondissement*, and so forth. Territorial analysis will—

(1) Indicate to the management where and how much marketing assistance is needed, identify provinces with poor and good sales, and establish an order of these provinces from the best to the worst, with the national average in the middle.

(2) In the provinces performing below average, cause one to take steps toward improvement, after having found and studied the reasons for bad performance.

(3) Assess annual sales quotas per each province on the basis of the real market potential. Checking against history may be done by establishing trends through hypothetical quotas computed for the past several years, but provinces containing large cities will probably need further research refinement.

(4) Enable one to reward the agents of provinces with good performance and to explore the reasons for their success.

EXHIBIT 10

Marketing Map of Portugal
(Purchasing Power of Principal Political
Subdivisions by Population and Income per Capita)

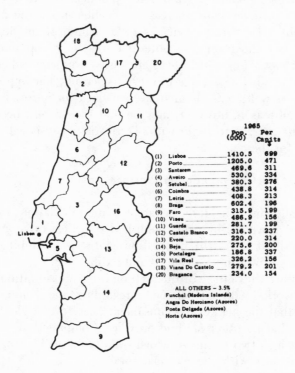

		1965 Pop. (000)	Per Capita $
(1)	Lisboa	1410.5	699
(2)	Porto	1205.0	471
(3)	Santarem	469.6	311
(4)	Aveiro	530.0	334
(5)	Setubal	380.3	276
(6)	Coimbra	438.8	314
(7)	Leiria	408.3	213
(8)	Braga	602.4	196
(9)	Faro	315.9	199
(10)	Viseu	486.9	156
(11)	Guarda	281.7	199
(12)	Castelo Branco	316.3	237
(13)	Evora	220.0	314
(14)	Beja	275.6	200
(16)	Portalegre	186.8	337
(17)	Vila Real	326.2	156
(18)	Viana Do Castelo	279.2	201
(20)	Bragance	234.0	154

ALL OTHERS – 3.5%
Funchal (Madeira Islands)
Angra Do Heroismo (Azores)
Ponta Delgada (Azores)
Horta (Azores)

Source: "World Marketing Survey," *Automobile International* (April, 1966), p 41; reprinted by permission of Johnson International Publishing Corp., (New York).

(5) In budgeting and planning, use the above findings for expenditure, store and equipment investment, personnel promotion, price policy, product mix, and the like.

(6) Perhaps cause the management to organize contests among the provinces, with escalating rewards corresponding to the current state of efficiency and goals above the average of the national market.

(7) Provide a realistic ground for practical day-to-day business strategies. For instance, any increase or decline in sales in a territory may, in reality, be either a success or a failure. It all depends on whether or not the economic potential was fully explored in that territory. Often salesmen's contests are easily won simply because the performance was below average in previous periods. The opposite cases are frequent as well; i.e., salesmen are penalized for a slow increase in sales. The real reason, however, may be that their recent performance was above the average to begin with. Territorial analysis will provide a proper basis for these judgments.

Calculation of Market Potential by Province

The following are three examples of calculation of market potential for provinces by using published statistics: (a) consumption statistics (Exhibit 11), (b) population statistics (Exhibit 12), and (c) purchasing-power index (Table 4 and Exhibit 13).

The primary advantage of the method using consumption statistics is that it works with actual facts regarding the amount of the commodity that the market has consumed. Therefore, it yields the sort of accuracy that no other method provides. Columns 2, 3, and 4 may each be split into two columns, which would thus enable a comparison of one's own sales with the national totals.

Not all territories can increase in regular proportion, however. The market potential should actually be determined by factors varying from one territory to another. Their weights should be applied to arrive at a potential conforming more accurately to the real situation on the market, as shown in Exhibit 12. The basic weakness of the weighted method lies in the arbitrary nature of selecting weights. Often what is called judgment is largely guesswork. There is no consistent and precise basis for the selection and weighting of the influencing factors. All this is left to human intuition.

Calculation of market potential using purchasing-power index statistics is illustrated in Table 4 and, graphically, in Exhibit 13.

EXHIBIT 11

Market Potential Derived from Consumption Statistics by Principal Political Subdivisions

(1)	(2)	(3)	(4)
Territory[a]	National Total Consumption[b]	Relative Potential (*percentage of national total*)[c]	Market Potential (*planned*)[d]
A	2,500	12.7	2,794
B	880	4.5	990
C	6,700	34.3	7,546
(etc.)	- - - - - -	- - - - - -	- - - - - -
National Total	19,550	100.0	22,000

[a] Territorial units: provinces, countries, sales territories, and so forth.

[b] Latest available data on sales, covering period of one year.

[c] Column 2 converted to percentages. Total equals 100 per cent.

[d] Column 3 multiplied by total anticipated sales (22,000) during period for which potentials are being planned.

EXHIBIT 12

Market Potential Derived from Population Statistics by Principal Political Subdivisions
(Weighted)

Territory[a]	Population		Dwellings		Occupations		Sum of Factors[d]	Market Index[e]	Market Potential[f]
	Percentage of National Total[b]	Weighted Percentage (x3)[c]	Percentage of National Total[b]	Weighted Percentage (x1)[c]	Percentage of National Total[b]	Weighted Percentage (x2)[c]			
A	13.5	40.5	14.0	14.0	11.8	23.6	78.1	13.0	91.0
B	6.0	18.0	7.2	7.2	6.0	12.0	37.2	6.2	43.4
C	35.0	105.0	39.7	39.7	21.3	42.6	187.3	31.2	218.4
(etc.)	----	----	----	----	----	----	----	----	----
National Total	100.0	300.0	100.0	100.0	100.0	200.0	600.0	100.0	700.0

[a] Provinces or other geographical units.

[b] Percentages of national total or area being studied for each factor.

[c] Columns 2, 4, and 6 multiplied by their weight.

[d] Items in Columns 3, 5, and 7 added horizontally.

[e] Column 8 divided by sum of weights. This is your market index; i.e., percentage of total sales possibilities assigned to each province.

[f] Products in Column 9 multiplied by total expected sales volume for entire market (700.0), with two places pointed off, since index is expressed as whole percentages. This is your market potential in money, units, cases, or other units used in total.

TABLE 4

Market Potential Derived from
Purchasing-Power Index in Portugal
(For Sales of X Product)

Province[a]	Purchasing-Power Index[b] (*per cent*)	Sales of X Product[c] (*per cent*)	Percentage Deviation from Potential[d]
Aveiro	5.18	6.16	19.0
Beja	1.88	1.56	(17.0)
Braga	4.99	5.24	5.0
Braganca	1.85	1.33	(28.0)
Castelo Branco	2.73	2.51	(8.0)
Coimbra	3.99	4.47	12.0
Evora	1.87	1.65	(12.0)
Faro	3.08	3.08	0.0
Guarda	2.22	2.13	(4.0)
Leiria	4.58	4.98	8.7
Lisboa	30.12	41.57	38.0
Portalegre	1.49	1.22	(18.0)
Porto	15.81	21.11	33.5
(etc.)	- -	- -	- -
National Total	100.00	100.00	

[a]Provinces listed by name.

[b]Purchasing-power index per province, in per cent, when not available from government or private research firms, derived from elementary statistics on population and income, weighted by factors such as automobile registrations, which are frequently available. (In above example on Portugal, index was provided by GFK-Nürnberg, Gesellschaft fur Konsum-, Markt- und Absatzforschung e.V.8500 Nürnberg, Burgschmietstr. 2.)

[c]Percentage of sales or any other business performance quantified and listed by province.

[d]Differences of sales data over (or under) purchasing-power data, listed by province in percentages.

EXHIBIT 13

Graph of Market Potential Derived from Purchasing-Power Index

Current Order	Portuguese Provinces [a]	Previous Order	Percentage Difference
1	Lisboa	1	
2	Porto	2	
3	Santarem	4	
4	Aveiro	6	
5	Setubal	7	
6	Coimbra	5	
7	Leiria	3	
8	Braga	9	
9	Faro	8	
10	Viseu	13	
11	Guarda	12	
12	Castelo Branco	10	
13	Evora	11	
14	Beja	15	
15	Portalegre	14	
16	Vila Real	16	
17	Viana Do Castelo	17	
18	Braganca	18	

[a] Listing of provinces rearranged in order, from best- to worst-performing province, presented graphically. If

Market Saturation and Market Potential

Market saturation (the amount of certain articles in use) may determine the complementary market potential (the number of households that do not use the article as yet) in the most logical way. Market saturation can, therefore, be the most acceptable and revealing indicator for managements' marketing policies. A certain amount of historical statistics and a number of good judgments are necessary, however. When making a market-saturation computation, one has to estimate the yearly amounts of retired or newly added items under study to arrive at the size of the stock in the hands of the users at the end of the period corresponding to the service life of the items, as shown in Table 5 and Exhibit 14. Further, the number of consumers must be determined.

In the developing countries, one may have an advantage in determining the ownership more precisely than in the highly industrialized countries, in that more commodities of interest for marketing research are, or have been, wholly imported; thus, the yearly additions to the market are evident from the government statistics of the importing or exporting countries. Local production for the given article is generally easy to estimate in the developing countries.

Market-saturation data are particularly useful when comparable standards in other economically similar countries are available, for the latter make the findings more meaningful. But, in general, a product with a higher saturation level means a larger number of replacement sales for this product, as well as sales growth from a growing population and new family formations. Conversely, a product with a lower saturation level means fewer replacement sales, but greater sales potential from an untapped market of likely new owners.

An example of sewing machine marketing in Portugal is shown in Table 5 and Exhibits 14 and 15 and is used to demonstrate the procedure in determining the market saturation. The formula is as follows:

$$\% \text{ market saturation} = \frac{\text{stock in hands of users}}{\text{number of households}}$$

The number of units in users' hands in a country is arrived at by adding all units sold yearly ("New Added Units") for the assumed

TABLE 5

Market-Saturation Computation
from Sales History and Survival Rate
for Sewing Machines in Portugal up to 1969

Period[a]	New Added Units (*thousands*)[b]	Still in Use (*per cent*)[c]	Stock in Hands of Users (*thousands*)	
			Amount[d]	Cumulative Amount
1925-29	114	5	5.7	5.7
1930-34	119	15	17.9	23.6
1935-39	69	30	20.7	44.3
1940-44	63	54	34.0	78.3
1945-49	109	74	77.7	156.0
1950-54	159	84	133.6	289.6
1955-59	141	91	128.3	417.9
1960-64	148	96	142.1	560.0
1965-69	102	100	102.0	662.0

Net households

Portugal population (1968), 2,570,000 households (9.2 million people), less 42 per cent for households that are not potential users = 1,490,000 net households.

Solution

Stock in hands or users $\dfrac{662,000}{1,490,000}$ = 44.5 per cent
Net households

Market saturation is 44.5 per cent at end of 1969.
Market potential, therefore, is 55.5 per cent or, in units, 827,000 (55.5 per cent of 1,490,000).

[a]Note reduced sales during war period 1940-44. From 1930 to 1934, depression years throughout world, sales increased slightly, however, due to subsisting nature of article. These sales had obviously been borrowed from future, for sales dropped markedly during postdepression period 1935-39.

[b]Represents sales.

[c]Represents survival rate.

[d]Column 2 multiplied by Column 3.

EXHIBIT 14

Graph of Market-Saturation Computation
(For Sewing Machines in Portugal up to 1969)

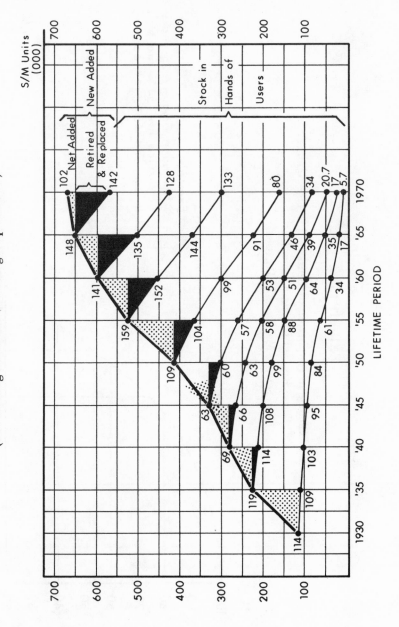

EXHIBIT 15

Example of Change in Proportion of Units Still in Use Against Those Retired During Service Life

(For Sewing Machines in Portugal)

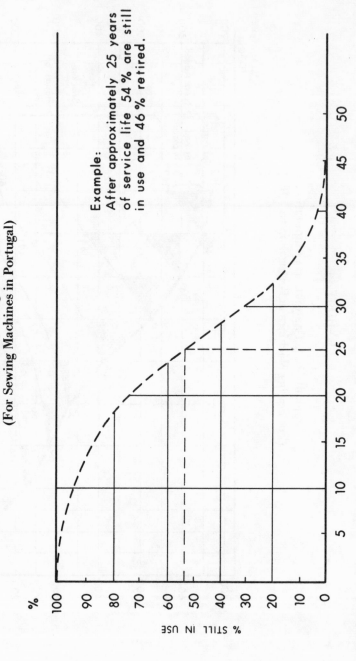

useful lifetime period of the article under consideration. In each year, deduction is estimated for gradual and progressive retirement due to use, obsolescence, destruction, emigration (such as Indians from Kenya and French from Algeria), and a survival quantity at the end of each year, or period of several years if preferred, is reached. Cumulation then results in "Stock in Hands of Users" for the entire useful lifetime period or any part of it.

To determine the extent of retirement due to use and obsolescence, the rate of trade-in sales and the age of the traded-in articles, if obtainable, are most helpful indicators. To determine the extent of destruction due to fire, calamities, war, and the like, a revision of the history of the useful lifetime period must be undertaken, and the number of dwellings destroyed should be estimated. (For instance, London had about 60,000 home fires, with 13,000 dwellings totally destroyed, in 1968.)

The number of households is arrived at by taking the total population, adjusted to the number of households. (Households, unlike families, include unattached individuals. In Portugal, for instance, there are 3.6 members per household.) Next, reductions are made to obtain "net households." This means that households that would not be potential buyers because of income, age, sickness, nonwired houses, and the like are deducted. This also applies to families who do not live in houses and flats. Income and whether the family lives in a house or a flat are, of course, the most significant factors in the developing countries. The influence of income may be obtained by proceeding along the outline in Exhibit 9. In some of these countries, the statistics of families who do not live in registered houses and flats are obtainable (Brazil, for instance). These statistics then should be used instead of using the estimating method shown in Exhibit 9.

One may be tempted to ignore the determination of "net households," but planning for households that cannot afford the price of the article is a basic mistake and causes the planning of overcapacity of production and waste of effort in marketing. In fact, projecting findings—for example, ownership of a household article—from an otherwise correct sample to the unadjusted official national total population number is one of the frequent mistakes in quantitative research in the developing countries.

The rate of replacement demand can easily be determined once market-saturation computation has been accomplished. In Exhibit 14, the section "Retired & Replaced" indicates at the same time the portion of the replacement. Knowledge of the extent of replacement is important for management, because marketing policy changes in many respects depending on whether the prospect is a first-time buyer or an old user of the item.

In order to estimate the size of the replacement demand during the coming years, one must know the amount of yearly additions and retirements of the given item that occurred on the market during the period corresponding to its service life. Exhibit 15 graphically represents an example of change in the proportion of the percentage of sewing machines still in use, as well as the complementary percentage of units retired during any point in the service life of sewing machines in Portugal. The size of the replacement market in forecasting is then obtained by extrapolating the latter proportion. Determination of the shape of the curve representing total market is an indispensible tool in long-range forecasting.

The process of market-saturation calculation also helps in estimating the market share of competitive brands for imported items, if yearly additions are broken down by country of origin. It is often sufficient to establish the market demand pattern by consulting elementary components, such as countries of origin—for instance, Japan, European countries, or the United States. The brand names and types of merchandise can then be established more easily, if needed at all. Granted, the market share by brand is usually a by-product of a consumer survey. Undertaking a survey in the developing countries may be difficult, time-consuming, and expensive, but establishing the competitive market-share pattern, as described above, may take only a few hours' work if the information is extracted from published statistics on importing countries or, preferably at times, on exporting ones. These statistics are available in the commercial consulates of the principal capitals.

FORECASTING

The marketing researcher will most often be asked to prepare three types of forecasting: a quantitative forecast concerning future sales, an economic environment forecast, and a measurement of trends of economic factors that cause changes in consumer demand in the sector to be forecast. In order to prepare a good forecast, the basic rule is to know and understand the past and the present of the subject to be forecast. Proper forecasting techniques combine this knowledge with skill in handling statistical data. These techniques may be classified as follows: (a) mechanical forecast, (b) lead series, (c) opinion and expectations, (d) causal forecast, and (e) business cycle.

Mechanical Forecast

An approach is classified as mechanical if conclusions are drawn on the basis of past experience, without any examination of past and current causal forces. If, for example, a forecast concludes that a particular series of data is going to move upward because it is now going in that direction, it is a mechanical technique of forecasting. This approach is sometimes called "naïve forecasting" or a "persistence prediction." It simply projects the current situation into the future. It means forecasting that the future will be the same as the present is.

Lead Series

The idea here is that at any given moment there exist plans at various stages of completion. If these plans can be uncovered in their early stages, it is possible to tell what will happen during the later stages. The forecast of the future becomes a matter of summing up the effects of plans now under way. Business plans for purchase of new plant and equipment are examples of this classification. The number of people in certain age classes, birth rates, and percentage of population reaching marrying age can be forecast indicators based on relatively safe grounds that permit the forecaster to establish a lead series. This constitutes one or more trends in economic indicators that usually precede movement in the economy as a whole or in the sector to be forecast.

Opinions and Expectations

In this approach, the forecast is based on the opinions or expectations of others. It may be what businessmen expect their sales, orders, and similar factors to be, or what consumers expect to spend, or what other forecasters believe will happen. This approach may be based on existing facts, such as findings of consumer surveys or consumer juries. (See Case History 6 on the use of marketing research techniques in forecasting.)

Causal Forecast

This forecasting technique may be also called "historical." It involves many specific techniques, but all of them have one thing in common: An attempt is made to determine the causes of the fluctuations in the series to be forecast, and then these causes are measured and evaluated.

The following example of causal forecasting is taken from the apparel industry and illustrates a forecast covering women's dresses. It is a method used also by shoe, textile, and mail-order firms and provides a good example of the technique. Various types of dresses, with the waistline worn at the waist, above the waist, or below the waist—for example, Empire, Princess, A-line, Trapeze, and so on—are listed. Columns opposite each style are provided for checking the colors, such as black, white, blue, red, and the like. The result is a two-dimensional table showing the frequency of occurrence of two of the basic elements of fasion, style and color. By making a series of such counts through time, say twenty-thirty years, the rising and declining interest of the buying public in various types of dress design and color is plotted.

An amusing but also interesting indicator in women's wear forecast is the relationship between economic prosperity, on the one hand, and the hemline and bustline, on the other. To get short-tempered about short skirts seems a short-sighted view, for it is demonstrable from the historical evidence that the elevation of ladies' hemlines and the plunging of bustlines have gone hand in hand with economic booms, and the reverse fashion has always come back during hard times. As it was in the soaring 1960's, so it was in the gay 1920's of the Charleston era, in the period of Louis XVI, in prosperous Crete, and so on. This suggests a tentative conclusion that the less ladies have to spend on clothes, the more they are clothed. Whether this is a leading or lagging economic indicator still remains to be seen.

Business Cycle

This method has been the subject of a great deal of research by economists. Its research is concerned with both the description of past business fluctuations and an attempt to establish the reasons for these movements in order to forecast peaks and valleys in future trends. Ordinary consumption movements seem to be the effect rather than the cause of the business cycle; however, there is good reason to believe that the movements of the capital sector of the economy and of durable goods represent key causes in a more fundamental sense. But there are numerous theories explaining the causes of cycles.

The better-known business-cycle theories are the following: (a) the monetary theory—attributes the cycle to the expansion and contraction of bank credit (R. G. Hawtrey *et al.*); (b) the innovation theory—attributes the cycle to the clustering of important inventions, such as the railroad (J. A. Schumpeter, A. H. Hansen, *et al.*); (c) the psychological theory—treats the cycle as a case of people's infecting each other with pessimistic or optimistic expectations (A. C. Pigou, W. Bagehot, *et al.*); (d) the underconsumption theory—claims too much income goes to wealthy or thrifty people compared with what can be invested (J. A. Hobson, W. T. Foster and W. Catchings, *et al.*); (e) the overinvestment theory—claims too much rather than too little investment causes recessions (F. A. Hayek, L. von Mises, *et al.*); and (f) the sunspot and weather-crop theories (W. S. Jevons, H. L. Moore).

SOURCE OF STATISTICS

Statistics are the basis of all quantitative research. The knowledge of where to obtain statistics for any given problem is half the success in quantitative marketing research. It is important for an industry or a business in the developing countries continually to maintain adequate and up-to-date statistics on its own trade and some basic statistics on the national economy. The mere record of sales that is sufficient for accounting purposes—for showing profit or loss—is rarely adequate for marketing needs and forecasting. What these quantitative internal data should comprise will vary with the particular business, but generally the information should not be confined to mere total sales data analyzed by geographical area but should also include sales by size of packing, size of order, type of customer, season of year, and size and type of community.

Industry and traders in developing countries would be well advised to maintain also at least a minimum of quantitative statistical records of their own and of competitive trading—both local and export. Statistics on competitive performance, however, are probably the most complex and difficult commercial information to compile, in particular for a multinational corporation. The formula "competitive production plus import less export," by countries of origin and countries of destination, is the ideal competitive business barometer for commodities traded internationally, in both the industrialized and the developing countries.

Maintaining such a record may be easier said than done, but it pays to attempt to provide this statistic, even if it has to be less than up-to-date or with a considerable lapse of time. One has to wait for the official government statistics to be made available in all countries involved. In European countries, the time lag for official import/export statistics is three-four months. For local production, these figures are available from trade associations within one-two months. From about 180 countries, statistics covering national import/export for the previous year are usually available not later than August.

The return on such an investment may not be immediate, and the expenditure may seem at first sight, especially in developing countries, to be relatively heavy compared with the marketing costs of any one project. When compared with the continued wasted outlay that may otherwise ensue, in both marketing and production costs, on unsuccessful projects, however, it appears in a different light. Thus, for the long-term success of an expanding business, statistical systems on one's own and competitive trading are essential. (See Case Histories 3, 4, and 5 for information on the importance of statistics and methods of gathering them.)

Traders in the developing countries who intend to introduce statistical records without previous experience should contact a research agency well acquainted with reliable sources, rather than to try to collect data on their own. Many traders believe that occasional clippings from magazines may serve the purpose; however, that is the surest way to cause business data to accumulate without any system and to provide a confusing basis for business decisions.

A primary source used throughout the world today is the United Nations—with its flock of international agencies, commissions, and organizations. The quasi-regulatory activities of these bodies require that they gather, evaluate, and disseminate information on an international level. Their publications are available (in English, and some in English and French) to everyone at a modest cost. Among the U.N. publications, for instance, are the *Statistical Bulletin of Latin America*, the *Survey of Economic Conditions in Africa*, and the *Economic Bulletin* . . . (for Africa, Asia and the Far East, Europe, and Latin America). Generally, this information is made comparable, country by country, and to the international researcher today comparability of data is often the biggest single problem.

Here is a list of agencies publishing their own statistics, all of which may be used by the researcher in the developing countries:

ECA	(The Economic Commission for Africa)
ECAFE	(The Economic Commission for Asia and the Far East)
ECLA	(The Economic Commission for Latin America)
ILO	(International Labor Organization)
FAO	(Food and Agricultural Organization)
UNESCO	(United Nations Educational, Scientific, and Cultural Organization)
ICAO	(International Civil Aviation Organization)
IBRD	(International Bank for Reconstruction and Development)
IMF	(International Monetary Fund)
WHO	(World Health Organization)
UPU	(The Universal Postal Union)
ITU	(The International Telecommunications Union)
UICF	(The International Union of Railways)
IATA	(International Air Transport Association)

This group of agencies spans a great deal of the market place and many of the applications in industry in which firms in the developing countries are interested.

Other multinational organizations—such as the OECD (Organization for Economic Cooperation and Development), EEC (European Economic Community), and GATT (General Agreement on Tariffs and Trade)—gather and publish extensive and very valuable international

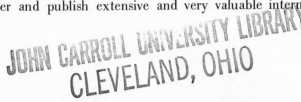

data. Excellent commercial information sources are the U.S. Department of Commerce, which offers the World Trade Information Service; the International Statistical Institute in The Hague, Netherlands; and the Pan American Statistical Institute in Washington, D.C. *Business International*, published in New York, and *Noticias*, published by the National Foreign Trade Council in New York, are good professional services.

Beyond these well-known information services are a host of services provided by manufacturers, trade associations, and banks for their members and customers. A good example is the service offered by the Chase Manhattan Bank in New York and by Barclays Bank, D.C.O., in London. Information on the subject of particular areas or sources—such as labor, productivity, foreign trade rules, arbitration, and national trade—can be obtained from the National Industrial Conference Board, Inc., in New York; the National Foreign Trade Council, Inc., in New York; and the International Chamber of Commerce in Paris.

No list of international data sources would be complete without *The Statesman's Year Book*, which is published by The Macmillan Company in London, and the *Exporters' Encyclopaedia*, published by Dun & Bradstreet Publications in New York. These works contain highly comprehensive information about virtually every country in the world. For advertising international marketing research, an excellent source is the *Concise Guide to International Markets*, issued by the International Advertising Association. The latter also lists advertising agencies in the developing countries.

The addresses of some of the organizations mentioned above are included here:

> Barclays Bank, D.C.O., 54 Lombard Street, London EC3, U.K.
>
> Business International, 757 Third Avenue, New York, N.Y., U.S.A.
>
> EEC (European Economic Community), 23 Avenue de la Joyeuse Entrée, Brussels, Belgium.
>
> GATT (General Agreement on Tariffs and Trade), Villa le Bocage, Palais des Nations, Geneva, Switzerland.
>
> International Advertising Association, U.K. Chapter, 15-19 Great Chapel Street, London, WIV 4AX, U.K.

International Chamber of Commerce, 38 Cours Albert I, Paris 8, France.

National Foreign Trade Council, Inc., 10 Rockefeller Plaza, New York, N.Y., U.S.A.

National Industrial Conference Board, Inc., 845 Third Avenue, New York, N.Y., U.S.A.

OECD (Organization for Economic Cooperation and Development), 2 Rue André-Pascal, Paris 16, France.

United Nations, Second Avenue, New York, N.Y., U.S.A.

U.S. Department of Commerce, Washington, D.C., U.S.A.

CHAPTER 5 PRODUCT RESEARCH

Usually packaging, trade name, trademark, label, and design are included in product research because of their close association with the product itself and the similarity of research procedures. Specialized techniques have been developed to solve problems in all product research areas. The following techniques will be considered here: (a) adapting existing product, (b) new product, (c) product-line analysis, (d) package research, (e) panel research, and (f) test marketing.

ADAPTING EXISTING PRODUCT

Since consumer preferences are constantly changing, progressive marketers periodically subject their products to marketing research. Minor product changes, due to supply shortages, changes of raw material, improved manufacturing methods, or keeping up with competition, are made from time to time in the normal course of business. Sound managerial judgment, combined with information from the field, is usually adequate for lesser changes and enables the product to keep in tune with current demand.

If, however, the merchant intends to revitalize sales with a stimulating campaign based on a substantially improved product or a new name and package, research should be done on the intended variations, and a probability of higher than fifty-fifty must be established to the effect that the change will be for the better. These tests invariably show how sensitive the public is to even small changes. For instance, dropping of the driver's ashtray and of the elbow rest as standard equipment has been found to be the leading reason for sales decline in a European automobile company. Change of color from green to baby blue on a small appliance has been found by motivational research as the reason for sales increase in certain Central American countries. Light blue appeals to the housewife in her thirties, for this age is symbolic of motherhood and the age when she becomes the prime buyer of household appliances.

Change of color is a typical product revitalization step. But only change to a better color will do. Color testing is an easy, fast, and inexpensive research procedure. A description of a color test follows in Exhibit 16.

EXHIBIT 16

Popularity of Colors for Home Appliances
in Central America
(In Per Cent)

White	22	Saffron	5
Light blue	22	Beige	5
Light green	20	Grey	4
Yellow	11	Others	2
Red	9		

Passing pedestrians were invited into a showroom and asked for their opinions or preferences regarding a set of colors. They were asked such questions as the following:

(1) If you were able to buy article X, which of the colors before you would you be most likely to choose?

(2) If your color choice were not available, which would you be most likely to choose next?

(3) Which of the colors would you be least likely to choose?

In countries where it is permissible, the tested object should be put on the sidewalk in front of the store windows to stimulate the cooperation of thy pedestrians. One interviewer may complete 80-100 interviews in a day this way. Such responses are broken down by age group and sex and are expressed in percentages.

The test results in Exhibit 16 clearly differ from the color preferences of western countries in leaning toward the bright, primary colors rather than the subdued ones. This inclination toward gay, bright colors is even more marked for house furnishings and clothing, especially among the young people in the developing countries. In these countries, one often has to take into account the cultural factors that may play a role in choosing and testing colors. Whereas with European men, for instance, blue is a favorite; red is more popular among European women. For reasons unexplained, yellow is exceptionally well liked by the Japanese, and white is a favorite among young Chinese. In western countries, white represents purity; whereas, in many eastern countries, purity is represented by yellow or saffron. (Hence the saffron robes of the Buddhist monks.) Similarly, in most temperate countries, black or purple is the color of grief and mourning; but, in some tropical and semitropical countries, white serves this purpose, as in India.

NEW PRODUCT

New-product marketing research is governed by whether the product is new to the firm but already in use by the consumer or whether the consumer is not yet aware of it and demand must be created. In any case, however, the firm, in launching a new product, must first concentrate on the question of whether or not the new field is associated with the one in which the firm is currently engaged. Diluting the company image may cause permanent damage, in addition to the failure of the new product itself, if such research is neglected.

Nielson Index records show a much higher proportion of failures than successes where companies established in one field have attempted to invade a new nonrelated field. For instance, the expansion of a sewing machine manufacturer in the production of refrigerators or washing machines is a related picture, as both of these items have one thing in common—liberating the housewife from backbreaking chores; therefore, they attract users who are governed by a similar motivation to buy.

Marketing research of a new product should ascertain, in the physical research stage before production and distribution are started, whether the product will appeal to consumers and whether they will think it equal or superior to competing products already on the market. Further, it must learn, by interviewing, about consumers' opinions on the product's various properties and thus find out which of these have the greatest appeal to buyers.

The Singer Sewing Machine Company used the three following methods of paired comparison to test consumer appeal of wooden cabinets for sewing machines in Portugal: a multiple-comparison test, a control-unit test, and a one-variation test. The cabinets to be tested, say ten-twenty units originating in different countries and being of various designs, are first of all grouped in three price groups—low, middle, and high price brackets. With such a grouping, the values of the product do not interfere with the priorities of physical properties to be tested. Each group is then tested separately by interviewing visitors in the store or pedestrians in front of the store. Two stores are selected in a city, one in high- and one in low-income consumer traffic, and three other stores are situated in the countryside.

In the multiple-comparison test, each cabinet is compared with each in the group, and votes are registered. The results from such tests, of say four cabinets with twelve comparisons, each with 50 votes and a total of 300 interviews, can be filled in on a two-dimensional table, as illustrated in Exhibit 17. The tests took two days for two interviewers and needed 500 square feet of shop space. This test is actually the most reliable, for the order of priorities can be determined considering each cabinet in its entirety.

In the control-unit test, one cabinet is selected as the control unit. This may be a product of the competition or the best seller of one's own line. Then the new cabinets to be tested are each compared separately with the control unit by again interviewing visitors in the store or pedestrians in front of the store. In that way, whether the new product will stand up on the market in comparison with the control unit will be established. The winner of such a test can be used again as a control unit, and the test can be repeated for confirmation. The advantage of this test is that it can be accomplished in a short period, but it does not supply as conclusive answers as does the multiple-comparison test.

EXHIBIT 17

Four-Product Paired Comparison
(50 Votes in Each Comparison)

Product	Number of Votes Compared with				Total Votes
	A	B	C	D	
A	- -	38	16	31	85
B	12	- -	10	32	54
C	34	40	- -	35	109
D	19	18	15	- -	52

The one-variation test is used when the object of the test is to discover the preference of one variation only, such as color, kind of wood, finish, or design. In testing, for instance, modern design against period or rustical design, two identical cabinets are used, differing only in the factor to be tested. By simple questioning of the respondent—"Which of the two cabinets do you perfer?"—one can construct a final product consisting only of the elements preferred. Additional details on marking and rotating the products tested are described in the section on panel research below.

Physical research as to the function, size, material, weight, and so forth, of a new product must seek a solution on the basis of marketing research findings. In technical and laboratory research, it is highly desirable that the marketers and laboratory personnel work closely together. A great deal of marketing judgment and experience is placed on physical qualities such as performance, design, size, taste, and ease of use. Hasty decisions in the laboratory stage of work are costly. Also, laboratory research unchecked by marketing people may develop into experimenting for the sake of experimenting alone and loses touch with the real needs of the market.

Psychological techniques have been developed for obtaining data concerning the underlying fears, apprehensions, need-fulfillment, social status, and the like associated with the use of specific products. They are especially valuable where the product is a "personal" one (such as soap, clothes, girdles, cosmetics, and other items relating to some facet of the user's personal appearance) or where the product is associated with the fulfillment of subjective needs (such as magazines, books, music, food, and beverages).

To determine the potential demand for a new product by the consumer, the present situation must be closely examined. For instance, when a new kitchen appliance is being introduced, the housewife must be asked how well she is satisfied with her kitchen duties, which of them takes most of her time, and which are most tiresome. When a washing machine is being introduced, the questions should not be "Would you buy a washing machine?" but "How long does it take you to wash your clothes?" and "How hard is the job?" Thus, the kind of clothes that are washed currently and the method and frequency with which this is done are to be examined, rather than the opinion of the prospective consumer when he is asked directly what he thinks about washing machines, for the consumer himself is not aware of the new possibilities and cannot picture abstract situations well.

PRODUCT-LINE ANALYSIS

The term "product line" embraces all variations of a certain article carried by the vendor. For instance, in men's socks, a vendor in Caracas declared that he had to carry at least as many as three quality grades, two lengths, three design patterns, three colors, and six sizes. It is easy to see how the line can wind up in a maze of complexity. Control of the product line is one of the critical and fruitful benefits of research, when strictly applied.

There is a natural tendency to add new items in order to satisfy apparent demand or to follow the competition blindly. Often new items are added to the line without any or without sufficient examination of the contribution they will make, and without an examination of the possibility of dropping a poorly performing item at the same time. The ability of dead items to survive is amazing. It is usually easy for the researcher to prove that 80 per cent of the sales come from a small number of items and to pinpoint items kept in stock because of tradition, sentiment, and lack of courage to weed out deadwood that is obsolete and articles that served their purpose a long time ago or never reached that stage.

In order to establish the most efficient concentration of items in the line, close cooperation between the researcher and the selling staff is essential. Some management consultant companies have acquired a very fine reputation for their ability to justify a product line. The product-line analysis steps are the following:

(1) Introducing a new product first in a limited area—for instance, only in certain sample stores or in certain provinces

(2) Maintaining up-to-date records of items arranged in the order of their contribution to profit, based on gross margin versus sales volume (see Exhibit 18)

(3) Checking the above arrangement at the time of adding a new product

(4) Dropping the least profitable product automatically when adding a new, successfully tested product.

EXHIBIT 18

Product-Line Analysis Through Comparison of Price, Sales Share, and Gross Margin

| | Article | | | |
Factor	A	B	C	D
Competition prices	10	30	45	50
Our prices	10	25	40	55
Sales share (per cent)	10	20	50	20
Gross margin (per cent)[a]	20	30	45	42
Gross-margin contribution[b]	2	6	22.5	8.4

[a] Net retail price less cost of goods.

[b] Sales share multiplied by gross margin and then multiplied by 100.

PACKAGE RESEARCH

Good packaging presents a great opportunity for stimulating sales. As a result of the increase in mass merchandising, such as the self-service supermarket, package design has become one of the outstanding considerations in marketing. In view of the increasing emphasis placed upon the package as a vehicle for selling commodities, this is often a fruitful and rewarding area for the researcher to pursue. A well-conceived, well-researched, well-executed package is often sufficient to guarantee instant success.

The techniques of package research involve far more than merely the testing of current or proposed package designs. Package research is most commonly used in four stages: (a) predesign, at the outset of a packaging program; (b) interim design, during the design program; (c) postdesign, to test the effectiveness of final candidate designs; and (d) research evaluation of package designs currently operating in the market. Deciding on the objectives of packaging should precede all work on the design as such. A successfully designed package is one that is unique and aesthetically appealing, evokes pleasant anticipations and positive associations in all phases of consumer contact, and will thus ensure long-term repurchase.

Rules of Good Package Design

The degree to which package research is applied and the type of techniques that are utilized vary with the type of the product, the complexity of the specific problem, and the availability of the budget; but the criteria that have to be met by package designers may be summarized in several basic rules:

(1) The package must have high visibility, memorability, and legibility.

(2) The package should sell well off the shelf when it stands next to competitive packages and should be capable of being picked up from the shelf, carried home, handled, and opened for use easily.

(3) The package should communicate the unique characteristics of its contents, as well as any prime functional advantages that the package itself may possess, such as usage and reusage (as, for example, a drinking glass).

(4) The package must fit standard requirements. (For example, overseas shipping containers must be resistant to humidity and heat in overseas transportation.)

(5) The product and the package itself must be protected and made suitable for rough handling in inland transportation until it reaches the display window and the end user.

In each case, the purpose of package research is to aid the designer to see factors of which he must be aware if he is to reach a desirable synthesis of factors and to produce the optimum design solution. The researcher should always insist on being in direct contact with the "talent," i.e., with the person producing the actual package design, because the synthesis cannot be obtained through any intermediary or in a round-table conference. A good design requires the effort of one man—a single brain, rather than the collaboration of a group. A work of art has rarely been produced by a committee of artists, nor has a great discovery generally been made by a committee of scholars.

Mechanical Test Equipment

Package research techniques include numerous mechanical methods that are also common in advertising research for measuring the speed and distance at which recognition and correct identification take place and for discerning the dominant image components and the order in which they dominate when presented in varying combinations. Primary mechanical methods include the tachistoscope (which measures the speed at which a package is recognized), the distance meter, the eye-dominance meter, the eye-movement camera, and eye-pupil measurement. Some of these tests are made by hidden observers with movie cameras that register the emotional reaction to a package.

Test equipment to check package resistance, such as a humid cell, a drop-test console, and a vibrating table, are essential equipment for any packaging producer, in order to simulate transportation conditions, such as prolonged overseas transport, rail or tracking shocks and vibrations, and, before these, all the rough handling during loading and unloading.

PANEL RESEARCH

For ascertaining consumers' purchasing behavior and expectations with respect to current, new, or modified products or packages, marketing research has developed product tests by a consumer panel as a special technique. The consumer panel functions by investigating, through demonstrations and answering questions, all perceptible properties of a product, such as taste, flavor, scent, color, and package design. The answers and opinions of the group of consumers, who remain constituted as a stable group over a long period of time, are carefully registered. The members of such a consumer panel must be typical. This means they must be carefully selected to represent a cross section of all consumers. Besides consumer panels, there are studies involving panels of dealers, experts, doctors, and the like.

Good results are obtained through the use of paired comparison, in particular when the new product is presented along with an old product already in use. The comparison of a new product with a competitive brand will indicate to what extent the new product will stand up when facing the particular competitive brand. The respondents and possibly the investigator are not told which of the two is the new product or which is the control and which the research item.

The tendency to give priority to well-known brands must be carefully avoided. Also, the order in which anonymous products are shown and marked for identification by letters or numbers should be rotated, as respondents tend to give more weight to products that appear first. For the same reason, the order of the letters A, B, C and the numbers 1, 2, 3 are not suitable for describing products to be tested.

It is likewise important that only one single factor be tested at a time. The common mistake of an inexperienced researcher is to employ more than one factor or difference, so that votes obtained must be arbitrarily allocated to each variation. This may confuse the interpretation and often makes the test useless. All variables except the tested one should be held constant in each single comparison in order to arrive at conclusive findings. For example, a consumer panel appeal test of two salad dressings, one yellow in color with relatively oily consistency and another colorless with low oil content, will be inconclusive unless each characteristic is tested separately.

The advantages of panel research are the following:

(1) A continuous record of the behavior of the individual participants composing the panel can be maintained.

(2) Opportunities exist for measuring changes over a period of time, as well as changes brought about by specific influences.

(3) Since the group being used is relatively stable, smaller numbers of respondents are adequate for measurements of change through time.

(4) A panel obtains information on buying from all sources, whereas store-auditing procedures may miss some purchase sources, such as the house-to-house selling practiced in some developing countries.

The following disadvantages of panel research have been discovered:

(1) Panels often have a drop-out problem. A special difficulty arises with the participants who nominally continue, but whose cooperation has become so stereotyped and inaccurate that they are not helpful members of the panel. The difficulty of detecting such cases in the developing countries and determining their extent is obvious, due to limited personal contact.

(2) In practically all panels, it is necessary to offer either a cash payment or premiums as rewards for cooperation. There is danger that the sample will be distorted by overselecting those individuals who are particularly susceptible to premium offers. Thus, the incentive may produce distorted results.

(3) Panel members may report data inaccurately.

(4) Panel operations are expensive.

(5) In the developing countries, gaining and maintaining the cooperation of the members of the panel may prove difficult.

TEST MARKETING

A final step in product research is making a controlled sales test. Test-marketing activities have as their primary objective the following aims:

(1) Finding out quickly, economically, and with sufficient accuracy for decision-making whether, and to what extent, consumers will try the new or revised product or package being test marketed and will continue to buy it

(2) Evaluating the relative effectiveness, as compared with the cost, of a number of alternative marketing programs for their ability to secure (a) consumer trial, (b) consumer usage, and a (c) satisfactory, sustained rate of consumer sales

(3) Securing a picture of the marketing pattern, such as user's characteristics, priorities, distribution channels, advertising information, and the like.

Generally speaking, every detail secured by test-marketing research increases its cost. Therefore, decisions as to what details to secure are of importance. To make this decision, marketing management should determine, as each test-marketing situation arises, the kind of information that must be available about the brand. Care must be taken to select a representative market for the test; however, this requirement may be hard to meet in the developing countries. Test marketing assumes a well-organized market, one that is technologically evenly developed and thus enables the application of findings in one area to other similar areas. This condition rarely exists in the developing countries.

CONCLUSION

The following is a summary of product factors that may require research:[1]

(1) *Consumer practices and attitudes*: who uses product; how often used; brands being used; reasons for

[1] Presented at a meeting of the American Management Association (New York, 1968).

using; consumer "likes" and "dislikes"; who buys; how often; how much at a time; when they buy; size or amount bought.

(2) *Sales volume and trends*: in terms of money, units, cases, weight, and per capita; by market subgroupings, including package size, product type, price level; by geographic area, sales district, city size, individual markets; by type and size of retail outlet; by brand; by package type; by manufacturer.

(3) *Amount and trend of advertising expenditure*: total; by brand; by media; by country.

(4) *Promotional activity*: price deals; couponing; mail handouts; contests.

(5) *Opportunities for expansion of market*: distribution channels; size of potential market; by market classifications.

(6) *Brand name*: semantic considerations—ease of saying, understandability, memorability; associations—connotations, historical, effect on product acceptability.

(7) *Suitability of package*: design—shelf appeal, memorability, apparent generosity of contents, ease of use, opening device, reusage; size—economical for use, quantity sold related to size preferred by consumers, standards; protection—actual (under home-use conditions), storage before use, transportation, ability to stand solidly and also steadily when put on top of each other in the warehouse; label—color acceptability and connotations, design acceptability and connotations, visibility, readability, effect on product acceptability.

CHAPTER 6   PRICE RESEARCH

Not long ago the pricing effort of many companies was a trial-and-error proposition. Lacking dependable market analysis tools, managers often had to settle for intuitive or so-called reasonable prices. As a result, sales potentials were frequently left unexplored and entire price strategies were often misdirected. The importance of marketing research for determining pricing policy is one of the neglected potential benefits of marketing research in the advanced countries, and pricing policy is a hit-or-miss affair in the developing countries. No other error in marketing affects proceeds as directly and unnecessarily as price reduction or overpricing based on intuition or trial-and-error guesswork. Manufacturers and traders who use instinct or casual observation as a basis for pricing often price themselves out of the market or are cheapening their product in the eyes of prospective consumers.

It is almost universally recognized that, with given production facilities, the most important factor in determining prices in a competitive economy is the market demand for a product and the degree of price acceptance. But, in actual practice, most firms determine pricing policy primarily on the basis of cost. The common practice is to begin with variable manufacturing cost data and add fixed production cost, marketing cost, and a desired profit to arrive at the price to be placed upon a commodity. This cost-minded policy is unsound in that it ignores the circumstances in the market place. As soon as the demand shrinks to a point where the company consistently loses money or obtains only a very small sales volume, as during a period of recession or market saturation, business executives give major attention to the market-minded price, determined from the point of view of what consumers are willing to pay.

While it is, of course, obvious that production cost must be taken into account in the final decision on price policies, the basic facts that must be determined are the competitive price, price acceptance by the consumer of one's own product, and the quantities that buyers will take at different price levels. When the above have been determined by marketing research, they may be brought into relation with production cost at different volumes of output and with the price that will yield the maximum net profit that can be placed upon a commodity. Consequently, the following basic price research procedures may be used to determine the right price: a competition-price survey, a price-acceptance test, and a price-sales volume relation.

COMPETITION-PRICE SURVEY

Research should obtain not only the nominal list prices of the commodity but also the prices that are actually in effect in various types of outlets. Price variation by different types of outlets may hold the key to the solution of marketing problems. The extent of retail price-cutting and price-maintenance practices is often an important element in the marketing situation. The trend of competitive prices over a period of time should always be reviewed. Thus, in the investigation of competitive prices, the following data may be used:

(1) Competitive prices taken from catalogues (list price)

(2) Competitive prices obtained from retail advertisements and from price tags in stores (actual price)

(3) Wholesale discounts and gross margins of profit practiced in trade

(4) Estimates as to the best timing of price changes

(5) Published data that show the trend of prices.

The data that can be obtained from each of the types and sources listed must be carefully appraised, and the resulting prices must be carefully compared, in order to realize their meaning. Data from list prices in catalogues alone fail to reflect the effect of promotional price-cutting. Data taken only from retail advertisements probably overemphasize the cut prices placed on items used as leaders.

Competition-price surveys are usually started by analyzing the competitive prices from current advertising, prospectuses, or price tags in the retail establishments of the competition. Exhibit 19 indicates how these prices can be arranged in order to provide a clear indicator. This arrangement of competition prices may also be used for matching associate product lines. Thus, a middle-priced store advertising men's suits at approximately $60 would feature shoes at about $16 (probably $15.95); stores featuring suits at $85 would find their coordinated price level on shoes at about $20-$25.

Competition-price surveys for export may be conducted inexpensively when the item is advertised in the press of a foreign country. In all capital cities, embassies or consulates obtain and keep for three-six months copies of the important newspapers and magazines of their countries. The researcher may visit the consulate libraries and note the prices in the press. This service is one of the reasons for the existence of commercial consulates, and the researcher will find that consulate personnel are cooperative in this respect.

Price surveys alone will not determine the best price for a given commodity. A price survey is not an end in itself. It is, rather, a means of obtaining general price orientation and of using it correctly in the price-acceptance test, as described in the next section. Data obtained in such controlled tests are far superior to those obtained in price field surveys.

PRICE-ACCEPTANCE TEST

A mistake frequently made in an enterprise with little experience in marketing research, particularly in a price-acceptance test, is to try to find the price acceptability by asking the members of the office staff of the company, personal friends, members of the family, and similar people the direct question, "What price would you be prepared to pay for this product?"

The consumer sample for any product test, a price test in particular, must be strictly representative and selected according to

EXHIBIT 19

Example of Competition-Price Survey Indicators[a]
(New York, October, 1969)

	Prices		
Commodity	Low Half	Center	High Half
WOMEN'S WEAR			
Silk or Wool Dresses	$ 12.48	$ 21.60	$ 43.40
Sweaters	3.80	7.32	12.70
Hosiery	.73	1.02	1.33
Bras	2.59	3.94	5.56
Millinery	3.89	7.19	16.80
Shoes	7.60	12.60	17.58
MEN'S WEAR			
Wool Suits	46.60	61.60	85.00
Outer Coats	40.64	57.28	86.20
Shoes	9.31	16.35	23.60
Dress Shirts	2.57	4.16	5.64
HOME FURNISHINGS			
Made-Up Drapes	5.00	9.16	18.00
Bedroom Suites	142.00	183.60	270.00
Radio Sets	20.90	76.00	285.20
Television Sets	148.40	185.60	264.00
Refrigerators	189.80	230.40	295.00
Washing Machines	153.00	176.00	199.00
Gas Ranges	146.60	185.60	268.40

[a] The center column indicates the exact middle of prices for each commodity during the test period (median); Columns 1 and 3 show the low and high prices. A low-end store can use Column 1 as a guide; an average store can use Column 2; and stores in the higher bracket can use Column 3.

Source: Bureau of Advertising, A.N.P.A. (New York); reprinted by permission.

the rules of sampling. The respondents should be well informed about the product, its features, and its advantages. Whenever possible, a sample of the product should be handed to each respondent during the test. In the case of large and bulky products, such as refrigerators, all features should be described; pictures of the inside and the outside, in color, should be shown; and, if possible, a dummy model should be produced.

In an optimum price-acceptance test, the respondents are divided into two groups. To the respondents of one group, prices are indicated for the product, starting from the low end of the estimated price range and continuing upward, with the investigator naming prices and registering the number of respondents that consider each individual "price acceptance," or regard an individual price as "still reasonable," until reaching a "too expensive" response. The prices and the number of respondents, in percentages, per each price can be plotted on a diagram, as in Exhibit 20.

Then prices are indicated to the respondents of the other group, starting from the upper end of the range and continuing downward, with the investigator again registering the number of respondents considering the price acceptable, until those who do not believe the product to be good enough at such a low price are reached. The results are again presented graphically. When both curves are projected on a single graph, the price that appeals to the largest number of respondents will be revealed. (See Exhibit 20.)

In case such a test is made inside a store and random shoppers are interviewed in the developing countries, a check of the literacy and "price understanding" of the respondents must be made. It is desirable to produce large price tags with numbers 2"-3" high. In addition, the researcher should state the price loudly and distinctly. The price tags should be attached to the product or should be put in the hands of the respondents.

The method of optimum acceptance may be used for new products and for existing products as well, in order to check prices that have been in use for longer periods and whose attractiveness management has doubts about, provided the researcher can be sure that respondents are not influenced by existing prices on the market.

EXHIBIT 20

Optimum Acceptance-Price Test
(Graphical Registering of Response to Price
Graduation from "too Expensive" to "the Item Cannot
Be Good Enough for Such a Low Price")

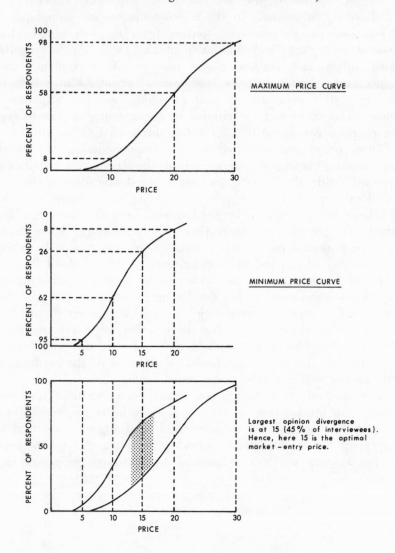

MAXIMUM PRICE CURVE

MINIMUM PRICE CURVE

Largest opinion divergence
is at 15 (45% of interviewees).
Hence, here 15 is the optimal
market-entry price.

PRICE-SALES VOLUME RELATION

Business people may have various attitudes toward marketing research. All of them, however, whether shopkeepers or industrialists, are intrigued by the question of how a change in price affects the quantity sold and the total revenue. They always pay concentrated, patient attention to this problem because they believe that, in this area, the theory of business may help to clarify to them this aspect of business strategy called "elasticity of demand."

In elasticity-of-demand investigation, market tests are set up in which a commodity is offered at different price levels and records of the volume sold at each price are made. In this way, the marketing research department uses the popular theoretical principle of elasticity of demand—the relation of changes in prices to changes in quantities sold—and translates it into a practical business reality. How can one decide whether the demand at a given point is elastic or not, and whether a borderline case represents demand being elastic or inelastic? The following are definitions concerning the elasticity of demand:

> Demand is elastic at any point where a 1 per cent cut in price, P, leads to a more than 1 per cent increase in quantity, Q, i.e., Q responds relatively "elastically."

> Demand is inelastic at any point where a 1 per cent cut in P results in an increase in Q of less than 1 per cent.

> Demand is at the borderline, called "unitary elasticity," if halving of P is matched by doubling of Q and a 1 per cent cut in P is matched by a 1 per cent rise in Q, i.e., where total revenue (P x Q) remains unchanged.

The way in which total revenue changes gives a quick means of testing whether one is at an elastic or an inelastic point. If a cut in P results in a cut of total revenue, the demand at this point is inelastic. A price increase should also be tested at such a point. If a cut in P raises total revenue, then demand is elastic and price reduction should be explored. If the total revenue remains the same whether P is raised or lowered, then demand is of unitary elasticity and price change would evidently not pay. Demand-elasticity experiments may thus lead to the discovery that greater returns will be obtained by increasing the unit price.

Carefully controlled experiments, conducted to yield reliable data on quantities taken at different price levels, must respect several difficult market-testing conditions. A basic assumption of this experimental method is that the economic environmental conditions of the test are essentially the same as those in the real market in which the results of the tests are to be applied. In the case of the physical sciences, this requirement may be met with comparative ease, because the scientist is dealing with relatively stable environments. In marketing research, however, one is dealing with the least stable of all elements—human activity. With personal inclinations, whims, fancies, and emotions playing an important part in determining market behavior, the whole subject matter of the analysis is exceedingly unstable.

Since markets are subject to so many conditions that affect the response to, and demand for, any given commodity and are in a state of constant flux, particular attention should be paid to the environment when this delicate experimental method is applied. But, as this method is, in principle, the most logical of all price-testing procedures, the researchers frequently seek to use and to develop this attractive experimental technique.

The requirement that environmental conditions during the test be the same as environmental conditions before and after the test is in conflict with the requirement that the public must learn, in some way, of the change in price made for the purposes of the test. Obviously, letting the public know by means of a striking advertisement may easily influence the steady flow of the forces of demand. Thus, a balanced demand must prevail on the market, not forced by advertising nor restricted by a lack of supply. For instance, in countries where import licenses are issued irregularly or where corruption in the distribution of import licenses flourishes, tests on imported articles would be a waste of time.

A further obstacle is that the experiment may prove costly to the company because prices in the test territory have to be cut, and losses may be incurred for the sake of the experiment. This disadvantage may be compensated for, however, by concurrent tests with opposite price changes in another territory. But often businessmen will lose patience and will not allow time to be spent on this complex testing. They will attempt, by trial and error, to obtain the highest possible price that is consistent with a reasonable volume of sales.

Many overlook the possibility of obtaining a much greater net yield as a result of testing price against volume. The common mistake is to accept the judgment of field salesmen instead of conducting a test on the "price versus quantity sold" relation. What is called judgment, particularly in this case, is largely guesswork, which invariably proves costly to the company.

Measuring Elasticity of Demand

The importance of measuring elasticity of demand rests in its ability to answer the question "How is total revenue affected by changes in P or Q?" This is what businessmen are interested in. In order to express this relationship, researchers often use a numerical coefficient called "E" to measure elasticity of demand. Elastic demand means that E is greater than one, and inelastic demand means that E is less than one. Unitary elasticity gets its name from the fact that E is equal to one. E is measured by numerical ratio in the following equation:

$$\text{Elasticity coefficient } (E) \quad = \quad \frac{\%\text{ rise in } Q}{\%\text{ cut in } P}$$

In these experiments, the changing amount of units sold at different price levels must be compared with the declining cost of production (cost of goods) and marketing (variable expenses) to arrive at the price and quantity that will yield the greatest, or guarantee a constant, earning for the manufacturer or merchant.

In practical business life, determining the per cent of discounts corresponding to the per cent of sales increase, thus maximizing or maintaining constant the money amount of the profit margin, is arrived at by means of various calculators, converters, and slide rules. These are produced in paper or plastic form and can be bought cheaply. (Two such calculators and their manufacturers are Profit-O-Meter, made in the United States by Eddy Rucker Nickels Co., Cambridge, Mass., U.S.A., and The Discount and Profit Calculator, made in Great Britain by Blundell Harling Ltd., 29 Sutherland Walk, London, S.E.17, U.K.)

CHAPTER 7 ADVERTISING RESEARCH

Advertising fills a vital and constructive role in our society in that it promotes national economic growth by promoting our individual enterprises. It is also a colorful, diverting aspect of our lives, since many of the advertising creations are helpful, tasteful, and honest works of art. Some ad men do not consider their audience as rational beings, however, since they have discovered that promise and hope can be manipulated with symbols affecting our personal desires and ambitions more successfully than with the advertised item itself. Soap nowadays promises beauty first and only then cleanliness; cosmetic manufacturers sell success in love rather than lanolin; we no longer buy oranges, we buy vitamins, vitality, virility, and so forth. These symbol manipulations are often just on the borderline of honesty, not only as far as the truth is concerned, but also because they capitalize mostly on the buying public's ignorance and desperate wishful thinking.

Still worse is the persuading technique that attempts to reach the unconscious mind of the customer. This approach has achieved a certain degree of success in the advanced countries. Besides revealing some amusing aspects of human behavior, it has aroused a great deal of aversion and has serious antisocial implications, such as psychoseduction of children in children's programs, exploiting our deepest sexual sensitivity for commercial purposes, and developing wastefulness toward national resources by encouraging psychological obsolescense.

The marketing researcher will often find that it is in his power to raise the degree of morality and honesty in advertising policy and that, by doing so, the selling effectiveness of the ad will be improved. This may start by judicious use of superlatives and claims of unbelievable value. The public soon educates itself to recognize tricks, with the consequence of permanent damage to the brand name. Marketing research should try to avoid putting on "research shows" or working in the service of tricky motives and dubious practices. If a researcher is hired to do such a job, however, and has no choice, he should try, whenever he can, to move toward improving morals in advertising. In the long run, he will be helping all parties involved—the manufacturer, the advertising agent, and himself.

The problems and research methods in advertising are many. (A survey of advertising methods is provided near the end of this chapter, in Exhibit 26.) Reduced to simple form, however, they fall into the following four categories of questions most frequently raised by management and the type of corresponding research:

Questions Raised by Management	Type of Advertising Research
What to say and how?	Copy-testing
Where to say it?	Media research
When to say it?	Timing
How much to spend?	Budgeting

COPY-TESTING

Checking of Advertising Message

Before testing the ad message by means of any of the research methods, it is advisable for the copy writer to make his own precheck. It usually improves the ad if the copy writer and the researcher compare the new ad with six-twelve similar successful ads and also compare it carefully with the following check list of basic ingredients of successful ads:

(1) An ad should be *easily recognizable*. It should be distinctive and different in appearance from the advertising of competitors. Its

appearance should be consistent and coordinated with the company image, store window display, and type of salesmanship.

(2) An ad should have a *simple layout*. It should not be a crossword puzzle. The layout should carry the reader's eye to every part of the message easily and in proper sequence, from headline to illustration, to price, and to name. The use of excessively decorative borders and lettering should be avoided.

(3) An ad should emphasize the product's *main benefit for the customer*. It should appeal to one or more of the basic desires of man: security, fun, leisure, beauty, health, popularity. It should refer to "plus" features that the competition does not have.

(4) An ad should have *room to breathe*. It should not be overcrowded. Generous space is important, for it attracts attention to the point being made.

(5) An ad should discuss *price or price range*, if relevant. Figures have a high attention-getting quality. There is no reason to be afraid to quote the price of the product, even if it is high. Why the item represents good value should be explained. One should not, however, go overboard on unusually low prices or clearance items. No advertising should rely too heavily or too frequently on apparently profitless clearances.

(6) An ad should mention *related items*, if feasible. Two sales can be made instead of one by offering related or matched items along with the featured one.

(7) An ad should *urge acting now*. Prompt action can be stimulated with phrases such as "limited supply," "this week only," and "until . . . ."

(8) An ad should *name the brand*. The brand name, store name, address and telephone number, and store hours should be included, all in lettering large enough to be read easily. One should double-check that these facts are present in the ad. It should not be forgotten that 74 per cent of adult people wear glasses (but only 53 per cent wear them in public). One should never assume that one's store is known in the town so that giving the address is not necessary.

(9) An ad should contain *everyday language*. Unusual or difficult words—such as "gourmet," "coiffure," or "synonym"—should not be employed. Nobody resents everyday language; it should be used. It should not be forgotten that, in the developing countries, 50 per cent of people who can read and write have had only one year of education above the obligatory elementary level.

(10) An ad should *not make excessive claims*. It should be fair and honest. Superlatives should be used sparingly. The surest way to lose customers is to make claims in advertising that cannot be backed up in the store.

Copy-Testing Methods

Many methods have been developed for copy-testing. They can be summarized as follows: (a) consumer jury, (b) coupon-return analysis, (c) recognition tests, (d) impact tests, (e) psychological tests, (f) sales-area tests, and (g) controlled experiments. Coupon-return analysis and recognition tests are frequently used in the developing countries.

Consumer Jury

In consumer jury tests, it is important that the usually small group of interviewed individuals is made up of genuine customers. This procedure should be controlled by sampling principles. Careful attention must be paid to various market segments; thus, members of the jury must be chosen and classified by such factors as age, sex, and economic status. The advantage of the consumer jury test is that it can be conducted before the ad is run. The disadvantage is that the reasoning of the members of the jury must be analyzed with considerable patience, and the interpretation of these results must be accurate. Neglect of these points may easily distort this kind of testing.

In the consumer jury, two aspects of reactions are most frequently evaluated: statements regarding the product and statements regarding advertising themes. Statements concerning the product may be the following:

(1) This brand is the most comfortable on your feet.
(2) This brand wears the longest.
(3) This brand is made of the finest English-type leather.
(4) Business executives, actors, and leading professional men use this brand.

These statements are then typed on small cards. Two at a time are placed in the hands of a member of the jury, a prospective buyer of the product, and he or she is asked a question similar to the following: "Please read each of these two statements carefully, and tell me which one would be most likely to cause you to buy this product." After the choice has been made, the respondent is probed for reasons for his selection. As to advertising themes, the test is usually conducted in such a way that a group of consumers are shown two or more examples of layouts, illustration, and slogans, and they are asked which appeals to them most.

Another typical example of research involving a consumer jury is the examination of the appeal of advertising material if it has been transferred from another country. Advertising appeals are not easily transferable from country to country. This may seem like a simple point, but it is surprising how often this is overlooked when dealing with foreign markets. The following is an example of typical failure that could have easily been avoided if the consumer jury research method had been applied.

A large U.S. coffee manufacturer, who should have known better, transferred to the Dutch market an appeal that had been very successful in Germany. It read "America's finest coffee." The Germans like foreign food products in general, were well accustomed to American products, and had a quality image of them. Thus, the appeal was persuasive in Germany. The U.S. coffee manufacturer did not realize, however, and did not bother to check, that, since Holland has a 300-year tradition of coffee-roasting and considers Americans amateurs, at best, in coffee-making, "America's finest coffee" meant nothing in the Dutch market.

Coupon-Return Analysis

The number of returns of ad coupons received in response to an offer contained in an advertisement is a direct indication of the ad's efficiency. The problem is the premium, or to what extent the premium may distort the coupon-return analysis, since certain people will be more attracted to one premium than to another. Further, it is difficult to estimate the "coupon hounds" who are interested in winning something rather than in buying something and who glance through the newspaper or magazine for free or inexpensive coupon offers. Coupons offering to supply more detailed information on the advertised item, and nothing more, may be more effective in detecting genuine customers.

Recognition Tests

Experiments designed to measure the ability of readers to recall accurately what they have read in the past have proved a high ability of readers to recall. In a recognition test, the interviewer makes certain that the respondent has read the magazines or newspapers containing the ad by asking him to name some facts he can remember. Then he turns to the page and checks the specific parts of advertisements that the respondent claims to have read. The data will then be analyzed to reveal figures such as per cent seeing and per cent not seeing one's own advertisements as against the competition's advertisements, broken down by types as to articles advertised, size of ad, layout, location of ad, and the like.

Because of the tendency of respondents to overclaim readership, singling out reliable data is bound particularly to tax the patience of the interviewer. The ever-present tendency of the interviewer to get a "quickie" interview through a half-open door and to influence results by hints and assumptions—in other words, to produce sloppy work—may make the recognition test particularly misleading.

Impact Tests

The impact test is based on the objectivity of experimental psychology rather than on reliance upon the reader's claims of recognition. The method assumes that the last thing anyone cares to admit is that he has been influenced by advertising. It is probable, because of the customers' self-defense and reluctance to admit that advertising may influence them, that a mistaken general opinion has developed that maintains that "people do not know what makes them buy."

There are specialized companies that have for many years employed a method based on psychological analysis of customers and that can retrace the mental steps that lead to purchasing. This analysis gives the researcher evidence as to the part that advertising did or did not play in the buyer's decision and which particular feature of the ad played an important role.

Psychological Tests

Since the whole process of advertising is psychological in character, it is natural that certain psychological procedures have been adopted for copy-testing. Such methods of analysis are used for testing attitude, readability, comprehension, and credibility. It is amazing how many things are done in advertising that result in the psychological effect of actually arousing hostility. Since the purpose of advertising is to create favorable attitudes and desires on the part of the reader, listener, or viewer, the detection and elimination of such hostile reactions is of vital importance.

Sales-Area Tests

Many researchers believe that area tests are the best procedure for measuring the effectiveness of advertising because the testing yardstick is the comparison of the actual preadvertising and postadvertising sales results. The disadvantage, however, is that it cannot be used before the copy has been run. There are justified objections that many variables influence the sales results, such as competitive activity, sales efforts, and weather. Furthermore, when these tests are made in limited geographical areas—such as provinces, counties, and cantons—with various ad copies, of which one is finally accepted for national advertising, the risk exists that the competition can benefit by this.

Controlled Experiments

There are countless measures of efficiency arrived at by experiments conducted on a small scale. For instance, there is simple advertising-efficiency measurement by sales results (see Exhibit 21), promotion of various themes in display windows, placing demonstrators in front of the shop or in the shop window, door-to-door selling in certain blocks or sections of a community, and circulars mailed to a selected group of people. The results from such measurements form the basis for the regular meetings between the ad agency and the sponsor to determine where to improve and increase advertising effort.

MEDIA RESEARCH

Circulation Analysis

The analysis of circulation as it affects potential sales is a very useful device. Where quantitative information is available, the

EXHIBIT 21

Advertising-Efficiency Measurement[a]
(Sales Result, Compared with Advertising
Expenditure by Commodity and by Month)

Department	Planned Percentage of Month's Sales	Monthly Advertising Space (*inches*)
Coats and suits	20	80
Dresses	15	60
Blouses, skirts, sportswear	15	60
Lingerie	10	40
Shoes	10	40
Accessories (gloves, handbags, hosiery, millinery, jewelry, etc.)	30	120
Total	100	400

[a]List major departments and approximate share of month's total sales that each contributes. Multiply by month's advertising space (400 inches in example given) to determine how much advertising each department should receive.

circulation of various media can be related to potential sales by provinces, sales territories, or population groups. (See Case History 10 on advertising media research.) This type of territorial coverage study can be an important form of media analysis, for it ensures against overspending or underspending in advertising. Such analysis for campaigns not previously planned in this manner often shows that the distribution of advertising dollars practiced in the past has been seriously out of balance with the market potential.

The problem of obtaining accurate data regarding the circulation analysis of the largest media, namely the press, has been solved largely in the developed and most of the developing countries.[1] In every industrialized country and in most of the developing nations, there are data available, issued by the government, trade associations, or private agencies, periodically in circulation, with socio-economic analysis of the readers. For instance, a print-media circulation survey covering Greece has almost the same standards of information as have similar surveys of any industrialized country. Typical reader classification includes geographic area, city size, age, sex, economic status, and education. In some countries, the statistics may also include marital status, composition of household, employment, type and size of home, and ownership or rental of home. (See section on source of statistics in Chapter 4 for sources of the above advertising data in the developing countries.)

Broadcast Media

As television advertising is new in many developing countries, it is useful to outline briefly the history of TV advertising in most states of the United States, because in many respects a similar evolution may be expected in the developing countries in the years to come. (See Appendix D for data on broadcast media sets in use in the developing countries.) Radio, in the meantime, has become a more or less stable background medium; information on radio media is adequately available in the developing countries, as is information on cinema advertising and on cinema-going habits.

In its early days, a television set was an exciting family acquisition. In the late 1950's, only one out of three families owned a set in the United States or Europe. Owning one meant having status. Viewers per set were many; attention was rapt, even during commercials; ratings were high. Television cast a kind of spell then; it was actually difficult to turn it off. Hence, TV values to both the consumer and the advertiser were high. Some programs were known by the name of the sponsor; singing commercials were popular; wrestling was a major

---

[1] Newspaper advertising has grown from almost $2 billion in 1949 to more than $4 billion in 1961 in the United States. There has been a steady growth in circulation: between 1940 and 1960, weekday newspaper circulation rose by 43 per cent, whereas the active adult population (21-64 years of age) increased by only 22 per cent.

attraction. Here was a pipeline to a mass market that exceeded an advertiser's fondest dreams.

But then the situation began to change. The excitement of ownership was over. As the novelty wore off, the owners treated their new possession more casually. Some members of some households drifted back to their normal pursuits. Nearly every family now has a television set; and more sets mean less status. One out of every seven families has two or more sets in the United States. Actually, there are more households with television sets than with refrigerators, bathtubs, or indoor plumbing. With more stations came more dial-switching. In the United States, there were ninety-eight stations in 1950; the number has grown rapidly, to more than 500 at the end of the 1960's.

The TV medium has admittedly been undergoing a cycle of changes in recent years, however, that indicates further changes in value, in proportion to other media, to come. They will bear close watching by the alert TV advertiser. There are other straws in the wind. For instance, program ratings are going down faster and faster. With more shows to select from, the viewer naturally becomes more selective. The average time spent watching TV has declined 20 per cent since 1963. Since 1958, the decline has more than counterbalanced the increased number of homes with television sets. Although more people are watching TV, they spend less time viewing. From three hours per day in 1958, the average viewing time dropped to two and one-half hours in 1962. In fact, the housewife cut her viewing time by one-third.

Broadcast Media Research Methods

Broadcast media research methods are many and sophisticated. The application of mathematics and psychology is particularly frequent in this area of advertising research. The most widely used methods are the recall method, the diary method, the audimeter, and the telephone survey. In the developing countries, however, only the first and possibly the second methods may be successful.

Recall Method

In the recall method, the respondent is asked which television or radio program he heard during a specific period. The information is marked on a roster that lists programs during the period. The disadvantage is that this produces inflation of well-established and popular programs.

Diary Method

The diaries have preprinted dates and a roster for information, such as how many and which members of the family have heard the program and commercials and which of them are usually attracted to the radio or television set. The disadvantage of this method is the constant neglect on the part of the respondent to make entries at the time the set is on and, even worse, his attempting to fill in parts of the diary much later on the basis of his memory. A mechanical reminder, like a bell tuned to the "on-off" switch, would improve the reliability of the information.

Audimeter

The audimeter is a mechanical device attached to the television set that records automatically the station to which it is tuned and the viewing time when it is in use. The Nielsen TV and Radio Index Service provides a large amount of valuable information on TV audiences, permitting analysis of audience per dollar, and so forth. The advantage of this method is that the research is based on data supplied by a mechanical device, thus eliminating human error. The limitations are the high installation cost, servicing, and the fact that the device records mechanical activity, not necessarily the state of mind of the viewers or the time that they actually spend watching TV.

Telephone Survey

Whereas in the developing countries this type of survey is not done at all, it is perhaps the most frequent broadcast media test in the advanced countries. Calls are made according to a predetermined sample pattern, usually at the moment or immediately after the program has been viewed. This provides more-accurate data for far less money than do other survey methods. It eliminates the necessity of relying on memory or making entries in a diary. The disadvantage of this method is that it is limited to homes having a telephone and thus results in an unrepresentative sample. The telephone survey procedure is described in Chapter 4 and in Case History 2 in Appendix A.

ADVERTISEMENT TIMING

Timing is the most important single factor in any advertising strategy. It is certainly a vital factor in the success of an ad. Timing of an ad means not only being alert to sales opportunities but also making profit days out of dog days. Many advertisers have found it a real eye-opener to subject their advertising effort to a simple "timing quick-check." Here is a hypothetical example of how quick-check records can bring promotion into line with a seasonal sales pattern.

The advertising timing quick-check consists of the following steps:

(1) List total advertising cost for money expended or lineage or time purchased during each month last year.

(2) Divide total amount for the year into each month's amount to determine per cent of total advertisement each month. Enter percentages in spaces for each month.

(3) Show the retail sales as monthly percentages of the entire trade for several previous years. Most likely it will be noted that the relative importance of each month has remained practically unchanged for several recent years, except possibly for a change around Easter or the like. If such is the case in a particular month, it is all right to use last year's percentage instead of averages.

(4) Plot on a chart both percentages obtained.

The four steps mentioned above can easily be visualized. (See Exhibit 22 for a table and graph representation of these four steps.) A timing quick-check permits comparison of selling opportunities for seasonal peaks with advertising pressure and permits the charting of a path toward more-profitable advertising by avoiding costly mistakes like premature promotion or underpromotion, as illustrated in Exhibit 23.

EXHIBIT 22

Four Steps in Advertising Timing Quick-Check
(Comparison of Percentage of Monthly Ad Expenditure and Sales)

Month	Step 1 — Ad Expenditure Space or Time	Step 2 — Step 1 as Percentage of Total	Step 3 — Monthly Sales as Percentage of the Whole Trade		
			1969	1968	1967
Jan.	1,300	10.0	7.2	7.2	7.4
Feb.	600	4.6	6.8	6.9	7.2
Mar.	1,800	13.8	8.1	8.1	7.9
Apr.	600	4.6	8.2	7.9	8.8
May	- - - -	- - - -	8.6	8.5	8.4
June	1,450	11.2	8.6	8.6	8.6
July	- - - -	- - - -	8.1	8.2	8.2
Aug.	600	4.6	8.5	8.4	8.3
Sept.	900	6.9	8.0	8.3	8.1
Oct.	1,350	10.4	8.7	8.6	8.5
Nov.	3,000	23.1	8.9	8.8	8.4
Dec.	1,400	10.8	10.3	10.5	10.2
Total	13,000	100.0	100.0	100.0	100.0

Step 4
Plotting Step 2 (Dotted Line)
Plotting Step 3, 1969 (Solid Line)

Note: See too early promotion in March and November and underpromotion in May and July.

125

EXHIBIT 23

Two Examples of Advertising Expenditure and Sales Trends

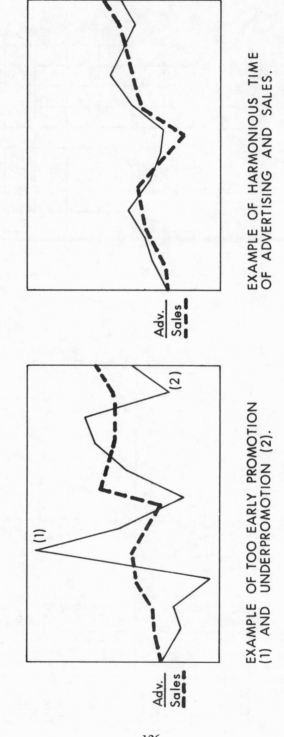

EXAMPLE OF TOO EARLY PROMOTION (1) AND UNDERPROMOTION (2).

EXAMPLE OF HARMONIOUS TIME OF ADVERTISING AND SALES.

An indispensable tool in the advertising profession and for the marketing researcher who tests advertisement timing is Table 6, which indicates the monthly seasonal sales pattern for a large majority of stores of various kinds in the United States. The difference in statistics between various countries may be significant; however, the differences should be in harmony with climatic conditions, local holidays, and the like in particular countries. Such a table is useful not only for scheduling advertising but also for store traffic measurements, studies of inventory-level control, and sales-forecasting.

BUDGETING

Management is requiring more and more objective evidence to prove that amounts spent on advertising are justified in terms of results. If sales are good, it is important to know why they are good, and, if sales are bad, it is even more important to know why. Although the funds spent on advertising and on promotion remain the backbone of a successful operation, the extent of spending on advertising has its own law of diminishing returns, as shown by the aversion of the buying public that may result from excessive, too aggressive, or tricky advertising.[2]

Deciding on the amount of advertising is extremely important in company planning. The basic requirement is finding out how much the competition is spending on advertising, broken down, possibly, by most significant competition and by media. It is one of the frequent and important activities of a marketing research department to collect such data in as complete detail as possible. In most countries, these data are available from trade associations or advertising agencies. Advertising

---

[2] On September 16, 1966, picketing against excessive advertising took place in New York right in the middle of Fifth Avenue. The response and positive participation of the public was such that emergency police troops had to be brought in to restore order. Some of the picket signs read: "Don't waste your dollars on silly television programs and expensive commercials"; "Advertising is a trap for consumers' dollars"; "Low-income consumers can't afford high salaried advertising parasites"; and "Incentive trading stamps mean: buy your own present." Some pickets showed brands and names of the companies that had spent most on ads in the past year, with the request not to patronize them.

TABLE 6

Monthly Percentages of Year's Sales for Selected Types of U.S. Stores[a]
(Used for Advertising Planning)

Type of Store	Month											
	J	F	M	A	M	J	J	A	S	O	N	D
All Retail Stores	7.2	6.8	8.1	8.2	8.6	8.6	8.1	8.5	8.0	8.7	8.9	10.3
Department Stores	6.0	5.4	7.2	7.9	8.1	8.0	7.0	8.0	8.2	8.7	10.1	15.4
Women's Apparel & Accessory Stores	6.6	5.7	7.6	9.1	8.5	7.4	6.7	7.6	8.3	8.5	9.4	14.6
Men's & Boys' Wear Stores	7.2	5.4	6.8	8.1	8.1	8.5	6.8	7.0	7.5	8.3	9.4	16.9
Family & Other Apparel Stores	6.3	5.3	7.4	9.0	8.0	7.5	6.6	7.7	8.3	8.6	9.5	15.8
Shoe Stores	6.5	5.7	7.7	10.4	8.4	8.3	7.1	8.4	9.2	8.3	8.2	11.8
Furniture & Home Furnishings Stores	7.0	6.6	7.6	7.6	8.3	8.3	8.2	8.9	8.6	9.0	9.4	10.5
Household-Appliance & Radio Stores	7.6	6.9	7.4	6.8	7.8	8.2	7.8	8.4	8.3	8.8	9.5	12.5
Variety Stores	5.6	5.9	7.3	8.1	7.9	7.9	7.2	8.2	7.9	8.1	9.0	16.9
Jewelry Stores	6.0	5.5	6.3	6.6	7.8	8.3	6.9	7.2	7.1	8.3	8.7	21.3
Drug & Proprietary Stores	8.1	7.7	8.2	8.0	8.3	8.3	8.0	8.2	7.9	8.1	8.2	11.0
Grocery Stores	7.8	7.5	8.7	7.8	9.4	8.8	8.2	8.7	8.4	8.3	8.5	9.0
Hardware Stores	6.3	5.8	7.4	8.5	9.3	9.1	8.4	8.5	8.3	8.5	8.2	11.6
Lumber & Building Materials Dealers	6.0	5.7	7.1	8.3	9.3	9.5	9.7	10.1	8.9	9.7	8.7	7.0
Eating & Drinking Places	7.3	6.8	7.7	7.9	8.6	8.9	9.1	9.5	8.7	8.6	8.3	8.6
Motor Vehicle & Other Automotive Dealers	7.3	7.1	8.9	8.8	9.4	9.2	8.3	8.0	6.5	9.6	9.1	7.8
Tire, Battery, & Accessories Stores	6.6	6.1	7.5	8.2	9.0	9.3	8.7	8.5	7.8	8.7	8.5	11.1
Gasoline Service Stations	7.8	7.1	8.0	8.1	8.5	8.7	8.8	8.9	8.4	8.6	8.4	8.7

[a]Compare overperformance and underperformance with monthly average of 8.3 per cent.

Source: U.S., Department of Commerce, 1968 Sales Reports (Washington. D.C.: Government Printing Office, 1968).

agencies and media owners themselves are usually willing to reveal the volume of the principal advertisers.

Table 7 shows a list of the average advertising budgets expressed in percentage of annual sales by types of various U.S. stores. It ranges from 0.3 per cent for candy and liquor stores to 5 per cent for travel agencies. In the developing countries, the budgets may vary to a considerable extent from country to country; however, the relation among the various types of stores will not differ significantly.

In using these figures as a guide, it should be remembered that, when a store is only average, it is as close to the bottom as to the top. Not only do the averages lump together the result of successful with unsuccessful companies or stores, but the average also includes stores that do not advertise at all. Needless to say, in order to achieve above-average success one has to do an above-aveage job of merchandising and advertising for a prolonged period.

Formulas have been developed by the advertising trade and operational research suggesting how much above the average a company should spend in order to achieve given sales goals in a given time. (The type of marketing research that attempts to determine rules of marketing strategy by using mathematical formulas is called operational research.) The controversy over such formulas suggests that they are not yet reliable. The best approach still seems to be sound managerial judgment on advertising expenses plus some basic advertising-cost algebra.

Exhibits 24 and 25 are examples of common procedures used to find out what it costs to reach the customer by two of the most significant media, the press and TV.

METHODS OF ADVERTISING RESEARCH

Advertising research is carried on by a variety of methods. The method or combination of methods used depend upon the question that management is attempting to answer, the element that is to be measured, and the goal that is set. Exhibit 26 provides a survey of these methods and of the various component factors involved in choosing them.

TABLE 7

Average Advertising Budgets in Percentage of Annual
Sales for Selected Types of U.S. Stores
(Range: From 0.3 Per Cent for Candy and Liquor
Stores to 5.0 Per Cent for Travel Agencies)

Type of Store	Percentage of Annual Sales
Appliance dealers	3.1
Auto accessory stores	1.2
Automobile dealers	0.8
Bakeries	0.6
Barber & beauty shops	1.7
Book stores	1.7
Camera stores	3.0
Candy stores	0.3
Children's & infants' wear stores	1.3
Department stores	2.8
Drug stores	2.2
Dry cleaners	3.0
Family clothing stores	1.5
Floor covering stores	2.9
Furniture stores	2.5
Hardware dealers	1.6
Laundries	2.0
Liquor stores	0.3
Lumber dealers	0.7
Meat markets	0.7
Men's wear stores	3.1
Music stores	3.0
Restaurants	1.9
Shoe stores	2.5
Supermarkets (food)	2.1
Travel agencies	5.0
Women's wear stores	3.4

Source: Bureau of Advertising, A.N.P.A. (New York). Based on
studies by individual trade associations and publications in each field;
reprinted by permission.

EXHIBIT 24

Example of Computation of Cost Per 1,000 People
Seeing Newspaper Ads
(Sample Figures in Parentheses Are for
Typical Market in 300,000-500,000 Population Class)

Newspaper Costs   Hypothetical
                                                                    Example

1. List the total circulation of your newspaper.   98,119
2. List that part of the total circulation that is in your local
   market area.   70,195
3. Divide the local market area circulation by the total
   circulation to determine what per cent of your total
   circulation is in the local area.   71.5%
4. List your minimum national line rate. $.38
5. Multiply this rate by the per cent of circulation in your
   local market area. ($.38 x 71.5%) $.27
6. Calculate the cost of a 600-line ad from your local area
   line rate. (600 lines x $.27) $162.00

Newspaper Audience

1. Adult persons
   For one 600-line ad, multiply the circulation in the
   local market area by the number of adult newspaper
   readers eighteen years and older per copy or 1.89.
   (The average number of newspaper readers eighteen
   years and older per copy is 1.89. An accurate figure, if
   you have one, would be preferable; otherwise, use the
   national figure in particular countries. The same
   applies to 17.1% in the next paragraph.) (70,195 x
   1.89)   132,669

2. Adult persons noting ad
   For one 600-line ad, multiply the adult audience in
   the local market area by the per cent of the audience
   noting a 600-line ad, or 17.1%. (132,669 x 17.1%)   22,686

Cost Per 1,000 Newspaper Ad Noters

Divide the cost of one 600-line ad by the adult persons noting
this size of ad and multiply by 1,000. ($162.00 ÷ 22,686 x
1,000) $7.14

Source: Bureau of Advertising, A.N.P.A. (New York); reprinted by
permission.

EXHIBIT 25

Example of Computation of Cost
Per 1,000 People Watching TV Ads

Television Audience	Hypothetical Example

1. List the TV homes in your local market area. 85,710
2. Obtain a TV program rating for the program under study. This is a per cent of the TV homes tuned to the program. The average night-time half-hour network television program has about a 20% rating in the United States. 20%
3. Calculate the number of homes tuned to the TV show under study. (85,710 x 20%) 17,142
4. Note the average number of adult viewers eighteen years and older per set. (The average national figure for evening viewing is 1.69 in the United States.) 1.69
5. Calculate the number of adult persons eighteen years and older tuned to the program by multiplying the number of homes tuned to the TV show by the adult viewers per set. (17,142 x 1.69) 28,970
6. Estimate the per cent of the adult program audience under study that receives an impression from the program's commercials:
   - (a) For the program as a whole 85%
   - (b) For a single commercial minute. 44%
7. Multiply the number of adult persons tuned to the program by the percentages receiving an impression from the commercial to arrive at the commercial audience:
   - (a) (28,970 x 85%) 24,624
   - (b) (28,970 x 44%). 12,747

Cost Per 1,000 Television Commercial Impressions

1. For the program
   Divide the cost of the TV program in your local market area by the commercial audience for the program and multiply by 1,000. ($210.54 ÷ 24,624 x 1,000) $8.55
2. For a single commercial minute
   Divide the cost of the TV program in your local market area by 3. ($210.54 ÷ 3 = $70.18)
   Then divide this by the audience for one commercial and multiply by 1,000. ($70.18 ÷ 12,747 x 1,000) $5.51

Source: Bureau of Advertising, A.N.P.A. (New York); reprinted by permission.

EXHIBIT 26

Survey of Methods of Advertising Research

Type of Research	Advertiser's Decision	What Is Measured?	Methods Under Study	Methodological Goal	Advertising Goal
Motivational research	What to say	Consumer motives	Nondirective interviews, projective techniques	Cheaper way of measuring buying motives	New appeals
Copy research	How to say it	Recall, recognition of ads	Mail questionnaires (posttests), theater tests (pretests)	Adequate pretest and posttests of ad memorability	More memorable ads
Visual research	How to show it	Response to visual displays	Tachistoscopic devices	Company-wide visual rating service	Higher impact for all forms of visual communication
Media research	Where to say it	Audience size and composition	Reanalyses of existing surveys	Accurate two-year forecasts	Best buys within and between media
Public-opinion research	To whom to say it	Attitudes, demographic characteristics	Personal interviews	Identification of definable attitude groups	Correct audience for institutional advertising
Operational research	How much to spend	Relationship between advertising expenditure and sales	Mathematical models	Successful prediction of sales in test markets	Optimal size and allocation of ad budget

Source: Presented at a meeting of the American Management Association (New York, 1968); reprinted by permission.

COOPERATIVE ADVERTISING

Cooperation between producer and marketer in sharing ad expenses is a justified approach to the ever-increasing cost of publicity. In the developing countries, the problem of extra cost is particularly difficult because of the limited purchasing power of the consumer. Cooperative advertising is one of the ways of helping to meet ad budgets of importers, dealers, and retailers in the developing countries. They should investigate the existing ad co-op programs or initiate one with their suppliers.

Probably more than half of all manufacturers who are exporters from Europe and the United States to the developing countries offer co-op advertisement plans. Strangely enough, in the United States, as in some European countries, the manufacturers report that their customers in foreign countries do not take full advantage of co-op advertising. It is used mostly for goods where competition is keenest, such as appliances, soaps, drugs, toiletries, clothing, tires, and gasoline.

Conversely, in foreign trade among European countries, co-op advertising is so frequent that the customs authorities automatically increase the value for customs purposes on goods imported from an associated company abroad. This is done because it is assumed that the supplier has prepaid part of the advertising done in the consuming country and so has increased the value of the imported goods.

The advantages of co-op advertising, besides the direct savings, may be found in the increase of consumer confidence by adding the extra prestige of the manufacturer's name or brand. It often gives the merchants in the developing countries the benefit of the manufacturer's art, advertisement copy, and advice. Co-op advertising may enable the importer or retailer to earn a lower rate for his own advertising by putting him into a lower contract-rate bracket.

CHAPTER 8 RETAILING RESEARCH

It is quite common for the marketing researcher to be well versed in the typical, traditional top-management aspects of marketing research, such as analysis of economic conditions and the technique of surveys and forecasts, yet he will avoid dealing with retailing. In fact, he may even be helpless when faced with a simple request for practical help on a down-to-earth retailing problem.

In the developing countries, retailing is a very backward area of marketing, and, therefore, particular attention has to be paid to retailing problems. For this reason, in this and in the following chapter, the most common aspects of retailing research will be described in somewhat greater detail. Retail problems most likely to become the subject of marketing research are site evaluation for store location, pedestrian-traffic measurement, sales-efficiency measurement, and display efficiency.

STORE LOCATION

History of Site

Considerable stress is often placed upon avoiding sites that have been unoccupied for a long period of time or sites in which a number of business failures or public evictions have occurred. To avoid such a site for this reason alone seems to be largely the result of superstition. A site with a favorable past history is certainly more desirable, other things being equal, than one marked by a succession of unfortunate ventures, but it does not follow that the latter condition is necessarily a detrimental site characteristic. Emphasis should be accorded to the importance of making sure that the conditions that were responsible for the downfall of earlier occupants do not apply to the new project.

Vicinity of Site

It is important to examine the nature of at least five shops around each site of the proposed location to ascertain the extent to which the articles or activities in the vicinity are of interest to one's own potential customers. For instance, for a store that sells sewing machines, the suitable neighbors are women's and children's clothing shops, food stores, beauty shops, jewelry stores, laundries, shoe stores, toy stores, sweetshops, and dry cleaners. For shops selling tobacco, however, the suitable neighbors would be men's wear stores, automobile accessory shops, barbers, camera stores, hardware dealers, liquor stores, sporting-goods stores, and restaurants.

In order to quantify findings concerning the store vicinity, one may assign 10 per cent to each favorable neighbor and zero to each unfavorable neighbor. Evaluation will then be expressed within a range of 0-100 per cent. A neutral store—such as a pharmacy, optician, bookstore, newspaper store, and art supply store—may be rated in accordance with the traffic and prestige that they generate in the area. Competitive stores may be found to be favorable where territorial concentration of trade is practiced, but unfavorable where trade dispersing through a town is the principle of the license-issuing magistrate.

Certain factors are generally considered detrimental site characteristics. Vacant buildings adjacent to, or in the immediate vicinity of, a site draw no trade and detract from the appearance of the area. The direction of prevailing winds and the location of particularly windy corners are matters to be investigated. Wind pockets sometimes result in continual deposits of dirt and trash on the sidewalks and at the entrances, no matter how many times a day the area may be swept.

Other disagreeable factors, such as smoke, unpleasant odors, and, in particular, noise from nearby shops or factories or congested vehicular traffic, tend to reduce the value of store locations. Poor sidewalks or those that are too narrow tend to discourage pedestrian traffic and cause people to take another route, especially when vehicular traffic runs too close to the sidewalk.

Business District

When a merchant enters into a long-term lease agreement or when he undertakes an extensive modernization program that must be amortized over a period of many years, it is important to consider the direction of growth in the business district. Growth of new residential areas, inauguration of new public transportation facilities, and the activity of property owners who desire to develop their holdings for retail purposes are perhaps the principal causes of such movement. The combnation of (a) the number of families, (b) the growth of sales per family over a period of recent years in a trading area, and (c) the distances between the store and residential areas are particularly revealing factors in site evaluation.

Several approaches toward developing a mathematical basis for trading-area delineation are being developed. One of these is Reilly's Law of Retail Gravitation, tested and developed by P. D. Converse. It has established the breaking point between two shopping areas on the basis of the following formula:

$$\frac{\text{Proportion of Trade to City A}}{\text{Proportion of Trade to City B}} = \frac{(\text{Population City A})\ (\text{Distance to B})}{(\text{Population City B})\ (\text{Distance to A})}$$

(See Case History 7, which deals with various aspects of measuring market potential, including store location.)

PEDESTRIAN-TRAFFIC MEASUREMENT

The calculation of pedestrian traffic is a basic aspect of site-selection practice within established districts, since quantitative characteristics of the traffic and its convertibility into sales volume are important considerations for most kinds of stores. The planning of a reliable traffic analysis poses surprisingly complex considerations. These include the definition of who is to be counted, the decision as to where the count is to be made in the case of a multiple-entrance facility, and the selection of sample time intervals for counting purposes. In some instances, depending upon the type of store, only men are counted; in others, only women. If significant to the kind of business, pedestrians may be classified by age groups.

A store chain once analyzed its present sites by counting only people carrying parcels that indicated they were shoppers. The latter approach revealed a closer correlation between traffic and sales volume than previous counts had done, and the organization subsequently based its analysis for new sites upon counts of women with parcels. In comparative studies for a chain-store enterprise, the length of store frontage may be used to calculate the time of exposure, i.e., the time it takes for the pedestrian to pass the store.

Noting the number of pedestrians who approach from both sides on a tally sheet or by means of an automatic push-button counter is usually adequate. But, when the volume of traffic is large, it may be necessary to have more than one person count at a given site, one counting men and the other counting women. Counts are often made by means of boards on which several automatic push-button counters are mounted, each used for different classes of traffic.

An evaluation of traffic is possible when the following information is available:

(1) The types of persons most likely to be customers of the store

(2) The number of such persons passing the site during business hours (obtained from traffic count)

(3) The percentage of those entering the store

(4) The amount of average sales (based upon trade experience)

(5) The number of buyers that a given article attracts, which results in a survey of articles in the order of their traffic-building ability.

In order to obtain a comparable standard, the pedestrian-traffic flow should be counted during five- to fifteen-minute periods at various times of the day; for instance, morning, noon, and evening on the busiest streets of the town in which the store site is sought or at a site actually being examined. In countries with a hot climate and late-evening business hours, an additional late-evening count is recommended. Counts are taken at the proposed shop site at the same hours. Traffic evaluation may be expressed in the average number of pedestrians passing per minute taken from all counts during the day. In general, thirteen-twenty potential customers passing the store in one minute as an average is considered the low limit of the range of pedestrian traffic.

Such counts, first establishing the local standards and then the actual traffic of possibly several proposed shop sites in the town, may be time-consuming. But having a standard-pattern table of proportion of traffic flow at given hours expressed in percentages may enable one to determine pedestrian traffic by interpolation from a single actual count taken at any time of the day and converted into percentages. For instance, in Palermo, Sicily, if noon traffic is taken as 100 per cent, the standard pattern of traffic-flow proportion has been found to be 115 per cent at 10 a.m., 100 per cent at 12 noon, 178 per cent at 6 p.m., and 235 per cent at 7 p.m.

The researcher will notice how sensitive pedestrian traffic can be to such things as construction work, road-digging, and prolonged truck-loading. Experience has shown that such work may reduce pedestrian traffic by one-half. It is not a rare experience for retailers to go bankrupt, without any possibility of recourse, due to such interference with pedestrian traffic. It is therefore advisable to check with the city authorities concerning intended work and construction when a location is sought for a new store.

Estimates of sales volume derived in this manner must be adjusted in accordance with usual variations in volume associated with days of the week and seasons of the year. Even so, they are only crude approximations. They may be sufficiently revealing, however, to indicate whether or not there is a reasonable probability of attaining a profitable volume of business.

SALES-EFFICIENCY MEASUREMENT

Space-Productivity Ratio

Space-productivity ratios are obtained by dividing sales by linear or square feet or square meters of selling area or shelf surface. This method is frequently used to determine the selling area needed for a new store or to evaluate selling performance in the existing store. But, if the store is a new business, there may be no sound basis for determining sales volume. The basic prerequisite for the application of this method is a knowledge of standards.

The method of computing departmental area requirements by this approach may be illustrated with a simple example. Assume that a new department store is being constructed and that this store is expected to have a sales volume of approximately $4 million. Sales volume for the hosiery department might be estimated as 2 per cent of this amount, or $80,000. As shown in Table 8, stores of this size typically realize sales of $173 per square foot for this department. The amount of selling area required for this level of productivity is 462 square feet. A similar computation can be made for all other departments that are planned for the store in question.

TABLE 8

Sales Per Square Foot of Selling Area for
Selected Store Departments in United States, 1968
(In U.S. $)

Department	Sales Per Square Foot of Selling Area	
	Typical (*median*)	Middle Range (*interquartile*)
Linens & towels	60	43- 83
Women's hosiery	173	129-211
Women's & misses' dresses	73	55- 86
Men's clothing	102	76-141
Furniture	19	13- 25
Major appliances	61	33-125
Television	103	74-149
Toys & games	31	20- 65
Candy	105	53-119

Source: *Departmental Merchandising and Operational Results* (New York: National Retail Merchants Association, 1969), published annually.

Rent-Paying Capacity

Merchandise with the highest rent-paying capacity is ordinarily placed in the most valuable store area. High rent-paying capacity is indicated by the ability to produce a large volume of sales in a small amount of space. Ratios of sales per square foot or meter of floor space or per linear measure of shelf or counter space reflect this characteristic when compared with rent per square foot or square meter.

Rental rates in percentage of retail sales is the basic evaluation of rent-paying capacity. (See Table 9.) A more refined approach is to determine the gross margin of profit per unit of space, which may be

TABLE 9

**Rental Rates in Percentage of Retail
Sales for Selected Types of U.S. Stores**

Type of Store	Range		Most Frequent Figures
	Low	High	
Automobile parts & accessories	3.0	5.0	3.0
Candy stores	6.0	10.0	8.1
Cigar stores	3.0	10.0	--
Clothing			
Children's	4.0	6.0	--
Men's	3.0	7.0	5 and 6
Men's furnishings	4.0	10.0	--
Men's shoes	6.0	7.0	6-7
Department stores	2.0	4.5	2.5-3
Electrical appliance stores	2.5	5.0	3.5-4
Furniture stores	2.5	5.0	4 and 5
Gasoline service stations	--	--	(1c and 2c per gallon)
Hardware stores	3.5	6.0	5.0
Restaurants	3.0	11.0	5.6

Source: Percentage Leases (Chicago: National Association of Real Estate Boards, 1969).

done by multiplying sales per unit of space by the gross-margin percentage for a particular line of goods. Some stores with similar sales productivities may be found to vary considerably in gross-margin realization when this is done. A still more refined approach is to determine a department's contribution after deduction of all direct (variable) expenses and then to reduce this to a unit-of-space basis. The ratio of selling space to total space may be revealing if standards are available for comparison.

Retail Shop Inventory Audit

The inventory audit method of assessing retailers' sales to consumers, commonly known as the Nielsen Index, is a measure of consumer sales conducted continuously by detailed audits of invoices and stocks of typical multiple and independent shops. These shops are selected on the basis of recognized sampling techniques.

The manufacturer does not generally know the amount of sales of his product over the counter to the consumer. He will, of course, know his sales to his customers, but, since these are wholesalers and retailers whose stocks may remain on their shelves anywhere from one to twelve months, factory sales figures will reflect changes in demand only a considerable time after they occur and then only partially.

This information is of value not only to participating manufacturers but also to the cooperating shops, as it permits comparison of their activities with those of all other shops in their group, city, province, country, and the like. The consumer sales figures thus obtained from individual shops are merged and expanded to total geographic areas. The basic statement of inventory audit employed is illustrated in Exhibit 27.

Since participating manufacturers use the data obtained as the basis for making decisions that may involve large sums of money, great care must be taken to ensure accuracy and uniform procedure. These requirements present the major difficulties to be overcome in the shop inventory audits procedure.

The information obtained by the auditors includes sales to consumers, purchases by retailers, retail stock, stock turnover, distribution (shops handling the merchandise), percentage out of stock, prices (wholesale and retail), retail gross profit, and direct versus wholesale purchases.

EXHIBIT 27

Example of Inventory Audit Statement of Nielsen Index

Listing	Number of Orders	Value (U.S.$)	Packages	Number of Items
Stock January 1st				172
Purchases				
From manufacturers	1	8.64	144	
From wholesalers	5	3.90	60	204
Available for sale				376
Stock March 1st				120
Consumer sales				256
Retail price per package		0.08		
Total sales		20.48		

Retailers' Market Share

The number of families in the vicinity of a retail establishment should be established, either according to the spread of actual addresses of customers or, when addresses are not available, by estimates. But the expenditure per family on items carried by the retail shop must be established by consumer survey. For example, a worldwide shoe producer and retailer calculates his share of a small shop in Port of Spain, Trinidad, as follows: "The average family spends $21.50 on shoes each year. In the vicinity of the shop, there are 11,000 families. Thus, the market potential is $236,500 ($21.50 x 11,000). Our yearly sales are $60,000. Thus, our market ratio is 25.3 per cent." Such periodic revision of the share may be used in measuring efficiency when other, more precise measurements are not feasible.

Personnel Efficiency

Most efficiency yardsticks are, in reality, measurements of human or personnel productivity, which cannot actually be measured alone without regard to some of the quantifiable aspects discussed in this and the next chapter. Sales statistics per selling employee, however, broken down as to, for instance, male compared with female, age, training obtained, full time compared with part time, in-store sales compared with outside sales and with sales leads from service organizations, may become an eye-opener in the evaluation of the efficiency of personnel as individuals or as a group.

Such findings can then be used to evaluate training programs; to establish incentives, contest conditions, bonuses, promotions; and so on. In larger selling organizations, the fraction of selling personnel over total employees is a valuable indicator if comparable standards for trade in the country are available.

Important, but hard to measure, is the behavior of sales personnel and their appeal to customers. A survey on "How the Customer Feels," conducted in 1969 in the United States by the National Retail Merchants Association, indicates the extent of undesirable attitudes and behavior of selling personnel expressed by customers. Of those queried, 57 per cent said that they preferred to be waited on by a woman, 13 per cent perferred a male salesclerk, and the remaining 30 per cent said that it depended upon the type of merchandise involved. Although 56 per cent of the respondents said that salespeople were better informed about merchandise than they used to be, 73 per cent noted that salespeople were less helpful than they used to be.[1]

DISPLAY EFFICIENCY

It may justifiably be asked whether design, color, lighting, and the whole question of display in the retail establishment belongs to the field of marketing research. If this subject is discussed at all, it is because marketing research, in general, should not be limited to traditional areas and should constantly try to enlarge its fund of objective information by applying quantitative research methods to all business activities, no matter how remote they may seem from the traditional field of marketing research. Display is eminently a field in which research can be of help, because it represents the most direct contact with shoppers and with the public in general. Finally, a good window display will brighten the shop, lend prestige, and improve the aesthetic aspects of the streets in the developing countries.

[1] Complaints, listed in order of frequency, included the following:

Not interested in what I needed (26%)
Didn't know the merchandise (18%)
Rushed me (11%)
Talked too much (9%)
Used high-pressure tactics or sold me merchandise I really did not want or need (8%)
Discourteous, rude, or unpleasant (8%)
Poor grooming, not clean (7%)
Chatting with fellow employees and ignoring me (7%)
Too opinionated and critical of my choice (6%).

Testing Power of Display

When a display has been on view for a few days, it will become obvious whether it is "pulling" or not, and one that does not sell goods should be reviewed immediately. To test the power of a display, check (a) the number of people who only glance at it and pass on, (b) the number of people who stop to examine it and then pass on, and (c) the number of people who examine it and enter the shop.

To succeed, a display must result in a reasonable proportion of people reacting as in point c, above. To achieve this result, a display must (a) attract and hold attention, (b) create interest in the goods displayed, (c) impress the public, and (d) induce the public to enter the shop with the intention of making a purchase.

Useful information can be gathered, at the same time, by noting and analyzing remarks made about the display by the public and by noting the area of the display that receives the greatest attention.[2] It must be remembered that factors quite outside the control of the display man, and sometimes intangible factors at that, can adversely affect the selling power of an excellent display.

Display Viewpoint

It is quite common to see display men viewing their work from a central point on the pavement. Although a display should be checked from this position, it is important to remember that few people see a shop window from this angle. The potential customer usually passes the window from the side, and, if the display catches his eye, it happens when he glances toward the side wall of the display window that is slightly ahead of him. This fact must be taken into consideration when

[2] A successful retailer in Frankfurt, Germany, used camouflaged microphones in the frame of his display window in order to hear or tape-record the comments of the pedestrians concerning his window display. This method, however, is open to criticism from the ethical point of view and may, in fact, be in conflict with the law. But it shows how much importance is attached to shoppers' comments by the successful retailer.

designing the display. If the passer-by has reached a central point of the display window without prior sight of the window, it is usually too late to catch his attention, for he is then already in a position to see the display next door! Attention is arrested usually by merchandise placed in the line of vision, i.e., by the display on the side walls of the window, placed at an angle, rather than parallel, to the window glass.

The goods should be placed as close to the window glass as possible. It is an error to arrange goods high up and at the back of the window, descending rapidly to a somewhat flat floor layout. This represents a loss of pulling power and a waste of valuable selling space. A similar error is sometimes made by arranging merchandise facing in one direction only or, still worse, by displaying the merchandise, such as small and middle-size articles, in the window on the shop-floor level. The center of attention is always on, or a little below, eye level.

Display Design

Good design is the essence of display. Without it, no display can accomplish its first purpose, that of attracting the audience to whom the sales message is to be conveyed. Design creates that audience, holds its attention, and links all those elements that make up promotion. The appeal to the consumer begins with the design of the merchandise. When a manufacturer employs a good designer, the result is a pleasing, functional article with high selling qualities. What applies to design of merchandise applies equally to window display, as display bears great responsibility in presenting the product to the public. Basic elements of design to be observed when evaluating a display are composition, color, and lighting.

Composition

Composition is the planned arrangement of display goods in accordance with the rules of balanced design. It is the arrangement of masses of lines and colors, the spacing of objects and their relationship to one another within a given area. Good composition is one of the most forceful means of holding the attention of the shopper, and, by the skillful use of harmony, repetition, and graduation, it can direct the onlooker's vision to the focal point of emphasis.

Harmony and contrast are both important factors in design composition. Harmony of line, form, color, and the like gives unity; contrast is needed to give interest and variety. Harmony is achieved by similarity of elements, i.e., similar shapes, similar colors, and similar lines. A series of straight lines at regular intervals, a graduation from a straight line through a series of increasing curves, or gradually increasing angles, provide harmony of line and direction. One of the most common causes of confusion in display is too frequent use of conflicting lines. The use of similarly shaped items, whether they are merchandise or decoration, produces harmony of form. Repetition, the equal spacing of objects, is harmonious. Frequent contrasts in spacing create chaos and produce a "jumpy" effect, which is disturbing.

Conversely, contrast is one of the most important elements in design. Without contrast, or variety, a design will be monotonous and will lack the power to attract. There must, however, be a careful balance between the harmonious and contrasting features. As an approximate guide, two-thirds of the features in harmony and one-third in contrast will provide the correct balance. A window-display design may need a lower proportion of contrasting elements; seldom will it require more. The basic elements of design can always be traced in nature, which has harmony and contrast, with both of these in unity. Snowflakes are an example; differing shapes provide contrast, whereas unity is achieved by the harmony of each individual, symmetrical design.

Repetition is one of the most striking factors in design. It is a sequence of identical units, evenly spaced at the same angle in any given direction. It has rhythm and it has a force that is almost irresistible. The technique is ideally suited to long, narrow windows where the units are either parallel or at an angle to the window glass. Unless the units or groups, and the spaces between them, are absolutely identical and placed with perfect precision, much of the effect is lost.

Graduation is the regular placing of similar objects, from large to small, or vice versa. False perspective is the regular placing of identically shaped units, graded from large at the front of the window to small at the back. This technique creates an illusion of depth and is particularly useful in very shallow windows. Graduation also applies to the arrangement of colors in their natural order, such as yellow, orange, red, crimson, violet.

The placing of price tags is particularly important. They form prominent points in the composition and must follow the general lines of the design. Hand-lettering is a job for the specialist and should be entrusted to the professional sign- or tag-writer. Nothing can more easily ruin the effect of an otherwise excellent display than the crude work of the amateur letterer or layout man. Although the display man need not necessarily be a lettering artist, he must be conversant with the subject and possess a good knowledge of lettering styles.

Color

The arrangement of the color masses, the relation and the proportion of one color to another, and the effect of colors on each of these is as important as is the basic composition of any design. A master of color, in the highest sense, is born and not made. Some display men can produce beautiful color arrangements, which, to them, are second nature. Many of us are not gifted with a sensitive appreciation of color, and a study must be made of this fascinating subject. Marketing researchers can, however, search for objective rules than can be applied to a good display.

A scrapbook of good color schemes resulting from successful experiments, together with clippings from magazines, samples of fabrics, and the like, should be kept. Experiments can also be made with samples from a paint manufacturer's catalogue by separating the leaves and observing the effects of various combinations.

Although a decorator must be conversant with the various color theories and must master at least one of them, he must not allow them to become his master. The decorator may develop his own color sense. Color theories should be used as a guide, a method of checking, by the researcher looking for the reasons for the success or the failure of a display. Even though the researcher and the decorator may not agree on any one color, the researcher may still offer useful suggestions garnered from the field of customers' preferences as ascertained by surveys and from the field of color theories.

Color theories in brief are the following:

(1) Rood's Theory: A reproduction of Rood's natural-order color circle should form part of every decorator's equipment. An excellent reproduction is now published by Reeves & Sons, Ltd., and can be obtained from most artists' suppliers.

(2) The Ostwald Theory: Wilhelm Ostwald has produced a theory whereby colors could, for convenience, be given a definite symbol.

Like Leonardo da Vinci, Ostwald has stated that there are four primaries, these being yellow, red, blue, and green.

(3) The Brewster Theory: Sir David Brewster supported the belief of Sir Isaac Newton that the solar spectrum consisted of three overlapping layers of red, yellow, and blue; that the orange was formed by the overlapping of the red and yellow, and so on.

(4) The Wilson Theory: This theory, developed by R. F. Wilson of the British Colour Council, suggests a great advance over that of Ostwald. Twelve principal hues are used to build up the color circle. These colors are illustrated in the Wilson Color Chart, produced for the Royal Horticultural Society in 1938.

Lighting

Good design, a good selling theme, attractive merchandise expertly handled—all can lose much of their sales potential through incorrect lighting. Less light, if properly used, is preferable to an abundance of badly placed lighting equipment. A hot-cathode fluorescent tube will give from about twice to about four and a half times the light of the same wattage of a tungsten lamp, depending on the color of the tube. Its efficiency is greater than that of the tungsten lamp, and it has about five times its life.

High-efficiency tubes, however, are not necessarily the most suitable for display purposes, and the choice should be made in terms of suitability of the tube in relation to the kind of goods displayed. Fluorescent tubes give good, over-all general lighting that is equal in all directions. But, without directional control, much of the light is wasted. Fluorescent lighting has a flat, shadowless effect when used without the addition of tungsten spot lamps.

Fluorescent tubes, however, particularly the white and blue ones, discolor the complexion and stress all irregularities of the skin. Thus, they certainly do not flatter women buyers. Fashionable stores, coiffeurs, restaurants, and the like should realize the discomfort that these lights cause women visitors and should use incandescent lights, possibly with pink-colored tubes, called "warm light." The use of the latter has increased enormously in the United States in recent years.

The source of lighting must be concealed. The glare of naked lamps or tubes serves only to detract from the display. Arcade and backless windows present the major concealment problems. Louvres recessed in the ceiling, spill shields, baffle boards, and recessed lamps are the most effective means of concealment. Black baffle boards are all that is needed to screen the lights from the pavement. The backless window must be illuminated from recessed lighting at the top.

Reflections in display window glass on bright days can reduce the effect of the display considerably. The bright sunny climate of the developing countries makes this problem particularly troublesome. Window-glass reflections occur when the external light is greater than the internal lighting. A white background, flooded with white light, helps to kill these troublesome reflections. The interior of a shop with backless windows must be well illuminated because of possible reflection. Unless interior lighting is increased to overcome the strength of the light outside, reflections can almost obliterate the display. This applies particularly on bright days and where light-colored buildings face the premises. One way to reduce the effect of reflections is to place the goods close to the window glass, so as to benefit from the direct daylight coming from the street.

Optimum-Location Measurement

Every location in the display window and every floor or shelf location within the selling space of the store, when measured in an experiment as to its productivity, will show a greater or lower efficiency in attracting the attention of the customer when compared with neighboring locations of the same display or shelf. An experiment with shelves usually shows that the priorities are equal in all horizontal locations and equal in vertical locations, so that an equal coefficient of priority in percentage of sales change may be attributed to each row. Exhibit 28 illustrates an example of optimum-location procedure that may be applied to strategies in location of merchandise within the shop or in windows.

LABORATORY SHOP

The laboratory shop is a device for obtaining market information used by manufacturers and marketers whereby they set up one or more

EXHIBIT 28

Application of Optimum-Location Measurement:
Experiment with Nine Shelves
(180 Average Units)

Sales in horizontal
shelves (*per cent over
or under average*)

1	2	3	+30
4	5	6	+10
7	8	9	−40

Sales in vertical   +10   0   −10
shelves (*per cent
over or under
average*)

Solutions:

Shelf 1: %   = 100 + 30 + 10
　　　Units = 180 + 54 + 18 = 252

Shelf 2: %   = 100 + 30 + 0
　　　Units = 180 + 54 + 0 = 234

Shelf 3: %   = 100 + 30 −10
　　　Units = 180 + 54 −18 = 216

Shelf 4: %   = 100 + 10 + 10
　　　Units = 180 + 18 + 18 = 216

Shelf 5: %   = 100 + 10 + 0
　　　Units = 180 + 18 + 0 = 198

independent shops in various localities (or part of an existing shop) for the purpose of discovering how various products sell. The points to observe when using this procedure are the following:

(1) The test nature of the shops is kept secret. Although the shops are owned by the manufacturers or marketers, they operate in exactly the same way as any other shop does. Usually, they are managed independently, and goods are received both from the manufacturer of tested goods and from competitors in the normal course of business and in accordance with the demand for them.

(2) The profit motive is subordinated to the research motive, even to the extent of the shop's being subsidized. Great care is necessary here to ensure that the manager of the shop does not become aware of anything unusual.

(3) Statistical records covering the test, pretest, and posttest periods are kept with the utmost care. They usually include, besides statistics on sales, statistics on customer traffic counts and reasons for entering the store.

(4) A diary is kept where comments of the customers are noted, as well as suggestions by any of the personnel in the store. The diary also contains a chronological copy of all ads placed in the media, as well as purchase analysis (sometimes by taping the dialogue between the customers and sales personnel), by dates or times of day, weather, the usual pay day of employees in the town, and the day when most rents are payable. These are all important data for the laboratory store and for retail strategy in general. Besides, they explain the usual erratic fluctuation of sales of a new product. This diary usually becomes the most important document when it comes to providing material for decision-making.

(5) The manufacturer or marketer should never attempt to use these shops for the purpose of. pushing his own lines, since such an attempt would immediately defeat the purpose for which such shops are set up.

This method has certain specific advantages to the tester:

(1) New product lines can be tried out, and consumer reaction noted, before full-scale manufacturing.

(2) A check can be kept of special terms offered by competitors.

(3) Local advertising prior to national advertising can be tried out in the area of these shops, and its effect can be noted.

(4) Statistics on ultimate customers can be broken down in terms of age, sex, class, and so forth. Their complaints and preferences may also be analyzed, particularly when competitive products are carried.

(5) The shops can be used as a practical method of investigating any problems that may interest the manufacturer.

The whole point of a laboratory shop is that the identity of the manufacturer or marketer behind it remains unknown. This is essential to the success of the method.

MAIL-ORDER CATALOGUE RESEARCH

One of the basic presuppositions for mail-order business, namely the dispersion of population and difficulty in reaching the retail outlet, exists in the developing countries. Also, the success in these countries of Sears Roebuck, the world's largest mail-order company, as mentioned in Chapter 1, permits the assumption that mail-order catalogue distribution may become an important factor in marketing in some of these countries, and the marketing researcher there may be called upon to study this type of distribution.

Mail-order retail policy may be studied by the following procedure, which consists of comparing catalogues from various mail-order companies for the following elements:

(1) Range and median of listed prices per product line

(2) Lower- and upper-half price medians

(3) Density of items offered by price classes of a product line (When this aspect is presented graphically, it is a revealing indicator, for it shows that the policy of competing companies toward various articles often varies considerably.)

(4) Order of prices for a product line as they appear in the catalogue. (Example: women's articles, such as

EXHIBIT 29

Example of Price-Quotation Comparison by Price Bracket of Three German Mail-Order Catalogues (Women's Coats)

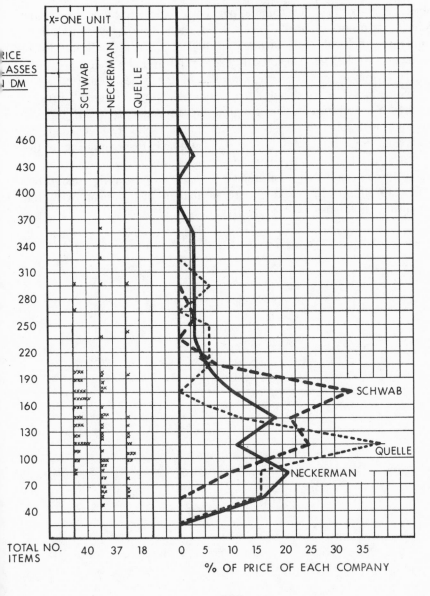

155

blouses, start with lower prices, whereas men's articles, such as shirts, start with higher prices.)

As to the catalogue itself, the researcher should be concerned with the comparison of the size, cover, weight, number of illustrations per product line, quality of printing, completeness and details of index, and cost to customers per copy. (See Exhibit 29 for an example of point 3, above. Note the contradictory policies of all three companies. Schwab concentrates in higher prices; Quelle in lower prices; and Neckermann is smoothly spread all over the scale.)

It is important to study a profile of the general characteristics of consumers periodically, as the catalogue must present merchandise and prices corresponding to the most frequent type of customer and must forecast what his income and taste is likely to be during the whole lifetime of the catalogue. Remember that the habitual catalogue customer examines the catalogues of all mail-order houses in the country. It is mandatory for the mail-order retailer to submit his catalogue to permanent comparison with the competing catalogues in the country.

The pilot of an airplane uses a number of gauges and dials to help him navigate and fly his machine. These instruments do not do the job for him, but by reading them he knows whether his course is right. If it is not, he puts it right. Similarly, there are a number of financial marketing ratios that can be used in business to measure its efficiency. It may be said that the ultimate profit is the one criterion by which the efficiency of a business can be measured. It may indeed be said as long as things are running smoothly and profit can be made without worrying about how it has occurred. But things do not always run smoothly, and it is advisable to have a system that will give warning as soon as difficulties start and that will show what progress is being made day by day and week by week when conditions are difficult.

The ratios and the break-even point analysis considered in this chapter are those that, although of a financial nature, have a direct bearing on marketing and sales. These ratios may be expressed in the form of a percentage, a time ratio, or an amount of money.

RATIOS

In most businesses in the advanced countries, the standard for each ratio can be established by experience if the business falls into a clearly defined industry. In the developing countries, however, inability to obtain these standards is a major weakness of financial retailing research. To provide these standards by a comparative study would indeed be a useful subject for research.

Asset Ratios and Gross Margin

Stock Turnover

Stock turnover is the relationship between sales and the stock normally held. If sales average 100,000 over a period and the stock averages 25,000 over the same period, the ratio is 4 (100,000 ÷ 25,000). This ratio of 4 is then a standard. If it falls below 4, then there is too much stock and, consequently, too much tied-up capital, and something must be done about sales. Conversely, if the ratio rises above 4, stock is falling too low, and action is again necessary to adjust it.

Capital Turnover

The capital turnover ratio is obtained by dividing net sales by total investment (total assets less current liabilities). What it does is to measure the number of times that capital is turned over during a business year. Comparison with the established standard will indicate whether the rate of turnover is increasing or decreasing. If it is decreasing, this means that the market conditions are changing; this may indicate that the firm's policy or product is not keeping step with consumer requirements. But before any change in policy is made, it is wise to investigate the market and discover the reasons for the situation.

Profit Per Unit of Capital Invested

Measurement of profit per unit of capital invested shows how much is being earned for every monetary unit invested in the business and is computed by dividing the net profit by the total investment. If the return on every unit is declining proportionately to the turnover of capital, the firm may well go out of business unless determined action is taken to readjust sales. This situation may be due to a variety of reasons, including falling sales or increasing costs.

Fixed Assets

Fixed assets are not trading commodities, and the more capital is invested in fixed assets, the less remains to be turned over by way of stock and sales. It is important, therefore, that the amount of capital invested in fixed assets be kept to a minimum. The ratio can be established by dividing total fixed assets by total investment, showing the result as a fraction or percentage. The trend can be established over a number of years and will indicate whether it is increasing or decreasing. If it is increasing, the firm's assets are less liquid, and action may be required to adjust the position.

Turnover of Receivables

A firm must know how efficiently its credit department is working. This ratio is obtained by dividing net sales by accounts receivable (debitors), and the resultant quotient is then divided into 365 (the collecting period). Thus, if net sales are 100,000 and accounts receivable average 10,000, the quotient is 10 (100,000 ÷ 10,000). This divided into 365 gives an average of 36.5 days. If the firm's credit policy is 30 days, then the credit department is falling down on its job, and the firm is financing its customers to a greater extent than has been allowed for.

Gross Margin and Mark-Up

Gross margin is arrived at by dividing the cost of the goods sold by total net sales and subtracting the quotient as a percentage from 100. Thus, if the cost of goods is 75,000 and the net sales are 100,000, the quotient is 75 per cent (75,000 ÷ 100,000). This subtracted from 100 gives 25 per cent. The gross margin is, therefore, 25 per cent, and the mark-up on cost is 33-1/3 per cent (25 ÷ 75). The importance of computing a gross margin and making comparisons with previous years is that a declining gross margin will reveal a trend that may be due to mark-ups' being too low, an unsound marketing policy, high costs, or slow-moving stocks.

Cost Ratios

Profit Per Currency Unit of Sales

The ratio of profit per currency unit of sales is obtained by dividing net profit by net sales, expressed in money. Since the profit is directly related to costs, this ratio will be useful in indicating, in general terms, the efficiency of the business. It is, in fact, one of the most common measurements that provides an immediate key to the state of the business. As long as the trend is one of increase or stability, there is little to worry about, providing it is up to the trade standard. A decrease in the figure, based on actual sales, will point to the need for market investigation or for an investigation into costs.

Cost of Goods Per Currency Unit of Sales

The cost of goods per currency unit of sales is obtained by dividing the total cost of goods by total net sales. It is a measurement of the proportion within each currency unit of income of fixed costs, labor costs, material costs, and distribution costs. It is an index that provides a direct indication of the efficiency of management.

Direct Selling Costs

Direct selling costs include salesmen's salaries, commissions, cost of demonstrations, traveling expenses, and the like, and should be shown as a percentage of the sales. By so doing, an immediate check on the efficiency of the sales staff is provided. Such costs should be broken down into separate expense items so that a check can be maintained on such things as car allowances and similar items.

Publicity Costs

Publicity costs are discussed in some detail in the section on budgeting in Chapter 7, above.

Physical-Distribution Costs

By establishment of the physical-distribution cost item as a percentage of the sales, it is possible not only to keep a general check on the cost of deliveries but also to work out immediately whether a particular delivery is profitable or not. Obviously, if 5 per cent is an allowable expense, a delivery of $10 worth of goods where the delivery cost is $1 is eating into profits. Periodic examination of rail and other carriers' invoices, as well as one's own tracking and handling expenses, often leads to fruitful renegotiation of freight rates, change of forwarding agents, or change in one's own means of transportation.

Total Operating Costs

Total operating costs per sales can easily be computed by adding all costs and dividing the result into total net sales. The resulting operating-expense ratio gives a general indication of the general health of a business. Any variations can be followed by a more detailed investigation into causes.

BREAK-EVEN POINT

Although everyone knows that a break-even point is a tool for profit planning, few realize the vital use to which it can be put as a price-planning device, and still fewer know what type of accountants' data are necessary and how to handle them in order to arrive at the break-even point by calculation or by constructing a graph. The break-even procedure permits one to obtain replies to such vital questions as which of the company's departments are most profitable; which store, product, line, customer, territories, or distribution channels are the most profitable; or which of them need assistance and how much.

In addition, break-even analysis brings to light all aspects of controlling cost and its components in relation to price, total cost, and profit. It also anticipates probable future performance by simulating, in advance, the impact on profits of a change in one or more of the decision variables. Through such an analysis, a number of questions can be answered, and certain decisions can be made more intelligently. (For more information, see the section on sales-efficiency measurement in Chapter 8, above.)

Writers of books on marketing research usually mention the importance of the break-even point, but seldom is its practical application explained in detail. It is useful for the researcher in a developing country to have handy a detailed explanation of the break-even point and examples of its use since, no matter in what field the marketing researcher may be engaged, he may sooner or later also be called upon to measure and give suggestions on how to improve the performance of a business enterprise in the numerous ways that the break-even point can be helpful. The break-even point, although it deals with accounting data, is actually a marketing research tool. It can be particularly useful in the developing countries because of its simplicity and the universality of its application, requiring only elementary accounting data.

Procedure

Break-even analysis consist of a relatively simple five-step procedure, which can be done on the basis of either actual or planned sales and expense data, as follows:

(1) Classify all individual operating-expense items as one of two groups: fixed or variable. Some writers call fixed expenses "indirect" and variable expenses "direct" because expenses vary directly or indirectly with sales.

(2) Determine the variable-expense ratio. This is done by expressing the total amount of variable expense as a percentage of sales.

(3) Determine the gross-margin ratio. This is done by subtracting the cost of goods from net sales. This may be an actual figure from recent experience, or it may be a hypothetical margin used for planning purposes.

(4) Calculate the marginal-income ratio, also called variable margin. This is done by subtracting the variable-expense ratio from the gross-margin ratio. This is the proportion of sales that is available to the business to cover its fixed expenses and profit.

(5) Calculate the break-even point. This is done by dividing the marginal-income ratio into the monetary amount of fixed expenses. The answer is the sales volume required by the business to break even. Below this calculated sales volume, losses may be expected to occur. Above it, profits can be expected in the operation.

Illustrative Application

Utilizing a hypothetical store as an example, Exhibit 30 provides a financial statement for break-even analysis. The break-even point can be established as follows:

(1) *Classification of expense items*: The total of all expenses for the store is $36,000. Each individual expense item must be classified on the basis of fixed (F), variable (V), or semivariable (SV); and the amount of each must be allocated between F and V and entered on the work sheet. (For example, the service personnel's salary of $8,200 per year is considered a fixed expense. The remainder of this item, $2,200, consisting of overtime hours and expenses incurred by service personnel, is considered variable in relation to sales.)

Some accounts, such as "all other expenses," contain a large number of different kinds of payments, some of which are fixed and others of which are variable. For purposes of this example, these items are divided in a 25/75 ratio among fixed and variable expenses.

(2) *Classification of operating-statement items for break-even analysis (gross margin of profit)*: The planned gross margin in the example is $40,000, or 40 per cent of projected sales ($40,000 ÷ $100,000).

(3) *Marginal-income ratio*: The variable-expense ratio of 16.0% is now subtracted from the gross-margin ratio of 40 per cent. This leaves 24.0 per cent as the marginal-income ratio. This is the percentage of sales volume that is available (after allowing for variable expenses) for covering fixed expenses and for making a net profit.

(4) *Break-even point:* The break-even point is now computed as $83,333 ($20,000 ÷ 24%). Thus, at a volume of $83,333, the marginal-income ratio of 24.0 per cent yields a marginal income of $20,000, which is just equal to the fixed expenses. Above this volume, the firm begins to operate at a profit; below this level, losses are incurred.

The idea behind break-even analysis becomes clear when plotted on a graph. (See Exhibit 31.) For accurate results, a sheet of graph paper must be used. Lines on the graph paper should be close enough to each other so figures can be plotted or read to the nearest thousand in

EXHIBIT 30

Example of Financial Statement for Break-Even Analysis
(Hypothetical Store)

Nature of Expense Items	Amount (*dollars*)	Classification of Expense Item[a]	Expense Distribution	
			Fixed	Variable
Net sales for year	100,000			
Cost of goods sold	60,000			
Gross margin of profit	40,000			
Operating expenses total	36,000		20,000	16,000
Owner's salary	5,000	F	5,000	
Salesmen's compensation	10,500	V		10,500
Service personnel's wages and expenses	10,400	SV	8,200	2,200
Delivery, vehicle maintenance, and depreciation	2,800	SV	1,800	1,000
Rent	2,300	F	2,300	
Other occupancy	900	F	900	
Advertising and promotion	1,700	SV	1,200	500
All other expenses	2,400	SV	600	1,800
Profit	4,000			

[a] F = Fixed, V = Variable, and SV = Semivariable.

EXHIBIT 31

Break-Even Chart

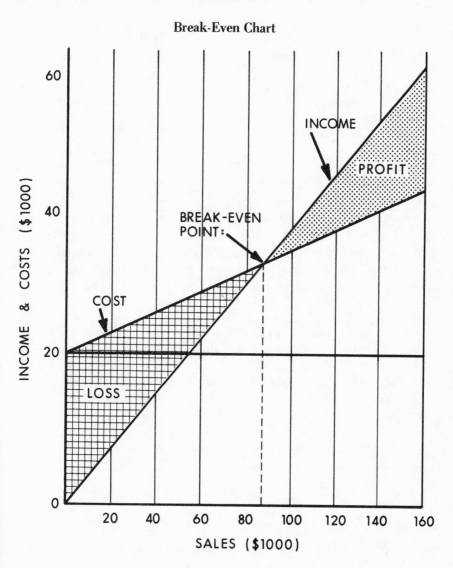

monetary units without difficulty. A scale for sales volume is set up along the X, or horizontal, axis. Margin and expenses are read along the Y, or vertical, axis.

After the scales are established, the following steps are taken in charting the break-even point:

(1) *Fixed expenses*: A line for fixed expenses is plotted on the chart. By definition, this is a constant factor. In the example, the fixed expense line is plotted at $20,000.

(2) *Total expenses*: At zero sales volume there would be no variable expense, so this line should be started at the left of the graph at the level of fixed expenses. At a sales volume of $100,000, total expenses are $36,000, which is plotted accordingly, so that the line can be drawn representing this value.

(3) *Break-even point:* The point at which the total expense line intersects the gross-margin line is the break-even point. Usually, it cannot be read as accurately from a graph as it can be computed. It is apparent, however, that the graph yields the same results. The break-even point, previously calculated at $83,333, appears at the same location in the graph in Exhibit 31.

Below this point (to the left of it), the margin is not adequate to cover total expense. Above it (to the right), the margin is above the total expense line, and profits are realized. The principal attribute of the graph is that it gives a picture of probable conditions over a range of sales volumes. For example, the retailer can read from the graph about how much profit would be realized if sales were $160,000 instead of $100,000, as is planned. He could also tell approximately what losses would be incurred at a volume below the break-even point.

Questions Answered by Break-Even Analysis

The following are examples of popular questions that may be answered by break-even analysis:

What will be the profit or loss at a given sales volume?

What additional sales volume will be required to cover the additional fixed costs arising from a store-modernization program?

What sales volume is required to earn a designated profit?

What sales volume is needed to cover additional variable costs resulting from a change in salesmen's compensation rates?

How will a given reduction in gross margin make a change in the break-even point?

If a change is made from a lease that involves a fixed amount of rent to a lease that involves a "per-cent-of-sales" rent, how will this affect the break-even point?

How will a revision of product mix affect the range of profitable sales and over-all profits? Which product mix will give the greatest profit and least vulnerability for the same sales level?

What additional sales must be made at the same profit, and/or how much must costs drop, to offset an increase in the administrative staff or an increase in equipment or space?

How much should be spent on an increased selling effort to bring about an increase in sales volume?

Which are the critical profit areas on which to spend management time fruitfully?

How much must various costs drop to justify expansion, or by how much must a price be cut, while maintaining the same profit, if sales cannot be increased?

What additional sales must be made at the same profit to justify a price cut? How much will profits drop if these sales are not realized?

CHAPTER 10 THE REPORT

PREPARING REPORT

Tabulation

Field-data analysis involves two separate operations: tabulating the data and interpretation. The process of tabulation, per se, is essentially that of counting the data. The process of interpretation is that of manipulating the data to bring out the best possible forms of quantitative summary.

The counting of data may be done by machine, as shown in Exhibit 5, or by manual methods on the counting sheet, as shown in Exhibit 32, and on the summary tables. The counting sheet is the form on which the tabulators record the number of items found on the questionnaires or schedules. Its form is determined largely by the tables that are ultimately to be produced. Summary tables are tables that summarize the results of the counting in such a manner as to obtain the most significant meaning from data by using cross-tabulations, such as the relation of brands used to age of respondents.

In order to ensure accuracy in tabulation work, as well as to conduct the work with a maximum of speed and a minimum of expense, there are several general principles that may be followed:

EXHIBIT 32

Example of Counting Sheet

Usually consists of three headings:

(1) Items counted are arranged in quantitative groups (class intervals), or items are indicated by names, as shown in questionnaire

(2) Tally for score marks

(3) Numberical and/or percentile totals.

(1)	(2)	(3)
4– 7.99	ᛉᚻ	5
8–11.99	ᛉᚻ ᛉᚻ ᛉᚻ	15
12–15.99	ᛉᚻ ᛉᚻ ᛉᚻ ᛉᚻ ᛉᚻ ᛉᚻ ᛉᚻ ᛉᚻ ᛉᚻ I	46
16–19.99	ᛉᚻ ᛉᚻ ᛉᚻ ᛉᚻ ᛉᚻ ᛉᚻ ᛉᚻ ᛉᚻ ᛉᚻ ᛉᚻ ᛉᚻ ᛉᚻ ᛉᚻ III	68
20–23.99	ᛉᚻ ᛉᚻ ᛉᚻ ᛉᚻ ᛉᚻ ᛉᚻ ᛉᚻ ᛉᚻ ᛉᚻ ᛉᚻ ᛉᚻ III	58
24–27.99	ᛉᚻ ᛉᚻ ᛉᚻ ᛉᚻ ᛉᚻ ᛉᚻ II	32
28–31.99	ᛉᚻ ᛉᚻ ᛉᚻ ᛉᚻ II	22
32–35.99	ᛉᚻ ᛉᚻ	10
36–39.99	II	2
40–43.99	II	2
44–47.99		0
48–51.99	I	1
Total		261

(1) The data should be tabulated separately by major groups.

(2) Base totals should be established at the beginning of the operation. If there are 427 questionnaires in a given survey, for example, every tabulation should total 427, regardless of the subject tabulated.

(3) Counting sheets should be standardized. The person in charge of the tabulations should decide the exact form to be used for counting sheets and then prepare these forms so that, when the tabulator begins his work on any unit, he is provided both with

schedules and a complete counting form. One common error is to make these counting forms too small, so that it is necessary to run the check marks over into the wrong column. Obviously this fault leads to inaccuracy.

(4) All forms should have clear, complete, descriptive titles. It seems a very simple rule, but in actual practice it is necessary to check constantly to make sure that the titles are satisfactory. The title placed at the top of a counting sheet or table should indicate clearly the exact nature of the data recorded thereon.

(5) Serial numbers should be assigned to schedules and other forms used in the tabulation. If these sheets are not properly numbered, they may easily get out of order, very much to the embarrassment of the person in charge of the tabulation work. Assigning serial numbers to the counting sheets and tables also makes it easier to determine just how much work has been completed.

(6) Class intervals should be mutually exclusive. This is a very simple rule, but one that is frequently violated. An example of classification that is *NOT* mutually exclusive follows:

0-30
30-40
40-50
50 and over

Having mutually exclusive class intervals is especially important in handling survey data because people tend to report data in even numbers. In such cases, the even numbers should be made the midpoint of class intervals, for, in this respect, the distortion of the original data through summarization is held at a minimum. A correct form for the same data is then as follows:

under 25.9
26-34.9
35-44.9
45 and over

Interpretation

The function of the interpretive stage in marketing research is to explain meaningfully the factual conclusions developed after having tabulated a set of specific conclusions and recommendations. The two fundamental requisites for the proper development of these interpretations are (a) using sound reasoning from facts to conclusions and recommendations (making logical interpretations) and (b) constructing the recommendations so that they will be adopted (making practical interpretations).

Since interpretation is primarily a problem of straight thinking, it is impossible to develop a mechanical formula by which any given type of statistic can be developed into a specific conclusion and recommendation. It is suggested that the following criteria be used as a basis for testing the logical foundation and practical use of any interpretation:

(1) *Is the relationship between the facts and the recommendation real or imaginary?* The whole process of research is essentially a "thinking" process. Everything that is done while the research project unfolds must be controlled by clearheaded and tough-minded thinking on the part of the researcher. In the interpretation stage, he must, in effect, review this entire thinking process to make sure that unwarranted assumptions do not destroy any links in the chain of his logic.

(2) *Is the interpretation supported at several points by the evidence?* In making a crucial interpretation, it is always advisable to check the evidence carefully to see whether the general conclusion on which a given interpretation is to be based is true in different localities, for different types of dealers, or for different periods of time. The more uniform the evidence and the more it points in the direction of one recommendation, the more confident the researcher can be in making such a recommendation.

(3) *Are any crucial exceptions to the proposed interpretation found in the evidence?* When one has hit upon a suggested recommendation, he does not usually find that all the evidence bearing upon it points clearly in one direction. In such a case, the researcher is presented with the problem of determining whether the exceptional cases destroy his proposed interpretation or merely modify it.

(4) *Has the probable opposition of executives been taken into account?* One should not submit a plan without first determining the opposition likely to be encountered and then taking the necessary steps to overcome this opposition.

(5) *Have company officials been given an active part in the interpretation?* The most obvious way to overcome successfully most

resistance to a proposed policy is to enlist the aid of those who are likely to oppose it while it is still being developed. Many researchers make it a policy to show executives individual findings during field work as they are received and to suggest interpretations that the latter may well come to regard as their own.

(6) *Has the required course of action been clearly stated*? If any research is to be worth its cost, it should recommend or point directly to a course of action. Unless this is stated in such form that the executives understand it clearly, the benefits of the study are likely to be lost in a maze of general discussions. One should remember that businessmen tend to think in terms of concrete instances and specific cases. They distrust abstractions and generalizations. Recommendations stated in general terms lead to involved discussions of the reasons why they are or are not true. A specific proposal, such as one to establish a new factory, to set up a test store, or to undertake a demonstration program, suggests immediate action.

(7) *Are recommendations interpreted as concrete gains*? The number of additional outlets, number of new customers, additional business, potential size of new markets, savings in marketing expense, or other results should be estimated if practicable.

WRITING REPORT

The writer must not only be conversant with the techniques of marketing research, but he must also be an expert in the art of conveying technical information to the inexpert. He must teach without the appearance of teaching. He must have the knack of imparting knowledge in an interesting manner, so as to hold attention, and he must be able to use words convincingly.

Sorbonne Method of Reporting

Marketing research reports are generally based on the Sorbonne method of reporting and are normally in four parts: (a) introduction and explanation of the problem, (b) conclusions and recommendations, (c) body of the report, and (d) supporting material and appendixes.

There is scope for variety in presentation since the requirements of individual studies will vary.

In general, the points to pay attention to in a report are:

(1) *Introduction and explanation of the problem*: The title page is most important because it is the first part of the report to be seen. A report is more likely to succeed if the first impression it makes is good rather than bad. All pages throughout the report and appendixes should be numbered and properly indexed at the beginning of the report for easy reference. The problem must be clearly stated because a market survey takes some time to complete, and it is necessary to remind the reader of the exact nature of the problem so that his mind will be in tune with the situation.

(2) *Conclusions and Recommendations*: Whatever information the top-level executive urgently requires should appear at the beginning of the report, so that he need not wade through such detail as purpose, scope, and method and can leave this task to subordinates. It must be remembered that a managing director or board of directors will be more interested in the findings and recommendations than in the way in which they have been arrived at.

(3) *Body of the report*: In the body of the report, the analysis of the problem is developed in detail, showing how the nature of the study was determined and the natural sequence of objectives. Here, the findings of the study are again stated in detail to show how they led to the development of the conclusions. The body of the report will, of course, be by far the largest part of it. There is no place for mere summaries here.

(4) *Supporting material and appendixes*: Although the findings are generally described in the body, the detailed breakdowns should be collated separately. The same principle applies to the use of graphs and charts, although in a number of cases it will be found useful to show some salient features graphically in the body of the report or even in the conclusions. The appendixes consist of such things as maps, diagrams of products, plans, case histories, statistical tables, lists, bibliography, and other items that are included to lend weight to the arguments or for interest.

Popular Report

Writing a successful popular report, whether as a written document or for oral presentation to an individual or a group, is largely a matter of following a few principles. The chief qualities it should possess follow:

(1) *It should be brief.* The popular report "high-spots" the outstanding findings of the study. Even though the presentation may last an hour or more or the report may have over 100 pages, conciseness should characterize the writing so that the reporting moves at a fast pace.

(2) *It should be accurate and correct.* Being accurate means being right in a number of ways. Accuracy requires correct use of terms and accurate statements, as well as correct numbers. Faulty rounding, improper addition of percentages, misuse of averages, confusion between percentages and percentage points—i.e., percentage differences vs. differences in percentages—and, above all, making statements that cannot be proven true (although these are sometimes necessary ingredients) are the most frequent causes of inaccuracy and incorrectness.

(3) *Emphasis should be placed on the practical use of the findings.* The report should talk in terms of action and should use conclusions and data as evidence to support recommendations.

(4) *Statistical terminology and concepts should be avoided.* They are kindergarten terms to the statistician, but they are new to the businessman. Many a popular presentation has lost much of its effectiveness because of interruptions caused by "the necessity" of explaining some statistical technicality.

(5) *The arrangement should be psychological, rather than logical.* The report should begin with material that will immediately arouse interest, then cover less important material, and finally work up to a climax containing the most significant findings.

(6) *It should be dramatized.* To do this, one employs many so-called dramatic devices. As long as there is no violation of the truth or distortion of facts, there is no reason why the report should not go far in this direction. The dramatic presentation should have a central idea or plot, like a good motion picture or stage play.

(7) *Use visual devices liberally.* In the popular presentation, words should be kept at a minimum. Here, the researcher applies the Chinese proverb "One picture is worth 10,000 words." Very often, rather expensive art work is employed to make some of the examples as dramatic as possible. "Blow-ups" (very large pictures, charts, and maps) are often freely used.

(8) *Advertise your report.* The report may well be preceded by short letters or occasional memos to the right people mentioning the most dramatic findings. The purpose of these is to get the man who really controls final decisions to urge further information. This procedure is good psychology, for, if one can get these men to ask for the findings, they are half sold before they ever see them.

(9) *Be prepared to be brief, if need be.* The researcher must always be prepared for the executive who wishes to "get the report over in five minutes."

GRAPHIC PRESENTATION

A graph is a method of presenting statistical data in visual form. There are many varieties of graphs. The type of graph used depends upon the data and upon the purpose for which the graph is constructed. The basics of graphical presentation follow.

Construction of Graphs

(1) Every graph must have a clear title, which is generally placed at the top center of the graph. As a rule, the title includes information as to (a) the nature of the data (units, weights, and the like), (b) the geographical location, and (c) the period covered. These elements of the title customarily appear in the order given above.

(2) Coordinated lines (the grid) should be held to a minimum, and curved lines should be emphasized so that the curves stand out sharply against the background.

(3) The source of the data should be indicated directly below the graph at the left.

(4) Footnotes, if any, should be placed below and to the right of the graph.

(5) If the graph is to be readily understood, the number of curved lines, segment lines, and other details should be as few as possible.

(6) Each scale must have a scale caption indicating the units used. The X-axis (horizontal) scale caption should be centered directly

beneath the X axis. The Y-axis (vertical) scale caption should be placed at the top of the Y axis. The Y-axis values are usually the function of the X-axis values (for example, sales: Y axis; income: X axis).

(7) The common zero point should be indicated on the scale.

(8) If lack of space makes it necessary, a scale break may be inserted.

(9) The scales of values should be placed along the X axis and the Y axis, thus giving a general indication of the size of the variations occurring in the graph. It is unnecessary to indicate fine gradations on the scales of value, since it is not intended that actual values be read off from the graph. Actual values can be obtained from the table of back-up data that usually accompanies the graph.

(10) If a space on the X axis is used to indicate time intervals, the point representing the value for each period should be plotted at the midpoint for the period.

(11) On the Y axis, the scale of values should run from zero on the bottom of the graph to the highest value at the top. On the X axis, the values should run from the lowest on the left to the highest on the right.

(12) The lettering should always be placed horizontally and done on a typewriter. The whole graph may sometimes be produced on a typewriter as well, as in Exhibit 33. When cross-etching or shadow areas are to be applied, they should be graded from the darkest shading at the bottom to the lightest shading at the top.

(13) Photographing of colored graphs is tricky. It should be remembered that, on black-and-white photographs, blue almost disappears and red becomes darker than black.

Graph Types

Graphs may be divided into the following types: line or curve graphs, bar charts, and area diagrams.

Line or Curve Graphs

The line or curve graph is distinguished by the fact that the variations in the data are indicated by means of a line or curve. This

EXHIBIT 33

Example of Typewritten Chart
(Personal Data Obtained in
Consumer Survey in Peru)[a]

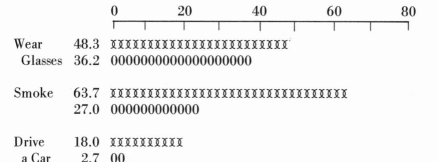

Men—XXX   Women—000

Per Cent of Adults

```
            0        20        40        60        80
            ┌───┬───┬───┬───┬───┬───┬───┬───┬───┐
Wear    48.3  XXXXXXXXXXXXXXXXXXXXXXXXX
Glasses 36.2  000000000000000000

Smoke   63.7  XXXXXXXXXXXXXXXXXXXXXXXXXXXXXXXXX
        27.0  000000000000

Drive   18.0  XXXXXXXXX
a Car    2.7  00
```

[a]Includes the provinces of Lima, Junin, Arequipa, and Ica.

type of graph is constructed by plotting points whose positions are determined by their respective values on the X and Y scales. The points are connected by straight lines. The line or curve type of graph is the most commonly used form of graphic presentation. The two types usually used are arithmetic rulings and semilogarithmic charts.

Arithmetically ruled paper has equal distances between the coordinate lines. Equal quantities then have equal distances. Thus, the distance between 1 and 3 on the background ruling will be the same as that between 8 and 10. An arithmetic progression (1, 2, 3, 4, 5, etc.) will plot as a straight line on arithmetic paper, since the differences between the successive values in this type of series are constant. Since equal amounts are assigned equal distances, equal changes indicate identical absolute differences.

Semi-logarithmic charts possess the following characteristics:

(1) Semilogarithmic charts have an arithmetic scale on the horizontal axis and a logarithmic scale on the vertical axis. (In logarithmic charts, both axes are logarithmic.)

(2) There is no zero or base line.

(3) Equal rises or falls indicate equal percentage changes.

(4) Equal parallel slopes denote percentage rates of change.

Thus, a slope from 2 to 4 will be parallel to the slope from 8 to 16, as the percentage rate of growth is the same, 50 per cent. Semilogarithmic charts may be used for (a) comparing proportional rates of change, (b) showing the relationship between two or more series that differ widely in amount, and (c) setting growth relation of one or several statistical series, for instance, in long-range forecasting (straight slope on semilogarithmic chart).

Bar Charts

Bar charts visually contrast quantities by a comparison of bars and subdivisions of varying lengths. Rectangular bars of the same width are erected from the same base line to proportionate lengths based on the data. The bars may be set up either horizontally or vertically; however, when the scale involves time, the vertical type of bar is recommended.

Area Diagrams (Pie Chart)

The most common type of area diagram is the pie chart. A pie diagram is a chart of circular shape, broken into subdivisions, or wedges. The size of the wedge indicates the proportion of each component part to the whole. Its construction consists of the following elements: the circle equals 100 per cent; each circle is divided into 360°; and, therefore, each per cent is equal to 3.6°.

The characteristics of the area diagram include the following:

(1) The arrangement of the size of the wedges is generally clockwise, according to size.

(2) A uniform arrangement of wedges must be made in comparing charts. Wherever possible, wording and percentages should be placed horizontally on the wedge.

(3) The effectiveness of the pie chart is enhanced by cross-hatching, colors, shading, and the like.

(4) If cross-hatching, colors, shading, and the like are used in place of wording on the wedges, a legend should be constructed to indicate their meaning. But try to avoid the legend whenever possible. For example, describe the areas directly on, or close to, the area. Use arrows if necessary.

(5) A pie chart should have a minimum of wedges.

(6) The zero point is on the top of the circle.

(7) The pie chart is difficult to construct accurately.

(8) It is difficult to estimate visually, with any degree of accuracy, the proportionate size of the wedges of a pie chart where percentages are not indicated.

Plotting Trend

Four methods are commonly used for plotting trends: freehand, semiaverage, moving average, and computed average.

Freehand Method

To fit a trend by the freehand method means drawing a line through a graph of the data in such a way as to describe what appears to the eye as the long-period movement. Advantages of the method are that it is simple and it may be used in place of a mathematical equation that may not describe the trend logically. If drawn with care, the trend line fitted by this method will be a close approximation to a mathematically fitted trend. Disadvantages are that the results vary according to personal estimate; thus, considerable practice is required to make a good fit.

Semiaverage Method

In this procedure, the data are split into two equal parts and the figures in each half are averaged. The averages thus obtained are plotted at the center of their respective periods and a straight line is then drawn through the two points. Advantages are that the method is simple and the result is entirely objective, i.e., it is not dependent upon an individual estimate. Disadvantages include the use of the arithmetical mean, which is greatly affected by extreme values. For this reason, the semiaverage trend line can be affected by such unusual occurrences as strikes and the like. The method is used primarily for the fitting of straight-line trends.

Moving-Average Method

In this procedure, the trend is described by smoothing out the fluctuations of the data by means of a series of successive averages secured from a group of items. By dropping the first item of the series and adding the next item to the series, the next average is obtained. (See Appendix B for a more detailed explanation.) Advantages are that only simple computations are involved; thus, it may replace the fitting of complex mathematical curves.

There are several disadvantages in the moving-average method. It cannot be brought up to date. Depending upon the number of items included, the last point in the trend must occur at a point before the time of the final data. A five-year moving average ends three years before the time of the final data; a seven-year average, four years; and so forth. A moving average fitted where the trend is that of a concave (upturning) curve will be higher than the true trend at all points, and lower in the case of a convex (downturning) trend.

The moving average is computed by using the arithmetic mean. As with the semiaverage method, this form of average is greatly affected by extreme values. Therefore, it will be pulled decidedly out of line by such unusual events as strikes, disasters, and the like. The number of items giving the smoothest moving average is equal to the number of years included in the average length of the cycle in the data. Since this average length must be estimated by the statistician, the estimate will vary from person to person and the method is, therefore, not purely objective.

Computed Average

A computed average is employed when one wishes to fit a trend by mathematical equation. (The least-squares method, for instance; see Appendix B for details.)

Correlation Graph

Although it is not proposed to enter into a description of the mathematical procedure used to establish the line or the correlation that exists between two or more factors (see Appendix B entries for correlation and scatter charts), it is appropriate to quote here a simple method recommended in "The Technique of Marketing Research," issued by the American Marketing Association.[1]

In most marketing problems it is not necessary to have an exact mathematical measurement of the degree of correlation between two or more time series, and for these cases the following simple expedient is recommended. The various time series are plotted on graph paper, each on a separate sheet. The dependent variable, that is, the time series which is presumed to be influenced in its variations by one or more factors, is plotted on heavy paper, and the factors whose influence is being studied are plotted on transparent sheets of paper. By placing the thin sheets over the heavy sheet, one at a time, the correspondence of the dependent variable with each of the factors can be judged by eye. This method is particularly useful in observing a time-lag which is done by shifting the transparent graph paper from left to right until the curve of the transparent paper corresponds best with the sheet underneath.

Even simpler than this is the very common method of plotting several curves on the same sheet, superimposed upon one another, on the same time-scale. Inspection by eye frequently gives all the information that may be necessary.

The graphical method for plotting curves for comparison is almost indispensible to a clear grasp of a situation. Even when correlations are to be computed mathematically, the curves should be plotted, anyway, if only for the purpose of obtaining a visual concept of their relationship.

A basic necessity in all marketing studies is that the investigator "keep his feet on the ground" at all times,

[1] Reprinted with permission.

understand the practical significance of every step in his analysis and interpret every mathematical conclusion in terms of the realistic problem at hand.

CHAPTER **11** ESTABLISHING MARKETING
RESEARCH IN A FIRM

In the United States, 77 per cent of industrial enterprises maintain one-six persons engaged full time in marketing research, and in the United Kingdom 56 per cent do so. In the developing countries, marketing research is practiced to the same extent only in certain fields, such as gasoline and mining. Probably for some years to come, one full-time or part-time employee will be the average for marketing research in larger firms of the developing countries. But describing now how to set up and operate a research department, as it is done in the advanced countries, will be useful for the future in the developing countries.

The principles of setting up and operating a marketing research department fall into the following major areas: (a) research personnel, (b) objectives, (c) efficiency control, (d) work load, (e) intellectual climate, and (f) budget.

RESEARCH PERSONNEL

Research personnel should have above-average mental capacity. This may be called ability to learn and, above all, to remember. A good memory is essential for building a mental portfolio of indispensable statistics on the national economy, trade, and one's company, which must all be remembered and considered together in a researcher's work. The popular short I.Q. (intelligence quotient) tests are an adequate measure of these abilities. But, in the case of some people, concentration is impaired during these tests. Furthermore, in some countries, testing techniques are part of the educational method, whereas in others they are not used at all. Thus, some candidates—especially foreign ones—may be handicapped by such tests, as well as by having to overcome the language barrier. Examination of previous written works and general knowledge of principles of national economy, government, and geography may provide a reasonable alternative.

Oral and written communication skill should be reasonably good. If a compromise has to be made, make it in favor of good writing ability, because the results of the researcher's work in their final form will be written most of the time. Knowledge of basic statistics is mandatory and should be examined and verified thoroughly. The researcher should also be able to operate calculating machines with ease and reasonable speed. The salary may vary; however, it should be in the top range of the company's personnel salary tables in appropriate classification.

The success of a marketing research department depends largely on the selection of its director. The director should have the abilities already enumerated for a researcher and analyst and, in addition, a good deal of business experience, as well as the ability to convert problems into quantifiable and practical suggestions for business use and to arrive in his conclusions at a "go" or "don't go" recommendation. He must be energetic, result-oriented, and aggressive, want to have things happen, and be impatient to see tangible business results from his department's work.

A reliable measure of his ability is his written work, published articles, and books. He may have been educated in any technical or literary field. It is important, however, that he completed his studies and that he have an academic degree. Knowledge of statistics and economics is mandatory. Particular attention should be given to his political and philosophical attitude toward the existing economic order in which the company operates. It is hard to imagine that skeptical, hesitant, or hostile attitudes toward the existing economic system can result in enthusiastic work.

A word of warning: The research director must exercise extreme prudence and tact when dealing with members of the divisions for which he is supposed to do research. He must bear in mind that often the object of his studies is, in reality, to discover the mistakes of others. It can be said that the success of the research department depends upon the proper, tactful personal approach. The director may soon run out of friends and isolate and immobilize himself if he does not think twice and weigh each word carefully when he states his opinions.

OBJECTIVES

The research department's objectives should be constantly changing. As each program is brought to an advanced stage (not completion), other objectives should be developed. A marketing research group should be willing and suited to solve the company's problems in the following areas:

(1) Measuring sales performance

(2) Assuming sole authority in sales and market conditions for forecasting

(3) Setting sales quotas

(4) Undertaking analysis of all existing or projected commercial ventures

(5) For multination companies, maintaining records on (a) economic and political development of foreign countries; (b) foreign trade regulations, including customs tariff rates; (c) international bodies, such as GATT and regional common markets; and (d) data on transportation, international routing, and basic freight rates.

The requirements under point 5, above, may not be the traditional records of the research department, but they often present basic information on the feasibility of a business project. It is of little help to establish by research that demand exists for certain imported goods, when the foreign trade policy of the importing country prevents the realization of such a project through, for instance, prohibitive customs duty tariffs.

The researcher will find that, in practice, no other department in the company keeps these records, and it is assumed that a research division procures this information as required. Thus, it may pay to keep permanent records at least of foreign trade regulations in the areas of frequent inquiry. For the developing countries, this inquiry may often go still further. The report on marketing opportunities will be complete only when current shifts in governments are described and the attitudes toward investment are covered.

EFFICIENCY CONTROL

Potentially, marketing research has large responsibility for the company's success or failure. The department director's positive initiative can make it a real factor in improving the company's performance. The rules of efficiency control are identical to those that would be employed if the director ran his own consulting shop. He would try to maintain top efficiency in all respects. A corporation should get the same attention. The rules may be outlined as follows:

(1) Analysts need firm direction and each should have at least two projects assigned to him with specific completion dates. Most major goals and projects should be attainable in six months. If a project takes longer than that, the department ceases to be responsive to the company's needs.

(2) The director should at all times have a list of major jobs being worked on in the department and estimated completion dates.

(3) As each project is brought to some degree of completion, the next project should be discussed with the analysts. The reason is not only to speed up but also that most projects need days of mulling over before the actual desk or field work starts.

(4) Regular department meetings should be held in which the director can review accomplished objectives and compare the performance of the analysts and their contribution to the performance of the department. This is helpful in result orientation. Follow-ups, checking, and updating of findings should be fairly frequent. In such meetings, implementation charts should be presented in order to figure out the past contribution of the department to the company's performance. This implementation chart is an important document for substantiating the reasons for the very existence of the department.

(5) The director must be interested in the details of each analysts's work and show at all times his willingness to assist in solving problems and doing away with bottlenecks. His interest will be regarded as a testimonial to the importance of the job. He should be able to tell the point at which there is nothing to be gained by seeking further information in a project.

(6) The director should see that time is allocated for the use of the company's own or rented computers to relieve the department of lengthy computation and tabulation of masses of data.

(7) The director can stimulate interest in the work by providing contact with the living business. The research department should be relatively free to contact customers, visit the field, or speak to members of any division of the company.

(8) Each analyst should be equally ready and equipped to handle any project from the beginning or take over at any stage of development. Specialization within the division, so that a particular type of project is assigned to certain persons, should not be practiced. Certain tasks, however, such as designing a questionnaire should be left to the specialists.

(9) The director should keep a close eye on the cost of his products. The object of the marketing researcher is to make money, not to spend it. Trips, phone calls, professional meetings, and outside services should pay off. Often they cannot stand close scrutiny.

WORK LOAD

The following three steps—systematic filings, temporary help, and outside research firms—may help in coordinating the work load:

(1) The researcher will find that over a period of time the management's questions become repetitious, often calling for precisely the same answers as were prepared some time ago. This is understandable, as the various divisions' problems are recurrent and no statistics are kept by the various divisions since they assume that this is the duty of the marketing research department. Systematic filing will help this situation.

Certain problems tend to arise at a given time of the year, such as seasonal variations in sales and advertising, budget, and GATT customs tariff changes. A well-organized file of closed projects, with quick reference to the replies and statistical information supporting them, may take care of a large part of such inquiries. It may pay to have professional advice on setting up the filing in larger divisions.

(2) The nature of the research department is such that periods of overload are followed by periods of less work. Engaging temporary help to handle the peaks is much preferable to being overstocked with statisticians and secretarial help, which breeds wasted time and prompts other divisions to ask for unnecessary clerical help. This is a sure way to discredit the department in the eyes of other divisions.

The permanent staff should be kept small and at a high quality level of performance. Students, teachers, and other helpers are usually available on a temporary, recurrent basis, with the advantage that they sometimes supply new ideas and a fresh approach to problems. Their productivity is invariably above the average of the permanent staff.

(3) The services of outside and marketing research firms on marketing problems should be the responsibility of the marketing research director and should be used strictly in specific, critical areas or areas of doubt. Because of their technical facilities to conduct certain types of surveys, they should not be assigned to vague tasks. Vague assignments usually result in boring volumes of studies representing reprinted official statistics and a restatement of the obvious.

Often the benefit gained from cooperation with consultants can be lost if top management goes directly to a consultant in an area where the research director has the responsibility. This may cause unnecessary frustration and be costly in terms of work, morale, and efficiency. To select and handle the outside research services is, to a large degree, a result of costly experience. It is described in the following section from a study by The National Industrial Conference Board, Inc., of New York:

The major reasons for turning to outsiders for marketing help are to obtain:
- Specialized skills, knowledge and resources
- Manpower and cost savings
- Objectivity and a fresh viewpoint
- Anonymity of the company in securing information
- Speed in completing a project

- Management acceptance of the results
- Exposure to outsider's ideas
- Better contacts available to the outsider.

Steps in selection. It is essential for the service buyer to define, at least tentatively, the project or problem for which help is needed, to consider what types of outside services are most suitable, and to put some value on a solution.

If the best choice is not obvious at the outset, the next recommended step is to develop a list of service suppliers who seem most capable of helping with the problem.

The best source of leads are said to be persons who have made similar use of such services or who are very familiar with them. Thus, companies often seek advice from business associates, advertising agency personnel, bank officials, trade association executives, university professors, etc.

Other sources of leads include: professional directories and journals; trade publications; promotional materials of service firms; solicitation visits by representatives of such firms.

References are checked as a matter of routine, not only to ascertain the reputation of the candidates, but also to seek firsthand reports from past clients who may be in a position to judge their ability to handle the project.

Proposals. It is common practice to request that the marketing consultant or research agency being seriously considered for an assignment prepare a "Proposal" which serves as a basis for agreement. A proposal usually contains these elements: restatement of the problem as the candidate agency understands it; description of the procedures it plans to follow; estimated time and charges for doing the job; reporting arrangements; and financial arrangement.

Working with research agencies. The research agency's primary mission in most instances is to obtain specified market data, with little in the way of consulting help required or expected. Sample design and questionnaire preparation most often are the agency's responsibility, subject to client approval. The field work phase, one of the most critical in a typical project, affords the client an opportunity to exercise certain checks and controls. Most marketing research directors in client companies prefer that the results of agency research be presented first to them or to designated members of their staff. The company's staff will sometimes rewrite the agency's report, giving summaries of findings of interest to executives who are to use them.[1]

INTELLECTUAL CLIMATE

The attitude of the director can do much to create a favorable climate. In this respect, he may follow these suggestions:

(1) Grant professional leeway to researchers. He must not supervise the staff so closely that it stifles creativity and initiative.

(2) In any specialized activity, there is a tendency to get involved in narrow problems and techniques that obscure the basic goals. The marketing director should permit the department to become a refuge for experimenting and pursuing programs of intellectual inquiry that do not directly or immediately reflect the company's good but that still have merit.

(3) In all studies and findings, the element of doubt should be admitted. When estimates are made, they should clearly be called estimates, and sources should always be named.

(4) The department should strive for solutions to problems that are not easy to solve and should make a systematic contribution to profit. It should avoid being overcharged in the collection of routine commercial data. This should be the task of particular divisions, such as advertising, product managers, accounting, planning, engineering, and the like. Only in the case of doubt should the research division assist in collecting commercial data.

(5) Reports should be well written and bound when suitable. Oral presentation should be clear and rhetorically prepared beforehand. Visual aids should be executed strictly in professional form.

[1] Paraphrased from *Using Marketing Consultants and Research Agencies,* "Studies in Business Policy," No. 120, (New York: National Industrial Conference Board, 1966), pp. 10, 11, 13, 28, 47, 55 *et passim.* Reprinted by permission.

(6) Researchers should be proud of their department, its contribution, and the people in it. Dirty linen should be washed at home, and it should be remembered that mistakes are human. Researchers should speak with confidence about their associates, their projects, and their findings and realize the damage done to their own reputation when they criticize the department inside or outside the company.

BUDGET

Marketing research is a commercial venture. It produces a product, and that product must be marketed like any other and should be able to stand close scrutiny and be accepted by its users. Thus, the cost must be in proportion to the dividend.

There is controversy as to how much should be spent on marketing research. Most writers on marketing research agree that, as a rule of thumb, to help establish an annual budget, the amount should be about 0.1 per cent of the annual sales volume. The administration of this budget should be left in the hands of the director of marketing research. If he is an effective director, the allocation of funds for marketing research is likely to bring a greater return than if the administering were done by persons not thoroughly familiar with marketing research.

CHAPTER **12** CONCLUSION

Marketing research is only about a quarter of a century old, but it is already beginning to function well in the advanced countries. It is, perhaps, partly responsible for the almost uninterrupted prosperity of these countries since the end of World War II.

Modification of marketing research methods from country to country and from continent to continent is, and probably will remain, a never-ending process. One should remember that marketing embraces the entire intricate task of getting goods and services from the producers to the consumer, and that there is no item in the average home today that has not been the object of at least some marketing research.

The markets of the developing countries of the world can be profitable, provided that marketers understand the real differences in these markets and are willing, when properly equipped, to search through them individually for business opportunities. In this book, marketing research methods have been described that have been found successful and have gained acceptance in the developing countries among marketing practitioners, both local citizens and businessmen from advanced countries.

An equally important aspect of the problem concerns the ways of dealing successfully with people from different countries with different cultural backgrounds. This is a matter of tactful human communication based on instinct, rather than on objectively determinable rules and techniques. A kind of sensitivity difficult to describe is needed when dealing with people in remote lands who have been brought up to respect and to adhere to their own traditions and customs. As in any human relationship, particularly when assistance and favors are asked for—such as, to cite an example, the close cooperation between consumer and researcher—thorough intimate knowledge of what to do or say, and when and how to do it or say it, will be an indispensable requisite.

To repeat, the new methods of marketing and marketing research are not only the great opportunity but also the grave danger of this age; catastrophe must result if the development of the poor countries cannot be realized to a modest degree at least. These techniques must be used carefully and with recognition of their potential for causing damage. In today's world, repeated marketing failures can easily turn the developing countries away from a free-enterprise economy, and they can invite in a centrally planned, state-oriented "command economy," with attendant social unrest, possible insurrection, and inevitable economic setbacks. It is in our power to prevent such developments.

As we look back upon history, we find, on the one hand, the clamor and turbulence of wars, revolutions, and insurrections; on the other hand, we find peaceful, constructive thought and effort directed toward achieving mutual help and understanding among nations. It is to the latter that this book hopes to have made a modest contribution.

APPENDIXES

APPENDIX A

**CASE HISTORIES OF SELECTED
ASPECTS OF MARKETING RESEARCH IN
THE DEVELOPING COUNTRIES**

1. USING MAIL QUESTIONNAIRES: COLOMBIA*

Many of the developing countries have a high proportion of illiterates, many dialects, poor postal services, and people with innate fears of putting anything in writing. Nevertheless, it appears that in Latin America, with proper selection of the areas to be studied (generally large urban centers) and limitation of the surveys to certain income strata, reliable information can be gathered quickly and cheaply by mail. This case history tells of experiments with mail surveys in Bogota, Colombia.

Test 1

The experiment began as a demonstration in a research methodology class. One hundred mail questionnaires were sent to a group of families living in a middle-income housing unit. They were randomly selected from a list of approximately 750 addresses obtained from the Housing Authority. The questionnaire solicited information about purchase and use of eggs. Fifty questionnaires contained a new 1-peso note (worth about 7.5 U.S. cents at the time). At the end of the test (twenty-two days after mailing), twenty-four questionnaires (48

*Material derived from: *Journal of Marketing Research*, V (February, 1968), 101-3; American Marketing Association (Chicago, Illinois); by permission.

per cent) had been returned by those who had received the peso and six (12 per cent) by those who had not. Ninety-five per cent of the replies came back within fifteen days after mailing.

Test 2

It was decided to expand the survey, and so 300 questionnaires were sent to families in the same housing project (but not to the original group). Half the letters contained a small plastic comb; the remainder did not. At the end of the test period, a response of 35 per cent was obtained from those who had received the questionnaire with the gift and 12 per cent from those without. Again, 95 per cent of the replies were received within fifteen days.

Test 3

The mail questionnaire was also used in two middle-income barrios (neighborhoods) in Bogota. This time 500 questionnaires about the consumption of milk were sent, half of which contained a new 1-peso note. At the end of the test period (twenty-two days after mailing), there was a return of 40 per cent from those who had received the peso and 22 per cent from those who had not. Seventy-five per cent of the questionnaires were returned within eight days and 90 per cent within fifteen days.

Test 4

Since all the previous tests had been done in middle-income barrios, a study was designed to obtain information from high-income areas. Five hundred questionnaires were mailed to homes in the highest-income area of Bogota. Half of these included a new 1-peso note and half did not. The percentage return was almost the same as that for Test 3 among middle-income families—a 39 per cent return from those who had received the peso and a 21 per cent return from the others. Of those returned within twenty-two days after mailing, 93 per cent had come back within fifteen days.

A simultaneous telephone and personal interview survey was conducted in the Test 4 barrio to test the results of the mail survey. The Bogota telephone company estimated that 70 per cent of the houses and apartments in the area had telephones. There were 194 completed telephone interviews and 217 completed personal interviews. The same questions were asked, and the same general order was followed.

A test of sample means showed no significant differences in size of family or weekly per capita consumption of milk with any of the methods used to obtain the information.

APPENDIX TABLE 1

**Consumer Response to Mail Questionnaires
in Bogota, Colombia**

| | | | | Percentage Returned[a] | | |
Test Number	Month	Number of Letters Sent	Product Queried	Sent with Gift	Sent Without Gift	Average
1	Feb.	100	Eggs	48.0	12.0	30.0
2	March	300	Eggs	35.0	12.0	23.5
3	March	500	Milk	40.0	22.0	31.0
4	May	500	Milk	38.8	21.2	30.0

[a]Within twenty-two days after mailing.

Conclusions

It seems reasonable to say that certain data can be obtained by mail questionnaires in large urban Latin American cities. It is apparent that the inclusion of a small gift is a desirable means of increasing the rate of return and reducing the cost per questionnaire returned.

This method of data collection is subject to many variables. Some areas within cities have low literacy rates; others have limited mail facilities. It appears applicable, however, if one wants to obtain information of a limited nature fairly quickly, at least in middle- and high-income areas.

2. CONDUCTING A TELEPHONE SURVEY: KENYA

In Mombasa, the second-largest town in Kenya and the largest port on the East African coast, a Singer Sewing Machine Company store had been located for 18 years on a street that, in the course of time, had deteriorated in relation to the neighborhood as a whole and in terms of distance from the new city center. Some members of the store's management believed that it should be relocated.

A choice had to made between relocating the store or leaving it at its present address and modernizing the façade and the interior of the shop. Because of budget and fund appropriations, the decision was due within two weeks. No research facilities could be mobilized in Mombasa. Research agencies in Nairobi proposed making a survey, for a fee ranging from $1,000-$2,000, that would have taken two months to complete.

In order to get quick results a telephone survey was organized by Singer personnel, using the company's own switchboard operator and an additional operator hired for the purpose. Both were local girls with a knowledge of English and Swahili. The instructions and procedures were those described in Chapter 2. The telephone book listed 2,800 telephones in Mombasa. Geographically, the whole city was covered by a random selection of 266 names from the telephone directory.

The question was a simple one—whether or not the respondents knew the location of the Singer store. Over 60 per cent of the interviews were conducted with people at work. The rest were people in households. About 12 per cent of the respondents were domestic help. Cooperation came close to 70 per cent.

The results satisfactorily indicated the wisdom of deciding to maintain the store where it was, despite the above-mentioned objections, rather than to move to some new location on a main street; for 86 per cent of the respondents were aware of the present address of the store. Relocation, therefore, would have meant a substantial loss during the coming year.

An additional factor was that a competitor had settled near the present store during the last years. If the Singer store had been relocated, the competitor would have benefited from the customers who would have been unable to find the Singer store at the old address when they got there.

3. COLLECTING STATISTICS:
CONGO AND SOMALIA

In order to demonstrate the amount of statistics obtainable from the developing countries, the author, in preparation for lectures on these countries at Pace College in New York, made the effort to collect as much data as possible on a hypothetical project. The project selected was the establishment of a plant for the production of bicycle tires in an African country. Any African country could have been selected, for the general census is available for each country, with the principal subclassifications, no matter what the standard of living is.

Soon after the first attempt to collect published data, it became obvious that the information obtained was surprisingly complete and referred directly to bicycles and tire production, import, and consumption. The following is a description of the method used for collecting the data. Two developing countries were selected: the Republic of Somalia on the horn of East Africa, perhaps the poorest country in the world, consisting of former Italian and British Somalia, and the Congo/Kinshasa, the former Belgian Congo, in the tropical zone of black sub-Sahara Africa.

In Somalia the elements that make a country poor are all strikingly present: very little fertile soil, unfavorable climate, not a single mile of railroad track, and no deep harbor to develop larger ports—the major geophysical problem of Africa. To complete the picture, the country is in a kind of permanent cold war with both of its stronger neighbors, Ethiopia and Kenya.

The tropical rain forest called the Congo is also a developing country—statistically and geographically—but the economic potential is enormous. There, the national treasury has always been rich because of the metal wealth in Katanga. The differences in the nature and the motives of the economy in the two regions were found suitable for comparison of the statistical material available.

A single visit to each of the Washington Commercial Consulates of these two countries with a request for statistics on the mentioned project was enough to produce whole volumes of statistical material and a detailed description of the national economy, including tires. The Somalian statistics showed, in seventeen headings, the trends of importation and production, including bicycles and motorcycles.

Further inquiry at such institutions as the United Nations, the U.S. Department of Commerce, the ministries in Brussels, Rome, and the capitals of both countries—Kinshasa and Mogadishu—provided truly complete material of the type needed to initiate most types of marketing research and adequately covered the need for information for the project mentioned. Desk research was undertaken on prices and customs tariffs so that landing costs could be derived. Information was also available on current wages and labor force, regulations on foreign investment, plant-location suggestions, taxation, government subsidies, and incentives.

4. THE IMPORTANCE OF STATISTICS
ON THE NATIONAL ECONOMY: ETHIOPIA

Immediately after World War II the Ethiopian Government requested, through the United Nations and, directly, in several industrially advanced countries including France, Belgium, and Czechoslovakia, that statistical experts from university or government circles be made available to modernize and validate Ethiopian statistics.

For Ethiopia the benefit of statistical data was instrumental in assessing the vast economic resources of the country, until then only superficially known. The number of cattle alone amounts to 27 million, not to mention sheep and goats. Then there is the fabulous virgin soil, estimated at 100 times that of Egypt's agricultural wealth. In Ethiopia barely 2 per cent of the food potential is being utilized and cultivated rationally, whereas throughout the world all arable land that can be cultivated rationally is already in use.

Without thorough statistical information it is hard to imagine that American, British, and Israeli foreign capital, for instance, would be so strongly interested in the Ethiopian economic potential. Good agricultural schools to explore the vast food resources are a remote but still direct benefit of the development of the nation's economy after the war.

The United Nations still gives such assistance to any member country in need of improving its statistics.

5. GATHERING WORLDWIDE STATISTICS: THE EXAMPLE OF SEWING MACHINES

Sewing machines are a suitable example for exploring the availability of statistics on yearly unit sales and stock in the hands of users, in the developing countries particularly. Sewing machines are sold in 182 countries and have penetrated into the most primitive and isolated communities during the postwar period. The intensity of demand increases (in terms of unit sales per 1,000 population as per cent of income per capita) faster in the developing countries than in the countries with high incomes. Thus, it is essential to obtain statistics on a regular, periodic basis from the developing countries in order to gain a worldwide picture of the industry.

Considerable effort has been made by the Singer Sewing Machine Company to provide a unifield yardstick of sales, and the territorial economic market potential in particular, in the developing countries. Further measuring of the performance of the competition was needed on the basis of the formula: local unit product plus import and export (by countries of origin and countries of destination). These methods were consistently applied in each country of the world, no matter what the economic standard of the country, so that today the United States and Afghanistan, for example, both have the same kind of sewing machine statistics in the files of the Singer Company.

This goal was reached after several years of correspondence with statistical offices in the developing countries. Many rough estimates that had to be made in the beginning (during the mid-1950's) are being replaced with original source data. Experience has been gained in collecting, simplifying, converting, tabulating, and interpreting data but, in particular, obtaining the location and exact addresses where one can find the statistics of more than 100 countries. Such statistics are a priceless possession and of central importance in this continuing project.

6. USING MARKETING RESEARCH TECHNIQUES FOR SUPPLY AND DEMAND ANALYSIS: INDIA*

Hindustan Lever Limited has carried out a series of surveys on groundnut oil to provide not only information on the demand in their home market for this and other oils and fats but also, through crop forecasts and other crop surveys, information on the likely supply of the groundnuts. Marketing research techniques figure prominently in this case history.

Supply Side

The main object is to obtain, as early in the growing season as possible, reliable estimates of the likely crop. Two methods are used: trade and market estimates and crop survey. The former are obtained through opinion surveys among the trade and the officials of the Agricultural Produce Market Committees and other organized bodies. Although these estimates are useful in getting a rough idea of the expected crop, they cannot be precise because of their inherently subjective nature. Crop surveys are the only way to get an objective estimate of total production, and they constitute the major part of this research on groundnuts. (Groundnuts are any of various plants with edible tubers, such as the peanut.)

The ideal method for accurate estimates would be to take frequent cuttings from small specific areas, chosen at random from all regions, and to make appropriate laboratory measurements of these cuttings.

*Material derived from the International Chamber of Commerce (Paris), Report No. 247, "How Marketing Research Helps Developing Countries"; by permission.

This is impractical, however, because of the costs and administrative difficulties involved. A simple route-survey method was, therefore, developed, which works briefly as follows. The investigators hire a taxi and ride along motorable routes through groundnut-growing tracts, stopping every five miles or so to interview farmers along the roadside. In all, over 1,500 farmers are interviewed. The emphasis is not so much on the number interviewed as on the quality of the information gathered. This is made as reliable as possible through proper training and supervision of the investigators, to ensure that they are well informed on agricultural practice.

Checks on the estimates so obtained are provided by discussions en route with the trade, market officials, and research officers at the government Agricultural Research Stations in India. The margin of error in the forecasts, as compared with the government's subsequent estimates of actual crop, is, on the whole, about 5 per cent and, compared with crop cutting surveys, when these have been attempted, about 2-3 per cent.

Other crop surveys can also be carried out. Acreage and crop progress surveys are aimed at estimating acreage as soon as sowings are over and establishing the exact dates of sowings so as to predict the expected time of crop arrivals in the market. Since it was found that acreage changes did not have as important an effect on the eventual crop as yield per acre, all that was really needed were the sowing dates, broad trends in acreage, and crop progress. These are simple enough to obtain through inexpensive mail surveys. From 1963 onward, this information has, therefore, been obtained through short mail questionnaires to a number of merchants, oil millers, commission agents, and government Agricultural Research Stations in India.

Stock-movement surveys are important because price depends not only on the total amount of the crop but also on the time pattern of its arrival at the markets, on the stocks held by farmers (the sellers) and by traders (the buyers), and on the trade's ideas about, and general attitudes toward, the stock position. Sample surveys to record these factors are made by representatives at regular intervals from the point of time at which most of the crop has been marketed and the prices are on the increase. Farmers, merchants, and millers are interviewed by representatives at important centers, and local records of groundnut arrivals are obtained wherever possible. Returns of stock are also obtained from some wholesalers and retailers to give a picture of the "pipeline" position.

Both the quantity and timing of rainfall throughout the growth cycle has an important bearing on the final yield. Rainfall charts are, therefore, kept for a properly chosen sample of fifty centers. By comparing these with the "ideal" pattern of rainfall, the progress of the crops in the different regions can be assessed, and early forecasts of their likely total can be made.

Demand Side

As regards the demand side—not only for groundnut oil but also for competing oils and fats—the research covers consumer panels and desk research.

Consumer panels involve random samples of households. In eighteen large towns of India these households are visited regularly by research investigators, who investigate monthly purchases of oils, fats, and, among other items, soaps and toiletries. In all, the total sample contacted is approximately 4,000 households.

The data collected in these panels form the base for much useful analysis. The monthly statistics on household consumption of oils and fats throw light on the movement of stock between the retailer and consumer and thus add useful information to the stock-movement surveys conducted among the farmers and the trade. Calculations can be made to show the extent to which demand would be expected to increase or decrease with changes in income and price. The trend in total household consumption of oil can be obtained in relation to population, urbanization, and other factors to form the basis for long-term projections of demand for oils and fats.

Demand projections are made both for short and long terms. The former are based mainly on likely price changes, due either to the supply or to the demand position. The long-term studies are made in relation to the development of the national income and take into account the likely changes in demand for the particular uses of the oil, e.g., as edible liquid, in soaps, paints, and other miscellaneous domestic uses, and as exports.

Using available data on the average weekly, monthly, and yearly prices of groundnut oil, studies have been made with the object of relating these fluctuations to the various factors that influence them. It was found that the factors examined in these studies explained about

75 per cent of the variation in average yearly prices, with the remainder due to intangibles not yet identified.

Generally, the use of mathematical techniques, some quite complex, for these problems is constantly expanding, in particular for coffee and cocoa futures in Ghana, Brazil, and Equador.

7. MEASURING MARKET POTENTIAL
FOR SUPERMARKETS: ARGENTINA*

Under certain circumstances the problem facing a businessman may require that a single survey contain research not only into the relevant marketing factors (i.e., attracting and satisfying consumers) but also into factors that are normally the subject of separate studies by management (e.g., cost and administration). This survey by the International Basic Economy Corporation was concerned 'with the potential for introducing a form of distribution new to a country—supermarkets in Argentina—and is an example of such circumstances.

The material for the survey was compiled from personal observations in the area itself and from such few statistical sources as were available. The findings and their interpretation comprise what is really an all-embracing descriptive economic report—a technical study of a possible distribution system, covering both the need for it and the practical issues to be faced in meeting this need.

The report, therefore, grew out of a detailed examination of the following elements:

(1) The economic situation in Buenos Aires: the cost of living as opposed to earnings during the previous five years, the factors contributing to this, and the effect on the distribution of food supplies

(2) The buying public: the various income groups, their habits of spending money, where they shop, who buys the

*Material derived from the International Chamber of Commerce (Paris), Report No. 247, "How Marketing Research Helps Developing Countries"; by permission.

family food and how often, and the value of average purchases and expenditures for food per week

(3) A general description of existng retail food outlets: mainly small shops offering credit and delivery, with very little variety of merchandising or food distribution (almost a forgotten industry compared with the modern shops for clothing, household goods, and so forth), supermarkets almost unknown, general conditions unsatisfactory, and prepackaging virtually unknown

(4) Gross margins for existing food outlets: data for each of a wide range of food items in various parts of the city

(5) Store location: estimate of proportion of the middle class living in the neighborhood—typical customers for supermarkets and highest spenders for food per capita—and availability of selling personnel. (The last two factors were found to be in conflict, as younger female selling personnel were harder to get because the retailer was open for six days weekly, whereas industry and offices worked only five or five and one-half days. Thus, the closer a selected store site was to the middle-class areas with factories and offices in the neighborhood, the harder it was to obtain selling personnel.)

8. HANDLING THE SHOPLIFTING PROBLEM IN A LARGE STORE: VENEZUELA

A recently established large general store in Caracas complained to its company about obvious and increasing pilfering, "We cannot afford to ignore it any more," they wrote, "not unless we are willing to have our store stolen from right under us." Surprisingly enough, the management was unable to give an accurate estimate of their losses. The marketing research department in the consulting company was charged with obtaining information to deal with the problem.

Venezuela is by no means the only country suffering from this growing epidemic. In the United States this problem has been dealt with statistically, and additional U.S. research information was available that was helpful in solving the problem in Venezuela. Information from the United States provided the following facts. Shoplifting by customers and employees and accounting "mistakes" account for 6 per cent of the yearly sales, about equal to the amount of profit. (In slums, black or white, pilferage runs 25 per cent or more, a main reason for retail merchants' prices being high in slums and ghettos.) The most common shoplifted items are food, liquor, books, clothing, and foodware. Larger stores are hit more often than are neighborhood retail establishments. Half the shoplifters are teenagers. Of these, 65 per cent tell their parents about their shoplifting. The chances are twenty to one that a teenage thief is a girl. Only 5 per cent of the latter come from bad family situations at home or are mentally ill.

The most frequent reasons given for shiplifting by teenagers were that they stole just for the fun of it; all the other kids did it, so why shouldn't they; and "the shops often consciously sell us damaged, spoiled, and overpriced things. It is a natural impulse for us to try to compensate ourselves for this."

The solutions suggested for the Caracas store were similar to those taken in the United States: hiring shop detectives; posting warning signs, such as "THIS STORE IS PROTECTED AGAINST SHOPLIFTING. VIOLATORS WILL BE PROSECUTED"; and insisting on police arrest, prosecution, and prison sentence when an adult person is caught, including informing the public by available means about such cases (through the local press, for instance).

For the teenage shoplifter problem in Caracas, however, the general approach selected was education. Colleges and parents' committees were invited to cooperate. Pamphlets were printed and distributed to the young people and their parents, emphasizing the following points:

(1) Pilfering is another name for stealing.

(2) The shoplifting impulse can have serious consequences; for example, with a police record it may be difficult or impossible to pursue certain professions.

(3) One must realize the great mental damage such petty acts of stealing can do to a young person.

At the same time a campaign in the local press was introduced. The result was amazing and showed what a little education can do. Shoplifting was measured by shelf-goods inventory control, and it had dropped 75 per cent during the week of the campaign. In several cases stolen goods were found in front of the entrance in the morning or were returned by mail.

9. MARKET SURVEY FOR THE
ESTABLISHMENT OF MACHINE-TOOL
MANUFACTURING: EAST PAKISTAN*

The research was divided into a survey of likely users within the market (i.e., East Pakistan) and a study of the consumption of machine tools in various countries at different stages of industrial development.

In the survey of the East Pakistan market, the interviewers questioned the main users and others interested in machine tools. Distinctions were made among workshops using machine tools in the course of their main activity; maintenance workshops attached to factories of all kinds, together with workshops attached to the main public services (e.g., railways, water); industrial workshops (schools, technical colleges, and the like), and miscellaneous workshops.

It was thus possible to determine the existing number of machine tools, the short-term needs of replacement, and the short- and medium-term needs of development. In interpreting answers given by the wide range of users interviewed, care was taken to check the characteristics of new users and estimate financial and other resources needed for full development. Subject to these two reservations, the estimates derived from the opinions obtained in the survey indicated an upper limit to the possible market in East Pakistan.

In the study of other countries' experience, statistics were obtained from international bodies and trade groups to show the relationship in both developed and developing countries between per capita income and the consumption of machine tools. From this relationship it was possible to forecast—quite independently of the survey of the East Pakistan market—what the total demand for machine tools in East Pakistan might be, given the levels of industrial income set out in that country's five-year plan. Information was obtained by examining statistics of exports of different types of machine tools to other countries at stages of development similar to that of East Pakistan and at lower and higher stages.

*Material derived from the International Chamber of Commerce (Paris), Report No. 246, "Export Marketing Research"; by permission.

10. ADVERTISING MEDIA
RESEARCH: CEYLON*

The Market Research Department of Lever Brothers Ltd. (Ceylon), conducted for the audit Bureau of Circulations Ltd. of that country the first comprehensive island-wide inquiry of its kind ever undertaken there. It exemplifies a joint effort in media research by advertisers, advertising agencies, and media owners.

The objectives of the survey were to establish the proportion of adult men and women in the major socio-economic groups in Ceylon that read/buy a newspaper or periodical and to study the relationship, for men and women in each important socio-economic group, between the readership of newspapers and periodicals and those who listen to the radio and go to the cinema. The methods that were used follow.

Readership

Respondents were shown a booklet in which the titles of twenty-five publications were produced in black and white. They were asked if any of these or any other publications had been "looked at" recently. On the basis of this data, readership was defined as having looked at a publication within a specified period: yesterday for dailies, during the last seven days for weeklies and Sunday papers, during the last two weeks for semimonthlies, and during the last four weeks for monthlies.

After readership was established, further questions were asked, designed to secure data on the places where the publications were read, the regularity of readership, and patterns of buying, borrowing, and lending of these publications. The twenty-five publications listed in the booklet were chosen with regard for two requirements: They had a circulation of at least 10,000, as far as it was known, and they were regularly available at most newsstands.

*Material derived from the International Chamber of Commerce (Paris), Report No. 247, "How Marketing Research Helps Developing Countries"; by permission.

Radio-Listening and Cinema-Going Habits

Supplementary information on radio-listening and cinema-going habits was also obtained to give perspective to the findings on readership. This was obtained through a series of questions aimed at collecting data on frequency of listening to the radio and visiting the cinema, language types, stations/services listened to, listening hours, programs listened to in the case of the radio, and similar and other pertinent questions on cinema-going habits. An additional question also attempted to obtain information on exposure to advertisements shown in the cinemas.

Classification of Respondents

Information on this was collected at the end of each interview. It included age, educational qualifications, languages spoken, religion, and occupation of the respondent or head of the household. These data also helped the investigator to classify the respondent into his or her socio-economic group.

Sample and Distribution of Interviews

Since most of the interviews had to be conducted in Sinhalese and Tamil, translations of the questionnaire in both languages were used. To obtain, at reasonable cost, a completely random sample representing the total Ceylon population is virtually impossible, because no properly maintained lists of names and addresses are available. The problems of transport and locating the selected persons would be immense. It is possible, however, to obtain representative subsamples of the country's main socio-economic groups, each of which are fairly homogeneous, and then from these subsamples to calculate figures for the whole country by weighting their results appropriately. The total sample, i.e., all the subsamples, comprised 2,600 interviews.

The principal division of this total was first into rural and urban subsamples in the ratio of 80:20, respectively. The rural subsample was further divided into four subgroups: Wet Zone Rural, Estate Tamils, Dry Zone, and the Jaffna Peninsula. The urban subsample was further divided, not geographically, but by three socio-economic subgroups—namely, upper and middle class, lower middle class, and working class.

Selection among these subgroups was based on the following criteria: estimated level of income, type of home and surroundings, type of domestic capital possessed, and educational level. Thus, for example, the upper and middle class included all professional types, such as doctors, lawyers, college or university teachers; the lower middle class was mainly white-collar workers and primary- and secondary-school teachers; and the working class included both skilled and unskilled workers. Where subgroups were very small, a more than proportional number of interviews was taken and corrected in the final weighting.

The problem of interviewing men at home during normal working hours was overcome by interviewing a fair number of men at their places of work—in offices in urban areas and in the fields in rural areas.

Data Reported

All tables in the report gave totals for "all Ceylon," with separate figures for each of the four areas for the rural subsample and the three socio-economic groups for the urban subsample. Readership or audience in Ceylon was shown not only for each journal or medium but also for various combinations of these, e.g., those who read publications and listen to radio, those who read dailies and Sunday papers, and readers of any one paper who also read other papers. Radio-listening data covered frequency and place of listening, choice of stations, language preference, and exposure to advertising. Field work was done between April and June, and the full report was available in September of the same year.

In conclusion, a few examples will illustrate the type of information that was obtained. In "all Ceylon," 53 per cent of men and 23 per cent of women read at least one newspaper or periodical. In urban areas, the corresponding figures were 80 per cent for men and 65 per cent for women. (The figures rise to a full 100 per cent for upper- and middle-class men—a useful medium, therefore, for firms selling luxury goods.) In rural areas, only 45 per cent of men and 13 per cent of women read publications.

Radio had an even bigger audience and was more evenly spread over the country. In "all Ceylon," 58 per cent of men listened to the radio—73 per cent in urban areas and 55 per cent in rural areas. The corresponding figures for women were 33 per cent for "all Ceylon," 62 per cent in urban areas, and 26 per cent in rural areas. In buying radio time it was, of course, useful to know that, for instance, 12 per cent of men listened between 7:00 and 7:30 a.m., about the same proportion as listened at lunch-time and about half of the peak evening audiences between 7:00 and 8:00 p.m.

11. SAMPLING FIELD TECHNIQUES: PERU

This case represents one of six identical projects undertaken simultaneously by a Chicago marketing research firm in Mexico, Venezuela, Colombia, Brazil, Peru, and Argentina. The topics to be covered in the research were determined on the basis of consultation with the sponsor of the survey in New York and developed and refined by means of an intensive pilot survey in Peru.

A master questionnaire was designed for use in all six countries. Of course, slight differences in wording occurred, to conform to local usage in each case. (The Brazilian study was the only one not conducted in Spanish.) Topically and structurally the questionnaires were identical in all six countries. Only brand names and terminology varied, after careful pretesting in each country.

Data-processing was also conducted along closely parallel lines and followed a tabulation plan designed in New York on the basis of preliminary returns from each country. All tabulation was done in New York, with the most up-to-date computer equipment available.

Field work was conducted by citizens of each country specially trained for this project by personnel sent from the New York and Mexican offices of the research firm. All interviewing was carefully controlled by professional field supervisors who had trained the field personnel and later verified a minimum of 35 per cent of the interviews that they had conducted. Verification was accomplished by revisiting 15 per cent of the respondents and repeating all or portions of the interview to make sure not only that the interview had actually taken place but also that it had been conducted precisely according to instructions.

Personal-Interview Survey

A personal-interview survey was conducted among a cross-section sample of Peruvian women. A total of 1,502 interviews was completed during the course of the study. The universe of study, or population to be interviewed, was defined as all women between the ages of sixteen and sixty-five living in accessible areas of the country. Both urban and rural populations were included in the universe. Probability techniques were used in the design of the sample. The steps in the selection procedure are set forth below.

Urban Sample

Selection of Cities and Towns

Cities and towns were selected as the primary sampling units for the urban sample. The urban population was defined as residents in towns of more than 2,000 inhabitants at the date of the most recent national census. This does not accord precisely with official definitions that impose requirements other than size and permit some very small communities to be considered "urban," but it seems to represent a reasonable definition and one that coincides with criteria used in other countries.

All cities and towns of more than 2,000 inhabitants were divided into five strata, designed to group together communities of generally comparable levels of urbanization. A total of thirty-six cities and towns were chosen for the national urban sample.

Lima, because of its vital importance in the market, was classified as a stratum by itself and constituted Stratum I. On the basis of the same criteria, all three cities in Stratum II—Callao, Arequipa, and Trujillo—were drawn into the sample.

APPENDIX EXHIBIT 1

Marketing Map of Peru
(Showing Vehicle Registration by Principal Political Subdivision)

(2)	Piura	3.9%
(6)	Lambayeque	2.8%
(7)	Libertad	3.8%
(9)	Ancash	1.3%
(11)	Lima	71.6%
(13)	Junin	4.0%
(14)	Ica	3.1%
(19)	Arequipa	4.1%
(22)	Tacna	1.7%

Following all under 1.0%

(1)	Tumbes
(3)	Cajamarca
(4)	Amazonas
(5)	Loreto
(8)	San Martin
(10)	Huanuco
(12)	Pasco
(15)	Huancavelica
(16)	Ayacucho
(17)	Apurimac
(18)	Cuzco
(20)	Puno
(21)	Moquegua
(23)	Madre De Dios

Source: "World Marketing Survey," *Automobile International* (April, 1966); reprinted by permission of Johnson International Publishing Corp., New York.

APPENDIX TABLE 2

Urban Stratification for Consumer
Survey in Peru

	Strata	Number of Blocks Selected	Interviews Completed
I	1 city of 1,000,000 inhabitants or more	54	271
II	3 cities of 100,000-999,999 inhabitants	60	299
III	4 cities of 50,000-99,999 inhabitants	64	321
IV	13 cities of 10,000-49,999 inhabitants	65	177
V	15 towns of 2,000-9,999 inhabitants		
	V-A 10 towns of 5,000-9,999 inhabitants	20	60
	V-B 5 towns of 2,000-4,999 inhabitants	10	75
	Total	273	1,203

In Strata III, IV, and V, all communities were listed in geographic order within the strata. Their populations were cumulated, and specific communities were selected for inclusion on the basis of a random-start, fixed-interval mode of selection, which accorded to each a probability of selection proportionate to its population. In all, four cites were selected in Stratum III, thirteen cities were selected in Stratum IV, and fifteen towns were selected in Stratum V. To achieve greater precision, Stratum V was further subdivided into Stratum V-A and Stratum V-B.

In Stratum II, since all cites were included, the interviews assigned were distributed among the three cities in proportion to their relative populations. In Stratum I, Lima was undersampled, because of its relatively great size and homogeneous nature. This disproportion was corrected in tabulation.

In all other cases, since cities were selected with probability proportionate to size, workloads were constant for all cities within a given stratum, although they varied among strata. In Stratum III, eighty interviews were assigned to each city; in Stratum IV, twenty-five were assigned; in Stratum V-A, ten were assigned, and in Stratum V-B, five were assigned.

Selection of City Blocks

The selection of city blocks was made through the use of the up-to-date block maps available for larger towns and obtained from the Peruvian Census Department. In cases where no adequate maps were available, simple hand-drawn maps were prepared. The following procedure was employed:

(1) Blocks were numbered in serpentine fashion. (See Appendix Exhibit 2 for the application of this principle on an authentic hand-drawn map.)

(2) A random number between one and the total number of city blocks was selected, representing the first sample block.

(3) A skipping interval was added to that first block, calculated by dividing the total number of blocks by the number of blocks desired for inclusion in the sample. This block represented the second sample block.

(4) This procedure was continued, in circular fashion, until the desired number of blocks was selected.

Workloads were divided into clusters of five interviews per city block. A total of fifty-four blocks was drawn into the sample for Lima, sixty blocks were drawn into the sample for all cities in Stratum II, sixteen were selected in each city for Stratum III, five for each in Stratum IV, two for each in Stratum V-A, and two for each in Stratum V-B. The actual distribution of interviews over the blocks selected was made in proportion to the population resident in each block, with the stipulation that no single block could be assigned a number greater than three times the over-all average (fifteen).

Selection of Respondents

A complete list of all households in the sample blocks was compiled in each city by field personnel. Specific addresses were selected for inclusion in the same way the blocks themselves were

APPENDIX EXHIBIT 2

Block Numbering in Spiral Fashion on Hand-Drawn
Map in Consumer Survey in Peru

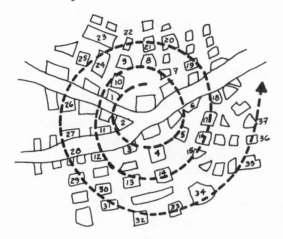

chosen, with a random-start, fixed-interval mode of selection. The number of households selected on any given block was thus proportionate to the number of households existing on all sample blocks in that city.

A single respondent was selected for interview within each household, regardless of the number of eligible respondents in that household. (Servants were not considered eligible respondents.) Field personnel compiled a complete list of all eligible family members, and selected one individual for interview on the basis of a table of random numbers that appeared on the questionnaire itself. Thus, the interviewer had no option in the selection of the respondent at any stage of the selection process.

A minimum of two visits was made in an effort to locate the designated respondent. A third visit was made in all cases in which there seemed to be a reasonable likelihood of success. The only deviation from rigid probability sampling methods occurred in those cases in which the designated respondent could not be located after repeated efforts had been made to find him. In such cases, interviewers were instructed to select a substitute of the same age group, economic class, and marital status living in the same or an adjacent block.

An attempt was also made to find substitutes with the same position in the family as the original respondent, where this was possible. In this manner the bias resulting from failure to locate all designated respondents was reduced to a minimum.

Rural Sample

Selection of Sampling Points

The rural population was defined as that population resident in towns of 2,000 inhabitants or less, or living in isolated homes along accessible roads. "Road segments" were selected as the primary sampling units for the rural sample.

Rural sampling points were generally selected within a radius of 10 kilometers from the communities that had been drawn into the urban sample. In several cases where the population was predominantly rural, however (such as the department of Cajamarca), sampling points were selected at great distances from urban areas. Interviews were assigned to each in proportion to the distribution of the rural population. Certain departments were omitted from consideration in this phase of the sample, however, because of limited rural population and inaccessibility. These were Amazonas, Madre de Dios, Moquegua, San Martin, Tacna, and Tumbes. Together, these account for only 2.9 per cent of the rural population of Peru.

Rural interviews were assigned in clusters of five to each road segment. The term "road segment" refers to a spot along a road, designated by a mileage indicator, at which interviewing commenced. Road segments were selected in the following manner:

(1) A circle was drawn with a radius of 10 kilometers from the border of an urban sampling point or other definable community.

(2) The number of roads leading from that point to the circumference of the circle was counted.

(3) The number of roads was then multiplied by 10.

(4) The resultant number constituted the universe within which sampling points were determined at random.

Numbers were selected by using the same random-start, fixed-interval mode of selection used for the selection of cities, blocks, and households in the urban sample. The number drawn into the sample thus indicated a specific sampling point—both a particular road and a particular point along the road.

Interviews were then conducted at the first five homes along a predetermined side of the road, extending up to 1 kilometer off the road, starting from the road segment thus selected. A total of sixty rural sampling points was drawn, distributed through thirty-eight different locations. Of these, twenty-eight were near communities of 2,000 inhabitants or more, and ten were selected in areas remote from all urban communities, no matter how small.

Selection of Respondents

Individuals within the home were selected for interview in the rural sample by procedures identical to those described for the urban sample.

Processing of Data

All questionnaires completed in the field were prepared for machine tabulation in Latin America and were processed by computer in New York. Disproportionate sampling was employed in certain instances in order to increase the efficiency of the sampling procedure. For example, the rural population, although important, does not approach the significance of the urban population as a market. Fewer interviews were therefore conducted in rural areas than would be called for in a strictly proportionate sample. By the same token, Lima, because of its size, would normally have drawn more interviews than were actually required to provide an accurate picture of the market situation in that city. It was also undersampled in order to permit broader coverage of cities and towns of the country other than the capital.

The disproportions that had thus been deliberately created to improve the efficiency of the sample were corrected at the time of tabulation by according a greater "weight" to interviews obtained from the undersampled strata. In effect, this procedure was equivalent to a physical multiplication of IBM cards for these strata. Appendix Table 3

APPENDIX TABLE 3

Urban and Rural Stratification for
Consumer Survey in Peru
(Weighted)

Stratum	Percentage of Population[a]	Completed Interviews	Weighting Factor	Weighted Interviews	Percentage Distribution After Weighting
I	14.5	271	x4	1,084	14.7
II	4.0	299	x1	299	4.0
III	4.2	321	x1	321	4.3
IV	9.2	177	x4	708	9.6
V-A	3.1	60	x4	240	3.2
V-B	4.4	75	x4	300	4.0
Urban total	39.4	1,203		2,952	39.8
VI[b]	60.6	299	x15	4,474[c]	60.2
Total	100.0	1,502		7,426	100.0

[a]1961 Peruvian Census.

[b]Rural; defined as any community with fewer than 2,000 inhabitants in 1961.

[c]One rural interview was given an incorrect weight of 4 rather than 15 by the computer. Since this discrepancy did not have any substantive effect on the data, it was accepted.

summarizes the distribution of interviews by stratum and the weighting procedure that was followed.

12. INSTRUCTING INTERVIEWERS: BRAZIL

Precise guidance is mandatory in order to obtain a random sample and to enable checking by the supervisor. A consumer survey in São Paulo (see the introductory section of Case History 11 for background data on this survey) used the following items as requirements in the sampling-field selection procedure: determination of the building; determination of the floor; determination of the residence; and, when feasible, determination of the respondent. Each interviewer was given a starting point, a code number, a number X corresponding to the last digit of the house number of the buildings in which the interviews were to be made, and a table of random numbers. The following instructions were also given to each interviewer.

Determination of Building

Place yourself at the starting point indicated to you by the supervisor (such as a church, a cinema, a municipal building). It may happen that for some reason this point is impracticable, due to rebuilding or the like. In such case substitute another starting point if possible, otherwise contact the supervisor by the most convenient means. He will direct you to another starting point.

Facing the starting point, start by keeping to the left. Turn into the first street on your left, then into the first on your right, then again on your left, and so forth, so that you alternate between left and right, left and right.

You should carry out interviews in every building you find along this itinerary where the house number terminates in the number X. Thus, if $X = 7$, you will carry out interviews in the buildings with house numbers ending in 7 that you encounter on either side of the streets on the itinerary. (Simple, but clear, hand-drawn illustrations may also be used in instructing interviewers. See Appendix Exhibit 3 for such an example and 3A for a sample itinerary map.)

APPENDIX EXHIBIT 3

Illustrations of Interviewer's
Itinerary in Consumer
Survey in Peru

A.

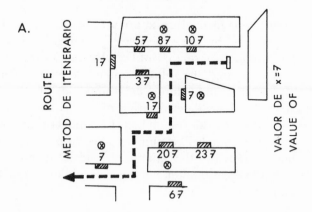

B.

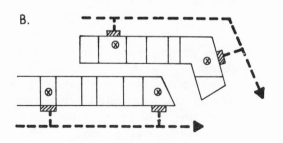

C.

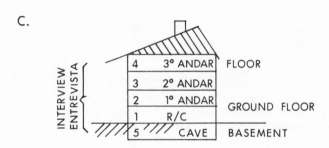

D.

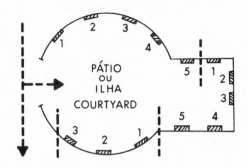

E.

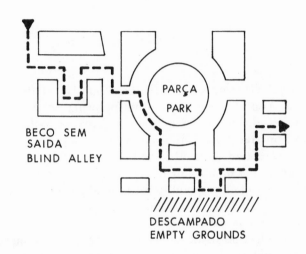

F.

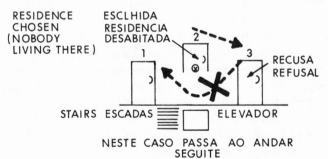

Note:
⊗ Indicates: Residence (nobody living there).

✗ Indicates: Do not continue on that floor because once an interview is refused other inhabitants on the floor may have heard the discussion and be inclined to refuse as well.

Never conduct interviews at starting points, even if the termination of the house number is the value of X. If you are forced to interrupt the interviews, start again at the point where you left off and proceed normally.

If the houses on the street are not numbered, select every fifth building, i.e., you will leave an interval of four buildings between the buildings where you try to conduct interviews. (See Appendix Exhibit 3B for a graphic example of this procedure.) But if the number placed on a window, gate, or side entrance on the same street happens to agree with the value of X, then select that building.

Determination of Floor

Start by taking note of the total number of floors in the building selected. You may use any of the following when you make a count: mail boxes, doorbells, asking the concierge, or looking at the building.

No matter how you make your count, be sure to include the basement, ground floor, attic, and the like, if they are inhabited. After determining the number of floors, number them in such a fashion that floor No. 1 will correspond to the ground floor, No. 2 to the first floor, and so on. The basement should be numbered last. (See Appendix Exhibit 3C for an example of floor numbering.)

The selection of the floor should be made by means of a table of random numbers that will be supplied to you. (See Appendix Exhibit 4 for such a table.) To determine the floor, all you need do is to cross that line in the table that corresponds to the code number with the column corresponding to the number of floors. Suppose that the code is 9 and the building has five floors: basement, ground floor, first floor, second floor, and third floor. By crossing line 9 (horizontal) with column 5 (vertical) you will obtain the number 2. Therefore, you will carry out an interview on the second floor. If the building has eight floors, you will conduct two interviews, one on the second floor and one on the third floor.

If you enter a courtyard because its door number corresponds to the value of X, you should number the residences facing the courtyard in groups of five, as if they were floors belonging to the same building, and proceed in the same manner as previously described. (See Appendix Exhibit 3D for a graphic example of this method of numbering.)

APPENDIX EXHIBIT 4

Table of Random Numbers for Selecting Floor on Which Interview Should Be Conducted

QUESTIONÁRIO Algarismo das Unidades	No. de pisos do prédio; No. de habitacões por piso																	
	1	2	3	4	5	6	7		8		9		10		11		12	
							1^a	2^a	1^a	2^a	1^a	2^a	1^a	2^a	1^a	2^a	1^a	2^a
0	1	1	3	1	3	2	1	5	3	1	2	1	5	6	4	2	2	1
1	1	2	1	4	3	5	2	6	4	2	7	9	9	8	11	9	6	6
2	1	2	2	1	4	6	2	7	4	6	4	4	2	2	8	3	10	3
3	1	1	1	2	1	3	3	1	6	7	3	3	4	3	7	6	4	12
4	1	1	1	4	5	1	3	4	6	8	8	5	7	10	5	5	8	5
5	1	2	3	3	4	2	1	2	1	5	5	6	10	5	1	1	7	7
6	1	1	3	1	2	5	5	5	7	7	9	9	8	9	3	4	11	9
7	1	2	1	4	5	3	7	7	5	4	6	7	1	1	2	7	3	10
8	1	2	2	3	1	4	6	6	8	8	4	2	6	7	6	8	1	4
9	1	1	2	2	2	4	4	3	2	3	1	8	3	4	10	11	5	2

Nota: Na contagem do no. de pisos são incluídas as caves, rés-do-chão, sub-caves, águas furtadas, etc.

Translation from Portuguese:

Questionário
Algarismo das Unidades

Questionnaire
Number of Units [Code number]

No. de pisos do prédio
No. de habitações por piso

No. of floors of building
No. of residences per floor

Nota: Na contagem do no. de pisos são incluídas as caves, rés-do-chão, sub-caves, águas furtadas, etc.

Note: Number of floors includes basements, ground floor, cellars, and attics, etc. [Attics and cellars should only be included if occupied.]

Determination of Residence

After having selected the floor, it is necessary to determine the residence, in case there is more than one, in which the interview is to be conducted. The first task is to number the residences, starting on the left, in a clockwise direction, as soon as you arrive at the top of the stairs. If you use an elevator, consider your position as if you had reached the floor via the staircase.

To determine the residence, use the table of random numbers (Appendix Exhibit 4) by crossing the code number with the corresponding number of residences on the floor. For example, if the code number is 6 and there are four residences on the floor selected, the number furnished by the table of random numbers is 1. Therefore, you will conduct the interview in the residence to which the number 1 was assigned.

Determination of Respondents

In the developing countries, the selection of the individuals to be interviewed cannot be governed as tightly by rules as can the rest of the sampling-field selection work. The rule that an interviewer should have no option at any stage of the selection process is most frequently violated in the selection of individual respondents in these countries. This selection depends on the kind of information to be collected. For example, in any survey concerning the household economy or readership, it is obvious who the interviewed person ought to be. In case an attempt is made to determine respondents in a survey conducted in a developing country, usually random selection is done by using a "contact sheet" and a "selection sheet."

On the contact sheet all members of the family or household are listed; these facts are obtained from the municipal authorities or by visiting the household selected. On the selection sheet the eligible members are relisted in order of age, indicating sex and relationship to the household. Then there are various ways of selecting the desired individual from all the eligible respondents—let us say, women from fifteen to sixty-four years of age. One commonly used method is to provide a column on the selection sheet with random interval marks indicating certain lines. The eligible respondent who appears at that line is the person to be interviewed.

Special Cases on Itinerary

Plaza, Square, or Garden

Enter such places as a plaza, a square, or a garden in conformity with the rules indicated and keep walking in the same direction until you find the first way out, proceeding normally afterward. (See Appendix Exhibit 3E for a graphic example of this procedure and those described in the remainder of this section.)

Blind Alley

Act as if a blind alley belonged to the same street. Conduct interviews first on one side, then on the other. Afterward, continue along the street from which you entered the blind alley.

Empty Grounds Within Limits of Town

If, upon reaching the limits of a town, you ascertain that there is no street for a distance of 100 meters, you should invert the route and continue along the street previously followed, in a way similar to that adopted in the case of a blind alley. If there is a street within a distance of 100 meters, continue along the route, get to that street, and continue the left-right procedure.

Empty Grounds in Heart of Town

If you meet up with empty grounds in the heart of a town, never cross them. Act as you did for empty grounds within the limits of town.

Substitution

Should an interview not be possible at one *residence* (an office or business establishment, premises not inhabited, and the like), go on to the next door on the same floor in a clockwise direction. Only in the case of a refusal on a given *floor* should you go on to the next floor. On the next floor you again determine residence by numbering the residences in a clockwise direction and use the table of random numbers to select the residence for interview. (See Appendix Exhibit 3 for a graphic example of this method of substitution.)

If the interview cannot be conducted in one *building*, go on to the next building along the route.

13. EXPORT MARKET RESEARCH ON
DEVELOPING COUNTRIES*

The following is a case history on export market research conducted by the Japan External Trade Organization (JETRO), a body supported by the Japanese Government. The JETRO surveys are conducted as part of JETRO's own program or at the request of outside organizations and various outside interests. For the purpose of conducting extensive surveys on export markets, JETRO maintains trade centers in various countries and also has agents in the leading countries of the world. The main aim of these surveys is to collect information that can be used to expand and increase Japan's trade.

This market survey was undertaken at the direct request of private businessmen, central and local government authorities, exporters' associations, and other organizations. The type of product involved was household electrical appliances (sewing machines, irons, cookers, toasters, fans, refrigerators, washing machines, vacuum cleaners, air conditioners, and the like). The countries regarded as potential export markets were Argentina, Pakistan, Venezuela, United Arab Republic, Ceylon, Peru, Ghana, Iraq, Spain, Chile, Nigeria, Turkey, Kenya, and Brazil.

Aim of Survey

Japanese electrical household appliances are exported mainly to advanced   countries—such   as   the   United   States,   Canada,   or

*Material derived from the International Chamber of Commerce (Paris), Report No. 246, "Export Marketing Research"; by permission.

Belgium—Southeast Asia, and the Near and Middle East. An accurate grasp of the market trends in the developing areas is needed if exports are to be drastically increased in the future. Only scanty basic information is available, however, concerning electrical household appliances that are closely related to the people's living habits in the target countries. The survey referred to here was aimed at filling this gap. Through the collection of data over an extensive area during a fixed period, it was hoped that comparisons of market trends could be made.

Survey Details and Method

In order to conduct extensive surveys simultaneously, efforts were made to complete the survey within one month. Actually, however, the task required more than the projected period.

In order to study the extent of popularization of household electrical appliances, the survey was conducted by classification into higher-, middle-, and lower-income groups; urban areas and farm villages; and fiscal year. Surveys were also conducted to ascertain the relation between fuel consumption (such as electricity, gas, oil, and liquefied petroleum gas) and income.

The request for the survey, once accepted by JETRO Headquarters, was relayed to more than seventy trade centers and special agents, and it was they who actually conducted the survey. The data were collected by examining various documents in different countries, requesting statistics, organizing direct interviews with businessmen, and carrying out a random sampling of individual consumers. Thorough efforts were made to obtain accurate figures.

14. RUSH RESEARCH ON EXPORTS TO DEVELOPING COUNTRIES

The following case history is an example of a "rush" research job, which may well turn out to represent practical advice for researchers on export to developing countries or possibly to any country.

A U.S. manufacturer of consumer goods needed a survey within two-three weeks on twenty-eight countries located in Latin America, Africa, and the Far East. The urgent business decision to be arrived at was whether to acquire a production facility to manufacture refrigerators centrally or, rather, to buy them from several local sources in the countries under study.

The data required, by country, were quantity sold; product characteristics of refrigerators sold; prices—average, import, retail; advertising—estimate of expenditure, copies, slogans; and import duties.

The consulates and the U.N. observers of most countries have offices in New York City. They regularly receive copies of the principal newspapers and magazines from their countries and keep them in their libraries from three to six months. These offices are concentrated in certain sections of the city, so that three investigators, each making two visits daily, were able to examine the libraries of these offices within a week.

The personnel of the foreign representatives' offices were cooperative and put the newspapers at the disposal of the visitors, except for three countries that do not have this material in New York but in their Washington offices. Ads for the prior three months were checked for the above-mentioned information requirements for most of the countries, so that a survey had been accomplished and orientation had been gained, as needed, for product characteristics, retail prices, and advertising.

Additional desk research was conducted at the same time on export statistics from major manufacturing countries to obtain quantities sold and average export prices from Italy, Germany, Japan, and the United States. Customs-duty information was obtained from the International Customs Tariffs Bureau in Brussels (at Rue de l'association 38).

A survey of this kind can be conducted in most capital cities. The embassies and consulates can be expected to permit any interested party to see the press advertising on imported products and other marketing factors of their home country. It should be remembered that a commercial consulate regards such service as one of the very important reasons for its existence. Therefore, one may rely upon this assistance when planning such a project.

APPENDIX B

GLOSSARY OF TERMS USED IN MARKETING RESEARCH

Like any other specialized field of activity, marketing research has its own vocabulary. Ordinary language and the accepted sense of everyday words and expressions are not capable of conveying every technical idea. For this reason, a technical vocabulary develops, through which it is possible for practitioners to convey in one word or expression ideas that would otherwise require the use of a score of words.

This glossary contains terms commonly used in the field of marketing research. Some of them have been borrowed from other fields, particularly statistics and economics. Others are terms used in allied fields. The texts are not intended to be exhaustive definitions but, rather, explanations that will help the reader to understand the meaning of the terms used. Several statistical notions are explained in more detail, so that they may be applied in practice.

The majority of these terms (those preceded by an asterisk) are translated into five languages in Appendix C to help communication in international dealings, which are frequent in marketing research in the developing countries.

ACCEPTABILITY. Worth accepting; received as adequate; in marketing research, may describe margin of error, as marketing problems are not solved in terms of absolute certainty or precision.

*ACTUAL MARKET. Sum total of consumers purchasing and using product in question; in terms of quantity, actual amount of product being sold.

AD HOC. That which is done by reason of circumstances obtaining at the moment; applied to marketing research, inquiries and surveys undertaken in light of particular circumstances or for limited purpose; usually single pieces of research that are not part of a continuous process.

*ADEQUATE SAMPLE. Sample size that is large enough to represent accurately group from which sample is drawn. Further increase in accuracy as result of increase in size of sample is slight relative to cost.

ADVERTISING. Paid-for and nonpersonal spreading of information about business concern or its products for purpose of stimulating demand and stabilizing flow of goods from production to consumption. (*Example*: press, TV, posters, direct mail, exhibitions, radio, public relations, and other forms.)

*AGE GROUP. Group of population belonging to certain age bracket. (*Example*: under 25.9, 26-34.9, 35-44.9.)

*AMBIGUOUS QUESTION. Question having two or more possible meanings.

ANALYSIS. Process by which complex thing is resolved into its elements; in marketing research, determines presence of certain factors and relative influence of each factor. *Qualitative analysis* reveals presence of certain factors; *quantitative analysis* determines numerical value of factors present. (*Example*: analysis of sales by territories to determine contribution that each sales territory makes to total sales.)

APPEAL (in advertising). Message or theme used in advertising for purpose of obtaining response from consumers or potential consumers by playing on their emotions.

*AREA SAMPLE. Sample selected on geographical basis, where territory to be covered is broken down into small but comparable areas, some of which are then picked out at random to form basis of sample. Within each small area, or cell, actual sampling units are then selected.

ATTITUDE QUESTION. Question that is designed to determine person's attitude or reaction to, or opinion on, pertinent point. (*Example*: to find out what person thinks about new feature incorporated in product or what he thinks about credit policy or advertising of competitor.)

*AVERAGE. Measure of central tendency, found by adding up values of several measurements and dividing that total by number of measurements recorded; also called common average or arithmetic mean.

BALANCE SHEET. Shows what, on particular day, company owes and owns, as well as who owns company. There is no one way of designing balance sheet, any more than there is one way of designing income statement. Particular items company lists, and way it lists them, depend on its legal form (proprietorship, partnership, or corporation) and type of industry it is in. Regardless of variations, however, will consist of three major headings: assets, liabilities, and net worth.

*BEHAVIOR. Responses to stimulation, especially those that can be observed.

*BIAS. Systematic error running through whole or part of sampling operation, essence of which is that it forms constant component of error recurring at each subsequent step; error that is not canceled out by errors in opposite direction in other elements of sample but is, rather, aggravated by occurring in same direction in these other elements. Can be due to variety of factors and can take place at any stage of sampling operation from planning of work to interpretation of results.

*BIASED ERROR. *See* Interviewer Bias.

*BRAND BAROMETER. Method of continuous marketing research enabling degree of, and changes in, brand acceptance to be measured and by which comparisons between different brands can also be made.

BREAK-EVEN POINT. Point at which income exactly equals expenditure. Use of break-even technique enables relationship between sales and various cost items to be established in terms of money and volume of transactions.

*BREAKDOWN. Division of sample or analysis of results according to specific factors. (*Example*: by income, by age groups, by sex.)

BUDGET. Statement of possible and desirable income for forward period of time and of various expenditures necessary to achieve that income.

CALL-BACK. Repeated attempt to interview respondent for purposes of completing interview; also, check call by supervisor.

CAPITALISM. Economic system based upon private ownership of all kinds of property and freedom of individual to contract with others and to engage in economic activities of his choice and for his own profit and well-being; also called free enterprise. Such government restrictions as are placed on private property and freedom of contract are designed for protection of public. (*Example*: zoning restrictions regulating building operations or land use and exclusion of agreements involving an illegal act.) In capitalistic economy, government plays relatively minor role in economic life, its functions being mainly those of maintaining order, preventing abuses, and carrying on such activities as private enterprise cannot pursue with reasonable assurance of profit.

*CELL. Smallest organizational unit of group. (*Example*: family.)

CENTRAL TENDENCY. Measure of summarizes number of values by providing one value that is expression of combined tendencies of all values. Some measure of this kind is essential to give meaning to mass of data. (*Example*: average or mean, median, mode.)

*CHECK INTERVIEW. Check call by supervisor for purpose of seeing whether interview has been made correctly.

*CHECK LIST. List of possible answers that can be elicited by question, one or several items of which are marked according to respondent's answer; list of points prepared at beginning of study for purpose of checking that all relevant points have been covered.

*CLOSED QUESTION. Question that limits respondent to brief precoded reply.

CLUSTER SAMPLING. Drawing together of sample units into groups, sometimes result of process of sampling. (*Example*: 100 consecutive names on list, three persons in household.) In such a case, all sample units in each group are observed or interviewed and not subjected to another sampling stage.

*CODING. Process of reducing answers to series of code numbers in order to facilitate tabulation.

COEFFICIENT OF CORRELATION. *See* Correlation; Scatter.

COMMUNISM. Economic system based upon government or community ownership of all wealth and abolition of concept of private property, with production by individuals, ideally, in accordance with capacity and consumption in accordance with need; sometimes used to describe temporary economic system of Soviet Russia, where private property in all capital goods has been abolished but has been retained in various types of consumer goods (Soviet theoreticians, however, usually refer to this system as socialism and suggest that actual communism is condition to be achieved in vague and indefinite future); also used to suggest social revolution by force.

CONCLUSIONS. Final deductions made from results of study, expressed in terms that leave no doubt as to these results and that point to action that is required.

CONSISTENCY. Degree to which data that measure same things or closely allied things agree among themselves.

CONSUMER. In widest sense, someone who purchases and uses a product (in this sense, consumer of product can be manufacturer who uses product for production of further product); in marketing research, usually refers to final consumer, i.e., the public.

*CONSUMER PANEL. Research technique that consists of selecting properly constructed sample of consumers (also dealers) for purpose of continuously reporting their day-to-day purchases. Reports of panel members are collected at regular intervals, and from their analysis changes in consumer demand and consumer attitudes can be established.

CONSUMER RESEARCH. External research consisting of direct questioning or observation of general consuming public, usually through sample surveys.

CONSUMPTION. Utilization of services or material goods for gratification of human desires (as thus defined, means destruction of utility and is one of main topics customarily included in study of economics); in popular parlance, also, use of goods and services for productive purposes. (*Example*: when it is said that raw materials are consumed in finished product.)

CONTROLLED SAMPLE. Sample that is verified according to known characteristics of universe or population. These characteristics are known as *controlling factors* and are included in sample in same proportions as they occur in universe or population.

COPY (in advertising). Material that is to be reproduced in type.

COPY-TESTING. Research for purpose of evaluating probable response to various kinds of advertising copy.

CORRELATION. Measure of dependence of two or more sets of numbers, one upon the other. (*Example*: distance flown by an airplane and amount of fuel consumed will have very close relationship, one being dependent on the other.) Where one variable increases in direct proportion to increase in another variable, *positive correlation* is obtained. *Negative correlation* occurs when one variable decreases as another variable increases. Degree of dependence is measured mathematically by *coefficient of correlation*. Two given factors may show high degree of similarity in their variations, however; this does not necessarily mean that correlation exists and that variation of one factor is dependent on variation of the other. It may well be that both factors are influenced by third factor that affects them both to same degree.

COSTING. Process of establishing cost of various constituents of industrial and commercial activities.

*CROSS SECTION. Segment of universe or population in which all characteristics of that universe or population are represented in their true proportions.

*CROSS-TABULATION. Process of establishing relationship among replies to various questions or among replies and questions and facts that are relevant to study.

CYCLICAL FLUCTUATIONS. More or less periodic variations in time series, caused by forces generating business cycle. There are various statistical methods for estimating cyclical fluctuations in time series. Curve may be computed by calculating secular trend using least-squares method, ascertaining seasonal fluctuations, and correcting trend values accordingly. Results are then subtracted from original data and differences are expressed as percentages of corrected trend values. Curve is finally smoothed by means of moving average.

*DATA. (Plural of datum.) Collection of facts or information.

DEALER. Trader; usually, retailer who sells direct to final consumer.

*DEALER SURVEY. Survey in which dealer, or retailer, is questioned or observed.

DEDUCTIVE METHOD. Process of logical reasoning starting with premise generally accepted as true and arriving at one or more conclusions based on such premise. This method was widely used by classical school and later challenged by historical school. Usefulness of method depends upon validity of basic assumptions, and these have often been found to be faulty. When properly used, however, it has recognized place in scientific investigation.

DEMAND. Schedule of amounts of product that consumers would be willing to buy at all possible prices at any given point of time; desire for product backed up by purchasing ability and willingness to use that ability.

*DEPTH INTERVIEW. Interview during which investigator probes mind of respondent in order to discover everything that he knows or thinks about particular subject and endeavors to uncover underlying thoughts or emotions of respondent. This type of interview is not normally conducted by means of formal questionnaire; investigator uses list of points to guide him during interview and allows interview to proceed as conversation, but guides respondent back to subject if he wanders away from point.

DESK RESEARCH. Deals with published statistics and trade records of own company, as distinct from *field research*, which deals with market characteristics collected through surveys, observations, or experiments. Such research on published information, statistical or otherwise, made within organization is quite inexpensive, simple, and very core of marketing research.

*DEVIATION. Turning aside from a course.

*DIARY METHOD. Broadcast media research method using preprinted diaries for information. (*Example*: which member of family has seen or heard certain programs.)

*DISPERSION. Degree of variation, or scatter, that occurs around average or typical value. Average or typical value is of little use unless this variation is given, for, if variation around measure of central tendency is very large, it is of little use as typical value. It is, therefore, necessary to develop quantitative measure of dispersion that occurs around the average.

DISTRIBUTION. Economic function involved in transfer of goods from production; in statistics, way in which factor or variable is dispersed throughout universe or population; used as synonymous with marketing.

ECONOMETRICS. Study of economics by means of mathematics and advanced statistics.

EDITING. Process of examining completed questionnaires and coding them or otherwise preparing them for tabulation.

EXPERIMENTAL METHOD. Research procedure designed as controlled experiment. Types of experiments most frequently used in marketing research are test markets, sales promotion tests, pricing tests, and consumer-preference or consumer-use tests.

EXTERNAL RESEARCH. Research where sources are external to concern for which research is undertaken. Two types: research for which sources are published data and original research among traders or consumers.

EXTRAPOLATION. Method of estimating unknown value that is either higher than highest or lower than lowest known value in series of numbers. (*Example*: from present record of population growth in country, estimate might be made of population, say ten years hence, by this method.)

*FIELD WORK. Work carried out by interviewers and supervisors among dealers in case of trade research or among consumers in case of consumer research.

FILTER QUESTIONS. Questions providing information that assists in formulating further questions or determines procedure of research, rather than information, for subject under investigation.

FIXED COST. Cost that does not necessarily increase or decrease as total volume of production increases or decreases; also called indirect cost, overhead, or supplementary cost. (*Example*: interest on borrowed capital, maintenance expenses, and fire insurance.)

FOCUSED INTERVIEW. *See* **Interview, Focused or Group.**

FORECAST OF SALE. Volume of sales that it is possible and desirable to achieve in given forward period, taking into account market conditions and predetermined level of sales effort.

*FRAME. Basic or skeleton structure of research project.

*FREQUENCY. Number of times particular value occurs in series of data.

FREQUENCY DISTRIBUTION. Classification of statistical data by class intervals according to size or magnitude, with number of items (frequency) applicable to each class interval. Sometimes called frequency table; when displayed graphically, using X axis for class intervals and Y axis for frequencies, called column diagram, or histogram. When midpoints of class intervals at various frequency levels join with straight lines, resulting broken line called frequency polygon. (*Example*: See Appendix Exhibit 5 for frequency distribution, in table and graph form, of weekly earnings of 200 employees.)

APPENDIX EXHIBIT 5

Example of Frequency Distribution

A. Frequency Table   *B. Column Diagram*

Class Interval (dollars)	Frequency
40-40.99	5
41-41.99	8
42-42.99	20
43-43.99	30
44-44.99	50
45-45.99	40
46-46.99	25
47-47.99	12
48-48.99	5
49-49.99	5
Total	200

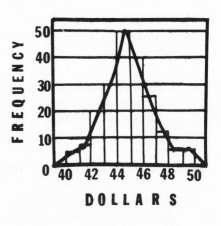

*GRAPH. Method of illustrating statistical data by means of squared paper on which data are represented by lines or curves.

GROSS NATIONAL PRODUCT (GNP). Total value at current market prices of all final goods and services produced by nation's economy before deduction of depreciation charges and other allowances for business and institutional consumption of durable capital goods. Principal components: net national product, national income, personal income, disposable personal income, and personal consumption expenditures. (*Example*: See Appendix Exhibit 6 for flow chart of GNP and its principal components.)

GROUP INTERVIEW. *See* **Interview, Focused or Group.**

*****HAND TABULATION.** Process of sorting, grouping, and counting data manually, as opposed to mechanically. Includes use of hand-operated mechanical or electrical adding and calculating machines.

*****HOUSEHOLD BOOK.** Booklet with printed dates and columns for recording data for survey purposes. (*Example*: for recording expenditure and consumption habits.)

HYPOTHESIS. Tentative statement setting forth apparent relationship among observed facts.

INDEX NUMBER. Figure that discloses relative change, if any, of prices, costs, or some similar phenomena between one period of time and some other period of time selected as base period, which is usually assigned number of 100.

INDUCTIVE METHOD. In economics, process of logical reasoning starting with observed facts and arriving at generalization, setting forth apparent relationship among observed facts; sometimes called realistic method. Such generalization called hypothesis; when repeatedly verified by same method, called theory. Usefulness of method depends upon validity of basic observations; when properly used, however, has recognized placed in scientific investigation.

*****INFORMAL INTERVIEW.** Form of depth interview used for obtaining information for purpose of building questionnaires.

INFORMAL INVESTIGATION. Preliminary investigation used for purpose of defining problem in research project where true problem is obscure.

APPENDIX EXHIBIT 6

Gross National Product and Principal Components Circulation

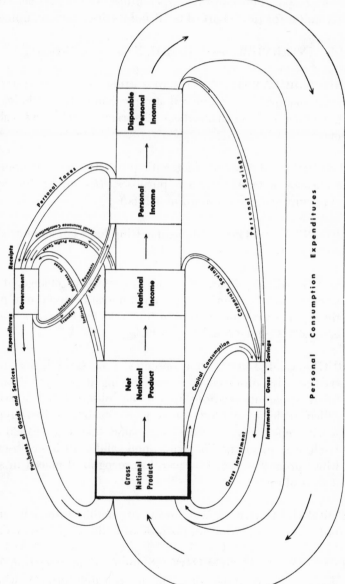

Source: Twentieth Century Fund (New York, 1968); reprinted by permission.

INTERLOCKING QUESTION. Questions in questionnaire that are linked to one another, or answers to some of which depend on answers to others.

INTERNAL CONSISTENCY. Extent to which answers to questions in survey support one another.

INTERNAL RESEARCH. Research concerned solely with sources of information confined to concern for which study is being carried out. (*Example*: records and personnel.)

INTERPOLATION. As applied to statistics, method of estimating intermediate unknown value in series of numbers by reference to known values in series or by reference to associated series, increments of which are proportional to increments of series for which intermediate value is desired.

INTERPRETATION. Process of giving meaning to statistical or other data resulting from research in form that enables information to be used for commercial purposes.

*INTERVIEW. Process of making personal contact with respondent and obtaining from him answers to questions.

*INTERVIEW, FOCUSED OR GROUP. Interview where respondents are assembled in groups of various sizes (see page 25) and complete questionnaire under supervision of researcher or in discussion groups where no questionnaire is used, but researcher takes notes or tapes discussion. Aids development of questionnaire and obtains group reaction to product, advertisement, and the like.

*INTERVIEW, PERSONAL. Interview where investigator is face to face with respondent, usually in respondent's home, at work, in street, or in stores. Used primarily where sample must be carefully controlled, where great deal of information is required, or where something must be shown to respondent.

INTERVIEW, SEMISTRUCTURED. Interview where greater control is given to interviewer than in structured situation and respondent has more freedom, is not limited in his choice of answers, and can explain his answers. Brings out more detailed information than does structured interview. Well-trained, experienced interviewers are required. Analysis is difficult.

INTERVIEW, STRUCTURED. Interview where questionnaire is conventional, interviewer is controlled as to wording and sequence of questions, and respondent is limited to precoded series of answers.

INTERVIEW, UNSTRUCTURED. Interview giving freedom of response relative to particular topic. Interviewer works from rough outline of topics, adopting sequence and wording of questions that will best bring out pertinent aspects of subject. Particularly useful in early stages of research to explore hypotheses; often used in helping to design conventional questionnaires. Well-trained, experienced, highly skilled interviewers are required.

*INTERVIEWER. Person who is employed to make contact with respondents and to interview them.

*INTERVIEWER BIAS. Systematic distortion brought about by personality or manner of interviewer in presence of respondent, often manifested in way in which he asks questions or reports results.

*INTERVIEWER INSTRUCTIONS. Instructions given to interviewer detailing procedure to be adopted during questioning, incorporating instructions that are included in questionnaire form.

JURY, CONSUMER. Jury surveys in advertising research that evaluate advertising themes.

*KURTOSIS. "Peakedness" of frequency distribution.

*LAYOUT. That which is laid out; design of plans, usually in advertising.

*LEADING QUESTION. Question worded in such a way as to suggest answer to person being questioned.

LEAST-SQUARES METHOD. Mathematical procedure for computing average relationship between two variables. Values that express this relationship most accurately are those that total to minimum sum when squares of their deviations from original values of two variables are added. Equations for obtaining this minimum sum are as follows:

$$\Sigma(y) \quad = Na + b\Sigma(x)$$

and

$$\Sigma(xy) \quad = a\Sigma(x) + b\Sigma(x^2)$$

where

$$x \text{ and } y \quad = \text{ variables}$$
$$N \quad = \text{ number of pairs of variables}$$
$$a \text{ and } b \quad = \text{ constants.}$$

Two equations are secured by substituting original values of x and y, as indicated above. These equations are then solved simultaneously for a and b, generalized equation for average relationship being:

$$y = a + bx.$$

This method is used extensively in economic computations for estimating secular trend and for calculating relationship between two or more variables for comparative purposes. (*For examples, see* **Scatter Chart.**)

*MACHINE TABULATION. Process of sorting, grouping, and counting data by use of punched-card machines.

*MAIL QUESTIONNAIRE. Questionnaire that is sent to respondent and returned by him through mail.

MARKET. In business sense, usually refers to aggregate demand of potential buyers for product or service. (*Example*: home market, African market, and small-car market.)

*MARKET ANALYSIS. Studies concerned with defining size and characteristics of market from business records and other sources—designed to show where, how, and to whom product is selling, as well as what seasonal and other trends exist.

MARKETING. Generally, that function of business concerned with ensuring production of right product and its transference from factory to consumer and including selection of method of distribution and price policy. Thus, impinges on both production and sales and is top-management function.

*MARKETING RESEARCH. Any form of research, internal or external, that is concerned with gathering, tabulation, and analysis of facts and information relating to transfer and sale of goods and services from producer to consumer, involving study of relationships between production and consumption, presentation of products, channels of distribution, market characteristics, market potentials, competitive position, advertising, pricing, and related financial problems.

MARKETING RESEARCH FIRMS. Firms that usually have large staff of field research and clerical personnel (such as teams of interviewers, tabulators, and analysts) supervised by limited number of experienced specialists in field marketing research and that perform primarily field research work. Must be distinguished from management consultant firms, which usually have several top-educated and experienced executives, maintain only limited number of research and clerical personnel, and do not usually engage in field research work.

MARKETING RESEARCH METHODS. Basically, survey method, observational method, and experimental method. *See under separate headings.*

*MEAN. *See* Average.

MEDIA. Collectively, various forms of vehicles that carry advertising or publicity. (*Example*: press, TV, cinema, posters, direct mail, and other forms; particular medium: *Daily Express, Nairobi Standard*, and the like.)

*MEDIA ANALYSIS. That part of marketing research concerned with evaluating advantages offered by various publicity media with respect to particular product. (*Example*: concern with form of media, such as press or posters, or with particular vehicle, such as *Daily Express*; although ascertaining circulation is important, attempts to do more, by evaluating readership of each medium.)

MEDIA RESEARCH. Research that is concerned with any form of advertising medium in its widest sense, including qualitative as well as quantitative assessment.

*MEDIAN. Form of average or measure of central tendency obtained by selecting middle value in series of observations. When number of observations is odd, median is value that has equal number of lesser and greater values in series. When number of observations is even, median is value that is exactly between two most-central observed values.

*MODE. Form of average or measure of central tendency obtained by selecting most frequently occurring value in series of observations.

MONEY INCOME. Income expressed in terms of monetary units, irrespective of its purchasing power.

*MOTIVATIONAL RESEARCH. *See* **Depth Interview.**

MOVING AVERAGE. Series of averages obtained by selecting fixed number of successive items in series, computing average, then dropping first item and adding next succeeding one, computing average of this second group, dropping second item and adding next succeeding one, computing average of this third group, and so forth, throughout series. In economic computation, frequently used in smoothing out irregular curves. (*Example*: See Appendix Exhibit 7 for moving average of three-item series.)

NIELSEN INDEX. Specialized form of marketing research for purpose of assessing competitive position of branded products, carried out by auditing retailers' stocks and purchases and based on statistically correct sample of retailers. This service is provided by A. C. Nielsen Company.

APPENDIX EXHIBIT 7

Example of Moving Average

Items	Three-Item Moving Total	Three-Item Moving Average
2		
6	9	3
1	15	5
8	12	4
3	12	4
1	15	5
11	24	8
12	27	9
4		

*NONRESPONSE. *See* Refusal.

NORMAL CURVE OF DISTRIBUTION. Hypothetical frequency curve, symmetrical about maximum ordinate and characterized by certain definite relationships between arithmetic mean and standard deviation (distances from mean).

OBJECTIVE. That which is striven after or which it is desired to attain. In marketing research, two kinds: *final objective*, which is ultimate purpose of study, and *intermediate objectives*, which are intermediate goals or steps leading to final objective.

*OBSERVATION. Method whereby investigator is placed in position from which he can observe and note actions and behavior of respondents instead of questioning them. Used to certain extent in normal question-and-answer interviews, such as for noting sex, age group, and type of dwelling.

OBSERVATIONAL METHOD. Essentially, method of watching people's actions and recording results of those actions. No conscious participation by subject is required; usually, no awareness of being under observation is desirable. Types of studies using this method are store audits and inventories, traffic counts, and shopper surveys.

OBSERVATIONAL TECHNIQUE. *See* **Observation.**

OMNIBUS SURVEYS. Continuous consumer surveys on large sample, but with limited number of questions. New questions are added when all are answered. Conducted usually by large research firm with permanent staff of interviewers.

*OPEN QUESTION. Permitting explanatory reply; not limited by precoding.

OPERATIONAL MARKETING RESEARCH. Research using mathematics to determine scientific rules for strategy in marketing.

*OPINION SURVEY. Survey designed to ascertain respondents' attitudes and opinions. Although marketing research surveys often attempt to evaluate attitudes and opinions as regard matters relevant to inquiry, opinion surveys are more common in public opinion research, such as Gallup Poll.

*ORAL INTERVIEW. *See* **Interview, Personal.**

OUTLET. Usually refers to distributor for a manufacturer's products. (*Example*: wholesaler, retailer, mail-order house, and the like.)

PACK. Immediate wrapping or container of product, which is essentially part of product and which is sold with it; also called package. (*Example*: paper cartons, boxes, jars, bottles, and the like.)

PACKAGING. Preparation of pack or package.

*PANEL. Group of people questioned at regular intervals. Essential characteristics of panel technique are that same group or sample of persons is interviewed or observed over period of time. (*Example*: consumer panel, dealer panel, and the like.)

PERSONAL INTERVIEW. *See* **Interview, Personal.**

*PILOT SURVEY. Exploratory survey that has following objects: providing information on components of variability to which material is subject and testing of questionnaires, which involves development of field procedures and training of investigators.

PILOTING. Usually refers to questionnaires and is process of testing questionnaire on small group for purpose of ascertaining respondents' reactions to questions and their wording, so as to bring out possible flaws that require correction before survey proper is begun.

*POPULATION. In sampling, entire data from which sample is drawn if all of it were available.

POPULATION PYRAMID. Graphic device for displaying composition of population according to sex and age groups. (See Appendix Exhibit 8 for population pyramid representing population of United States for 1950, as reported in census returns. Vertical axis is divided according to age groups in five-year intervals from 0 to 100. Bars extending to right and left from vertical axis represent per cent of total population in various age groups. Bars to left represent male population; those to right, female.)

*POTENTIAL MARKET. Aggregate of all those consumers who would be able and willing to buy product, given opportunity; hence, in terms of quantity, amount that may be expected to be sold.

*PRECODING. Technique whereby questions and answers are reduced to numerical code on questionnaire itself before survey takes place, which thus enables data to be transferred directly to mechanical punched-card system without intermediate step of coding questionnaire after completion.

*PRESTIGE BIAS. Error present throughout survey due to prestige prejudice or mental inclination.

*PRETEST. Usually refers to questionnaires and consists of first test to establish whether questionnaire fully meets purpose for which it is intended and whether it contains any flaws.

APPENDIX EXHIBIT 8

Population Pyramid

Population au 1er janvier 1965 suivant le sexe et l'âge

Source : I.N.S.E.E.

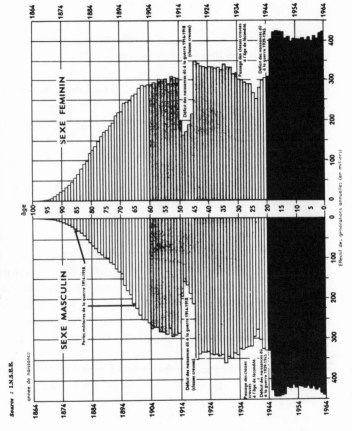

*PRIMARY DATA. Original information from which other information is derived; usually, official published statistics.

*PROBABILITY. Expectation of certain result based on past experience; statistically, measure of that expectation.

PROBABLE ERROR. Error that is likely to occur for given sample before that sample is actually put to test.

PROBING. Searching by questioning for thoughts that underlie respondent's superficial answers.

*PROCESSING. Counting, tabulating, and interpreting of survey data.

PRODUCER. Persons and undertakings engaged in extraction, processing, or manufacture of commodities, as opposed to those engaged solely in their distribution.

*PRODUCT-TESTING. Specialized form of marketing research concerned with measuring market's reactions to new product or to proposed changes in existing product.

PRODUCTIVITY. Amount each worker produces during given length of time. Depends upon technological developments, capital equipment, organization and management, working and living conditions, and many other factors. Changes in quality are not reflected in statistical measurements of productivity but might well be considered part of general concept.

PROFIT AND LOSS STATEMENT. Shows profit made or loss sustained by business over period of time; sometimes called operating statement. Two major parts: gross profit section and expense section.

PROPENSITY TO CONSUME. Keynesian statistical phrase denoting relation, expressed as percentage, between total income and total consumer expenditures.

Relation is expressed in following equation:

$$P = \frac{C}{Y}$$

where

P = propensity to consume
C = consumer expenditures
Y = income.

PUBLICITY. *See* **Advertising.**

*PUNCHING. Perforating of preprinted computer cards to identify classification and to sort data for counting by card sorter.

*PURPOSIVE SAMPLE. Deliberate selection of sample units made according to arbitrary criteria and not according to random principles.

QUALITATIVE DATA. Data that provide reasons for certain situations or evaluate, in terms of attitudes or opinions, respondents' reactions, as opposed to purely numerical measurements.

QUANTITATIVE DATA. Data that express respondents' reactions in purely numerical terms. (*Example*: number of times product is bought, quantity absorbed by market, and readership.) Qualitative data can also be expressed quantitatively. (*Example*: number of respondents holding certain opinion.)

*QUESTIONNAIRE. List of questions organized in particular way for purpose of market survey.

*QUOTA. Quantity of business allotted to particular sales area or salesman's territory, as expressed in sales budget; number of interviews of particular kind allotted to interviewer. (*Example*: number of interviews to be conducted with class A-B housewives.)

*QUOTA SAMPLE. Sample that is broken down into quotas according to factors it is intended to use as controlling factors and in accordance with their incidence in universe.

*RANDOM NUMBERS. Haphazard selection of numbers arranged on cards used in probability sample surveys to indicate, for example, which floor, residence, or respondent to select for interview.

*RANDOM SAMPLE. Sample that gives equal chance of selection to every item in universe; purely random, as opposed to quota or controlled samples.

RANGE. Simplest of measures of dispersion, i.e., difference between minimum and maximum items in series.

*RATIO. Relationship of one quantity to another, expressed as fraction.

RATIONALIZATION. Process of reducing varieties of goods in product line to those that are economical propositions by relating them to demand for them; also called product simplification.

*RAW DATA. Data before analysis; data before they are organized.

READERSHIP. Number of people of any particular advertising medium who read that medium. Not necessarily related to circulation of medium; for example, one copy of publication may be read by number of people apart from its original purchaser, as would occur with publications in hairdresser's salon.

REAL INCOME. Income expressed in terms of what it can buy, as opposed to its money value. *See also* **Money Income.**

*REFUSAL. Respondent declines to cooperate in research before investigation has started.

RELIABILITY. Of response: consistency of replies to question in questionaire; of sample: extent of inherent error in sample.

*REPEATED SURVEYS. Sometimes sampling survey of same kind is repeated at suitable intervals to constitute series of successive surveys, for example, for purpose of brand trend survey. In such cases, it is possible to choose entirely independent sample units in each survey.

REPRESENTATIVENESS. Extent to which sample is true miniature of universe from which it is taken.

*****RESPONDENT.** Individual who replies to questionnaire, whether by mail, telephone, personal interview, or depth interview.

SALES ANALYSIS. Breaking down of sales figures by products, areas, customer types, salesmen, and the like.

SALES BUDGET. Statement of expected sales income and sales expenditure, showing, on one side, sales forecast for future period and, on other, expected cost of achieving anticipated sales.

SALES PROMOTION. Any steps that are taken for purpose of obtaining or increasing sales; often refers specifically to selling efforts that are designed to supplement personal selling and advertising and, by coordination, help them to become more effective.

*****SALES QUOTA.** Salesman's objective in terms of quantity he is expected to sell. *See also* **Quota.**

*****SAMPLE.** Section of universe that is selected in such a way as to be a properly representative cross section.

*****SAMPLE MAKE-UP.** Composition of sample in terms of characteristics present in universe.

*****SAMPLING.** Process of using relatively small cross section of universe for purpose of ascertaining facts applicable to total universe; method by which sample is chosen—random, area, or quota sampling; process of inductive mathematical reasoning whereby qualified quantitative generalizations with respect to entire aggregate of phenomena, having certain characteristics in common, are drawn from comparatively limited number of observations.

There are various methods of sampling and various mathematical techniques for arriving at generalizations. A simple illustration may be cited in case of large aggregate, such as price per dozen of eggs in a city. Suppose random sample of 1,600 (N) representative prices is gathered, results are arranged in frequency distribution, and arithmetic mean and standard deviation (σ) are calculated at U.S. $0.80 and $0.05, respectively. From this one sample; it can be estimated what standard deviation, called standard error of mean, would be in frequency distribution constructed from means of indefinite number of samples, such as above, all containing same number of items. Generalized equation for standard error of mean ($\sigma_{\bar{x}}$) is as follows:

$$\sigma_{\bar{x}} = \frac{\sigma}{\sqrt{N}}$$

and, in above example,

$$\sigma_{\bar{x}} = \frac{0.05}{\sqrt{1,600}} = 0.00125$$

In normal distribution, 99.7 per cent of items fall within three standard deviations of mean. (See Appendix Exhibit 9 for normal curve.)

APPENDIX EXHIBIT 9

Normal Curve

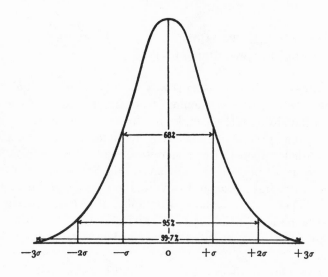

It may be assumed, then, in this example, that there are 99.7 chances out of 100 that obtained mean of $0.80 is not more than $0.00375 (3 x 0.00125) away, plus or minus, from unknown mean of total aggregate. Area between curve and two uprights shown at any two points gives fraction of total number of observations between those two points. Uprights have been drawn at points corresponding to one, two, and three times standard deviation of distribution on either side of mean. Area between $-\sigma$ and $+\sigma$ is 68 per cent of total area. This means that, in normal distribution, 68 per cent of observations lie within distance equal to one standard deviation on either side of mean. Similarly, from -2σ to $+2\sigma$ included 95 per cent of all observations and from -3σ to $+3\sigma$ includes 99.7 per cent. Hence, it is obvious that in normal distribution practically all observations lie within range six times standard deviation.

*SAMPLING ERROR. Statistical error that is present in particular sample and that can be ascertained with respect to particular question once pattern of replies to that question is known.

*SAMPLING FRACTIONS. If same sampling fractions are used for each stratum of population, method is *proportionate sampling*. But sometimes different sampling fractions are used for different strata (stratification with *variable sampling fraction*), and in this case results for strata are suitably weighted before being aggregated to produce results from complete sample.

*SCATTER. Way in which different values of variable lie around their average or mean; also called dispersion.

SCATTER CHART. Graphic device that displays actual relationships by mathematicallly constructed curve. In chart below (Appendix Exhibit 10), large black dots indicate actual relationships between GNP and private domestic investments in United States for years 1919-28 (as shown in Appendix Table 4).

Solid line in chart, called line of regression, indicates average relationship between these two variables during the same period. Its mathematical equation is as follows:

$$y = -2.58 + 0.2029x.$$

APPENDIX TABLE 4

U.S. Gross National Product and Private
Domestic Investments, 1919-28

	Billions of dollars	
Year	Gross National Product (x)	Private Domestic Investments (y)
1919	77.1	17.2
1920	86.2	18.5
1921	70.3	9.2
1922	72.5	10.3
1923	84.3	15.6
1924	83.4	13.3
1925	90.0	15.3
1926	95.3	16.8
1927	93.5	15.2
1928	95.6	14.9

Number of cases 10 (N)

Source: U.S. Department of Commerce, *Historical Statistics of The United States* (Washington, D.C.: U.S. Goverment Printing Office, 1957).

Equation is computed according to least-squares method. Standard error of estimate (S_y) measures significance of this line, i.e., extent to which spot markings are in close proximity to it. Standard error of estimate is standard deviation (σ) measured from line of regression. Its value in present example is 2.17. It may be computed by means of following equation:

$$S_v^2 = \frac{(\Sigma y^2) - a\Sigma(y) - b\Sigma(xy)}{N}$$

Scatter Chart

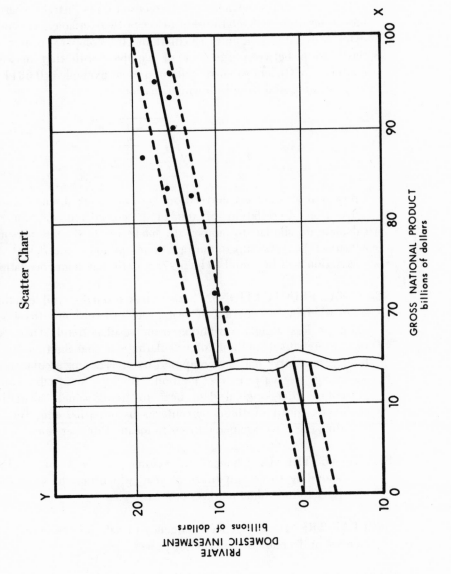

In same chart dotted lines show limits of standard error of estimate. About 68 per cent of cases are within these limits, this being approximate constant proportion of cases within one standard variation plus and one standard variation minus arithmetic mean. Coefficient of correlation (r) is abstract measure indicating degree of relationship between two variables. It is used extensively in economic calculations to compare degree of relationship between one pair of variables with that between another. Coefficient of correlation in present example is 0.6311. It may be computed from following equation:

$$ r = \sqrt{I - \frac{S_v^2}{\sigma_v^2}} $$

Unity indicates perfect correlation; zero indicates absence of any correlation. Correlation of 0.6311 is considered medium. If calculations similar to above are made for GNP and personal consumer expenditures during same period, coefficient of correlation will be found to be 0.9733, definitely high correlation.

SEASONAL FLUCTUATIONS. Characteristic often discernible in time series wherein, over period of years, each of twelve months shows more or less regular variations from secular trend. There are various statistical methods of calculating seasonal fluctuations in time series. Curve may be computed by ascertaining secular trend according to least-squares method, finding for each month percentage that original data bear to trend value, calculating arithmetic mean of these percentages by months, and, finally, adjusting these average percentages to mean of 100 per cent.

SEASONAL TREND. Changes in volume of sales of product corresponding to certain times of year, which may be general or may refer to individual markets or areas.

SECULAR TREND. Any general tendency of values in time series to increase or decrease over period of years.

*SERIES. Set of observations in statistical analysis.

*SHOP AUDIT. Measure of group of retail outlets by audits of invoices and stock.

SHOW-CARDS. Illustrations or listing of possible answers used in interviews to help respondents.

*SIGNIFICANCE. Usually refers to difference. Difference occurring between two results in sampling is said to be significant if its existence cannot be attributed to chance errors involved in sampling process.

SINGLE-STAGE AND MULTISTAGE SAMPLING. In *single stage*, sample units that are to be observed or interviewed are drawn directly. In *multistage*, units drawn are treated as population for further sampling (process that may be done more than once) until at last stage sample units that are to be observed or interviewed are drawn.

SOCIALISM. Collective system of ownership and operation of means of production (capital goods), usually by government. During course of nineteenth century, terms "socialism" and "Communism" reversed their meanings. Socialism at one time referred to ideas of certain social reformers who were called Christian Socialists and Utopian Socialists, some of whom established colonies in United States based on principles of Communism in various forms. Karl Marx, however, generally regarded as architect of modern socialism, at first referred to his program as Communism. As experiments of these social reformers gradually fell into disrepute, Karl Marx and his followers began referring to their program as socialism, and it is by that term that their own program is known today, although in popular speech socialism and Communism are very frequently confused.

*SOCIO-ECONOMIC GROUPING. Method of dividing population into groups representing various social and economic levels. Income and status of head of household are usually criteria by which the household is classified into one or other socio-economic group.

*STABILITY. In group, degree to which that group is liable to change. Normally, larger the group is, more stable it is likely to be as a whole.

*STANDARD. Situation or measurement that is accepted as normal and that can be used as measure of effectiveness of other situations or of measurements of similar nature.

*STANDARD DEVIATION. Measure of scatter of series, i.e., average by which values deviate from their mean.

*STANDARD ERROR. Inherent variation of sample or of answers to particular question, measurable and dependent on size of sample and pattern of replies to questions.

*STATISTICAL RELIABILITY. Degree of error present, measurable for any question in sample survey. (This is measure of statistical reliability of sample.)

*STRATIFICATION. Method of dividing universe into strata, i.e., into groups representing possession of various characteristics in various degrees. (*Example*: income groups, ages, sex, educational standard, and the like.) Where subdivision into strata is done according to one characteristic only, *single stratification* is employed; where it is done according to two or more characteristics, *multiple stratification* is employed.

*STRATIFIED SAMPLE. Sample in which population of sample units is subdivided into groups, or strata, before selection of sample; equivalent to set of random samples on number of subpopulations, each of ultimate subdivisions, or cells, being equivalent to one stratum.

*SUBSAMPLE. Part of whole sample. (*Example*: subsample representing 30-50 age group in total sample covering all age groups.)

*SUBSTITUTION. Use of person or thing in place of another. (*Example*: substitution of respondent, residence, or block in survey field work.)

SUPERVISOR. Person entrusted with task of supervising and checking work of interviewers in field.

SUPPLY. Schedule of quantities of commodity that would be made available at various price levels.

*SURVEY. Inquiry concerned with collection of data in relation to total universe. Two kinds: *census survey*, in which every item in universe is considered, and *sample survey*, in which only sample of item in universe is considered, but where results are related to total universe.

*TABULATION. Process of sorting, listing, and counting answers to questions.

*TALLY. Section of counting sheet for score marks.

TELEPHONE INTERVIEW. Interview conducted by telephone, as opposed to personal call or mailed questionnaire.

*TEST INTERVIEWING. Interviewing small number of respondents for purpose of testing questionnaire and ascertaining whether it contains any flaws. *See also* **Piloting.**

*TEST MARKET. Area that is isolated as far as possible from other areas and that is used for testing new product, package, advertising appeal, or particular marketing factor.

TRADE RESEARCH. Research that is conducted among traders, i.e., among factors, wholesalers, and retailers.

TREND. Direction in which situation is moving. (*Example*: continuous 5 per cent upward trend in sales.)

TURNOVER. *Cash turnover*: Income of business concern measured over period of time, usually a year; *stock turnover*: number of times stock is sold and replaced over period of time.

*UNIVERSE. Total number of items that are relevant to inquiry. (*Example*: total population, all housewives, all motorists, medium-income housewives only, all chemists in city or area.)

*VALIDITY OF SAMPLE. Extent to which sample truly represents universe from which it is taken, i.e., extent to which it possesses same characteristics in same degree.

VARIABLE COST. Cost that increases or decreases as total volume of production increases or decreases; also called direct cost. (*Example*: costs of raw material and labor.)

***VARIANCE.** Technical term for square of standard deviation.

***WEIGHTED AVERAGE.** Average of numbers that have been previously individually increased or decreased in order to give them their true importance in relation to each other; average in which numbers to be averaged are augmented by certain values called weights. (*Example*:

Weights (*w*)		Numbers to be Averaged (*m*)	
1	x	10	= 10
2	x	8	= 16
3	x	5	= 15
—			—
6			41

$$\text{Weighted arithmetic mean} = \frac{\Sigma wm}{\Sigma w} = \frac{41}{6} = 6.833$$

In economic computation, weighted averages are frequently used in construction of index numbers.

***WEIGHTED SAMPLE.** Sample in which small subsamples are increased arbitrarily to permit their statistical analysis, results being "weighted" during tabulation in order to bring them back to their true values.

***WEIGHTING.** Process of giving numbers their true values according to their individual importance.

APPENDIX C

MULTILINGUAL DICTIONARY
OF SELECTED TECHNICAL TERMS
USED IN MARKETING RESEARCH

The purpose of this dictionary is to help marketing research penetrate across national borders and language barriers. International dealings and the use of foreign languages are frequent in marketing research in the developing countries. Project proposals, report-writing, and personal negotiations in a new field such as marketing research are better understood in a foreign language when at least the key words are precise.

The terms indicated by an asterisk have been explained in the glossary (Appendix B); the rest are defined or explained in the text of the book or are self-explanatory.

English	French	German
*Actual market	Marché actuel	Tatsächlicher Markt
*Adequate sample	Échantillon représentatif	Adäquate/zulängliche Stichprobe
*Age group	Groupe d'âge	Altersgruppe, Klasse
Aided recall	Aide-mémoire	Erinnerungstest mit Gedächtnisstütze
Alternative question	Question alternative	Alternativfrage
*Ambiguous question	Question ambiguë	Mehrdeutige Frage
*Area sample	Échantillon par région	Flächenstichprobe
*Average	Moyenne	Durchschnitt
Average deviation	Écart moyen	Durchschnittliche Abweichung
*Behavior	Comportement	Verhalten
*Bias	Préjugés, déformations partis pris	(Systematischer Fehler durch) Verzerrung, Voreingenommenheit, Vorurteil u.s.w.
*Biased error	Erreur systématique	Systematischer Fehler
*Brand barometer	Étude de notoriété et d'utilisation des marques (baromètre des marques)	Marken Index
Brand trend survey	Étude de notoriété des marques	Marken Index
*Breakdown	Ventilation	Untergliederung
*Cell	Strate, groupe, cellule, classe	Zelle, Einheit, Unter-abschnitt
Check (verb)	Contrôler, vérifier	Überprüfen, vergleichen, abhaken

Italian	*Spanish*	*Portuguese*
Mercato attuale	Mercado actual	Mercado actual
Campione rappresentativo	Muestra representativa	Amostra representativa
Classe di età	Grupo de edad	Grupo de idade
Lista di risposte possibili, carte lino	Lista de respuestas posibles	Recordação ajudada
Domanda alternativa	Pregunta alternativa	Pergunta alternativa
Domanda ambigua	Pregunta ambigua	Pergunta ambivalente
Campione per aree	Muestra por áreas	Amostragem por área
Media	Media	Média
Scostamento medio, scarto medio	Desviación media	Desvio médio
Comportamento	Comportamiento	Comportamento
Distorsione, deformazione sistemática, "bias"	Distorsión, deformación sistemática	Deformação
Errore sistematico	Error sistemático	Erro sistemático
Barometro delle marche	Barómetro de marcas	Barometro de marcas
Studio della notorietà et difusione delle marche	Estudio de la notoriedad y difusión de las marcas	Estudo de notoriedade de marcas
Classificazione	Distribución o ventilación	Ventilação
Gruppo, classe, strato, categoria	Grupo, clase, estrato y categoria	Estrato, grupo, célula, classe
Controllare, verificare	Controlar, verificar	Controlar, verificar

(Continued)

English	French	German
*Check interview, control interview	Interview de contrôle, interview pour vérification	Kontrollinterview, Kontrollbefragung
*Check list	Check-list, aide-mémoire, listes de vérification	Kontrollliste
*Closed question	Question fermée	Geschlossene Frage
*Coding and classifying	Codification et tri	Verschlüsselung und Klassifizierung
Computation	Dépouillement, calcul, analyse, comptage	Auszählung
Consumer interview	Interview des consommateurs	Verbraucherinterview
*Consumer panel	Panel des consommateurs	Verbrauchergruppe
Continuity	Enchaînement	Zusammenhang
Coverage	Population étudiée	Erfasster Personenkreis
*Cross section	Fraction de l'échantillon	Querschnitt
*Cross-tabulation	Tri combiné	Kreuztabulierung
*Data	Chiffres, données	Daten, Zahlenmaterial
Dealer interview	Interview des commerçants	Händlerinterview
*Dealer survey	Enquête sur commerçants	Einzelhandelserhebung
*Depth interview	Interview en profondeur	Intensives Interview

Italian	Spanish	Portuguese
Intervista di controllo	Entrevista de control	Entrevista de supervisão
Lista di controllo, lista di questi	Lista de control puntos a considerar	Controle, verificação
Domanda chiusa	Pregunta cerrada	Pergunta fechada
Codificazione e classificazione (selezione)	Codificación y clasificación (selección)	Codificação e classificação
Spoglio	Escrutinio	Contagem
Intervista di consumatori	Entrevista de consumidores	Entrevista do consumidor
Campione permanente di consumatori, giuria dei consumatori, "panel"	Muestra permanente de consumidores, "panel"	Painel de consumidores
Concatenazione	Cadena	Encadeamento
Extensione della indagine campo dell'indagine	Extension del sondeo, campo del sondeo	Cobertura
Gruppo rappresentativo sezione rappresentativa dell'universo, campione	Grupo representativo, muestra	Fracção representativa do universo
Tabulazione a doppia entrata	Tabulación a doble entrada	Tabulação cruzada
Cifre, dati	Cifra, datos	Dados
Intervista di negozianti	Entrevista a commerciantes	Entrevista a commerciantes
Indagine tra i negozianti	Sondeo entre los comerciantes	Inquérito ao comércio
Intervista approfondita, . . . in profonditá	Entrevista en profundidad	Entrevista em profundidade

(Continued)

English	French	German
*Deviation	Déviation	Abweichung
*Diary method	Méthode du journal d'achats (livre de comptes personnels)	Tagebuchmethode
Dichotomous	Question dichotomique (ou fermée) par oui-non	Alternativfrage Ja-nein Frage
*Dispersion	Dispersion	Streuung
Evaluation	Évaluation, exploitation	Beurteilung, Auswertung
*Field work	Travail sur le terrain, sur le tas	Feldarbeit
Final summary tables	Tableaux récapitulatifs	Zusammenfassung der Resultate
*Frame	Base, schéma, modèle	Rahmen, Erhebungsgrundlage
*Frequency	Fréquence	Häufigkeit
General-purpose sample	Échantillon universel	Allzweckstichprobe
*Graph	Graphique	Graphische Darstellung
*Hand tabulation	Tri manuel	Manuelle Tabulierung
*Household book	Livre de comptes (du ménage)	Haushaltsbuch
*Informal interview	Interview sous forme d'entretien libre	Offenes Interview
Informant	Interviewé, enquêté	Befragter
*Interview	Interview, interrogation	Interview, Befragung

Italian	*Spanish*	*Portuguese*
Scostamento, scarto	Desviación	Desvio
Libro di casa, metodo del diario	Método del diario	Método de diário
Domanda alternativa, domanda dicotoma (si o no)	Pregunta alternativa	Pergunta dicotomica (sim ou não)
Dispersione	Dispersión	Dispersão
Stima, Valutazione	Estima, valoración	Avaliação
Lavoro estorno, rilevazione diretta	Trabajo "in situ" recopilación directa	Trabalho de campo
Tabelle sintetiche del risultati, prospetti riasuntivi	Tabla síntesis de los resultados	Quadros de sintese dos resultatos
Schema di riferimento lista di base, "frame"	Base, esquema de referencia	Bases de referencia
Frequenza	Frecuencia	Frequencia
Campione per tutti gli usi	Muestra para todo uso	Amostragem geral
Grafico	Gráfico	Gráfico
Tabulazione a mano	Tabulación a mano	Tabulação manual
Libro di casa	Diario de gastos de la casa familiar	Diário de gastos familiar
Intervista libera	Entrevista libre	Entrevista livre
Soggetto interrogato	Entrevistado	Entrevistado
Intervista	Entrevista	Entrevista

(Continued)

English	French	German
*Interview, focused or group	Interview dirigée	Interview über bestimmtes Thema
Interview outline, interview guide	Schéma d'interview	Leitfaden für die Befragung
*Interviewer	Enquêteur	Befrager, Rechercheur, Interviewer
*Interviewer bias	Déformation de l'interview due à l'enquêteur	Verfälschung durch den Befrager
*Interviewer instructions	Instructions aux enquêteurs	Befragerinstruktion
Interviewer's schedule	Trane pour les enquêteurs questionnaires formulaires	Auftragsschema
*Kurtosis	Profil (point de fréquence au diagramme)	Wölbung (einer Verteilung)
*Layout of final summary tables	Projet de tableaux recapitulatifs de résultats	Modell, Anlage des Schlussberichts
*Leading question	Question tendancieuse	Suggestivfrage
*Machine tabulation	Tri mécanographique	Mechanische Tabulierung
*Mail questionnaire	Questionnaire postal	Durch die Post versendeter Fragebogen
Mailing list	Liste d'adresses	Verteilerliste
Margin of error	Marge d'erreur	Fehlerspielraum
*Market analysis	Analyse du marché	Marktanalyse
*Marketing research	Étude de marché	Marktforschung
Master sample	Échantillon théorique	Grundstichprobe

Italian	*Spanish*	*Portuguese*
Intervista guidata, intervista messa a fuoco	Entrevista dirigida	Entrevista dirigida
Schema di intervista guida per l'intervistatore	Esquema de la entrevista guion para el entrevistador	Esquema do questionário, guia de instruções para o entrevistador
Intervistatore, rilevatore	Entrevistador	Entrevistador
Distorsione dovuta all'intervistatore	Deformación debida al entrevistador	Deformação devida ao entrevistador
Istruzioni all'intervistatore	Instrucciones al entrevistador	Instruções para os entrevistadores
Formulario per l'intervistatore, modello di rilevazione	Formulario para el entrevistador	Formulário para os entrevistadores
Curtosi	Curtosis	Curtose
Modello delle tabelle finali	Modelo de cuadros finales	Modelo dos quadros finais
Domanda suggestiva	Pregunta sugeridora	Pergunta tendenciosa
Tabulazione meccanica	Tabulación mecánica	Tabulação mecânica
Questionario per posta, referendum per posta	Cuestionario por correo	Questionário pelo correio
Lista di indirizzi	Lista de direcciones	Lista de endereços
Margine di errore	Margen de error	Margem de erro
Analisi di mercato	Análisis de mercado	Analises do mercado
Studio di mercato	Estudio de mercado	Estudo de mercado
Piano di campionamento	Plan de muestreo	Plano de amostragem

(Continued)

English	French	German
*Mean	Valeur moyenne	Mittelwert
Mean average	Moyenne arithmétique	Arithmetisches Mittel
*Media analysis	Analyse des supports publicitaires	Analyse der Werbeträger
*Median	Médiane	Zentralwert, Median
Methods of collecting data	Méthodes de rassemblement des données	Erhebungsmethode
*Mode	Mode	Modus, häufigster Wert
*Motivational research	Étude de motivation	Motivforschung
Multichoice question	Question à choix multiple	Auswahlfrage
Multiple stratification	Stratification multiple	Mehrfache Schichtung
*Nonresponse	Absence de réponse, sans réponse	Ausfall, Nichtbeantwortung
Normal curve of error	Courbe d'erreur normal	Normale Fehlerkurve
*Observation	Observation	Beobachtung
*Open question	Question ouverte	Offene Frage
Opinion scale	Échelle de comportement	Einstellungsskala
*Opinion survey	Enquête d'opinion	Meinungserhebung
*Oral interview	Interview orale	Mündliches Interview
*Panel	Panel (panneau)	"Panel" ständige Befragtengruppe
Personal interview	Interview individuelle	Persönliche Befragung

Italian	*Spanish*	*Portuguese*
Media, valore medio	Valor medio	Valor médio
Media aritmética	Media aritmética	Média aritmética
Studio dell'efficacia dei mezzi pubblicitari	Estudio de la eficacia de los medios publicitarios	Analise de médios publicitarios
Mediana, valore mediano, valore centrale	Valor mediano	Médiana
Metodi di rilevazione dei dati	Métodos de recopilación de datos	Métodos de recolha de dados
Moda, norma valore modale, valore piu frequente	Moda, norma, valor poco frecuente	Moda
Studio della motivazione	Estudio motivacional	Estudos de motivação
Domanda multipla, domanda a risposte multiple	Pregunta múltiple	Pergunta de resposta múltipla
Stratificazione multipla, stratificazione a più gradi	Estratificación múltiple	Estratificação múltipla
Mancata risposta	Falta de respuesta	Sem resposta
Curva normale degli errori	Curva normal de los errores	Curva normal de erro
Osservazione, sopralluogo	Observación "in situ"	Observação
Domanda aperta	Pregunta abierta	Pergunta aberta
Scala di opinioni	Escala de opiniones	Escala de opinião
Sondaggio di opinione	Sondeo de opinión	Sondagem de opinião
Intervista verbale	Entrevista verbal	Entrevista oral
Campione permanente di consumatori, giuria dei consumatori, "panel"	Muestra permanente de consumidor, panel de consumidores	Painel de consumidores
Intervista personale	Entrevista personal	Entrevista pessoal

(Continued)

English	French	German
*Pilot survey	Enquête pilote	Probebefragung
*Population	Population, groupe	Grundgesamtheit
Postal survey	Enquête postale	Erhebung im Postwege
*Potential market	Marché potentiel	Potentieller Markt
*Precoding	Précodifier	Vorverschlüsseln
*Prestige bias	Effet de prestige	Von Prestigerücksichten Beeinflusste, falsche Antwort
*Pretest	Pré-enquête	Voruntersuchung, Probebefragung
*Primary data	Données originaires, élémentaires	Urmaterial
*Probability	Probabilité	Wahrscheinlichkeit
Probability sample	Échantillon choisi au hasard	Zufallgesteuerte Stichprobenauswahl
*Processing	Mise en oeuvre, exploitation	Aufbereitung
*Product-testing	Essai du produit	Produktprüfung
Proportionate sampling	Échantillon proportionnel	Ausgewogene Stichprobe
*Punch (-ing)	Perforer (perforation)	Lochung
*Purposive sample (sampling)	Echantillon (-nage) à choix intentionnel	Bewusste (-s) Auswahlverfahren
Qualifying hit	Piège	Fangfrage
*Questionnaire	Questionnaire	Fragebogen
*Quota	Quota	Quote

Italian	*Spanish*	*Portuguese*
Inchiesta di prova	Encuesta de prueba	Inquérito piloto
Universo, popolazione	Universo, población	Universo, população
Indagine per posta, referendum postale	Encuesta por correo, referéndum postal	Inquérito pelo correio
Mercato potenziale	Mercado potencial	Mercado potencial
Precodificare	Precodificar	Precodificar
Distorsione da prestigio, risposta falsata per ragioni di prestigio	Distorsión de prestigio	Resposta falseada por razões de prestigio
Sondaggio preparatorio, sondaggio pilota	Sondeo preparatorio, sondeo piloto	Pre-teste
Dati originari, dati della rilevazione	Datos originales	Dados originais
Probabilitá	Probabilidad	Probabilidade
Campione casuale, campione probabilistico	Muestra casual, muestra probabilística	Amostra casual, amostra probabilística
Elaborazione dei dati	Elaboración de los datos	Elaboração dos dados
Prova del prodotto	Prueba del producto	Teste do produto
Campione proporzionale	Muestra proporcional	Amostra proporcional
Perforare (perforazione)	Perforar (perforación)	Perfuração
Campione (campionamento) a scelta ragionata	Muestra intencional	Amostra intencional
Domanda tranello	Pregunta control o testigo	Pergunta de controle
Questionario	Cuestionario	Questionário
Quota	Cuota	Quota

(Continued)

English	French	German
*Quota sample	Échantillon déterminé par quota	Quotenauswahl
*Random numbers	Chiffres tirés au sort	Zufallszahlen
*Random sample	Échantillon tiré au sort	Zufallsauswahl
Random sampling error	Erreur d'échantillonnage	Stichprobenfehler
*Ratio	Ratio, rapport	Verhältniszahl
*Raw data	Données brutes	Unaufbereitete Daten
*Refusal	Refus de répondre	Antwortverweigerung
*Repeated surveys	Enquêtes repetées	Erhebungsreihe
*Respondent	Interviewé, enquêté	Befragter
Rules for coding and classifying	Règles de codification et classification	Regeln für die Verschlüsselung und Klassifizierung
*Sales quota	Quota de ventes	Absatzquote
*Sample	Échantillon	Stichprobe
*Sample make-up	Plan de sondage	Stichprobenanlage
Sample unit	Unité de sondage	Stichprobeneinheit
*Sampling	Échantillonnage	Stichprobenverfahren
*Sampling error	Erreur d'échantillonnage	Stichprobenfehler
*Sampling fraction	Fraction sondée	Stichprobengruppe
Sampling survey	Enquête par sondage	Stichprobenerhebung
*Scatter	Dispersion	Streuung
Schedule	Questionnaire	Schema, Fragebogen

Italian	*Spanish*	*Portuguese*
Campione per quote	Muestra por cuotas	Amostra por quotas
Numeri casuali	Números aleatorios	Números aleatórios
Campione casuale, campione a sorte	Muestra casual, muestra al azar	Amostra aleatória
Errore di campionamento	Error de muestreo	Erro de amostra aleatória
Quoziente, rapporto	Cociente, relación	Coficiente, relação
Dati grezzi	Datos brutos	Dados brutos
Rifiuto di rispondere	Negativa de respuesta	Recusas
Sondaggi ripetuti	Sondeos repetidos	Sondagem repetitiva
Soggeto che risponde	Persona que responde	Respondente
Regole per la codificazione e la classificazione	Reglas para la codificación y clasificación	Regras para codifição e classifição
Quota di vendita	Cuotas de venta	Quota de vendas
Campione	Muestra	Amostra
Piano di campionamento	Plan de muestreo	Plano de amostra
Unitá di campionamento	Unidad de muestreo	Unidade de amostra
Campionamento	Muestreo	Amostragem
Errore di campionamento	Error de muestreo	Erro de amostragem
Frazione di campione	Fracción de muestreo	Fracção da amostra
Indagine campionaria inchiesta per campione	Investigación muestraria	Investigação da amostragem
Dispersione	Dispersión	Dispersão
Questionario	Cuestionario	Questionário

(Continued)

English	French	German
Scrutiny	Vérification	Prüfung auf Vollständigkeit
Selection of sample units	Désignation des unités de sondage	Auswahl der Stichprobeneinheiten
Self-weighted sample	Échantillon autopondéré	Selbstgewichtetes Stichprobenverfahren
*Series	Série	Reihe
*Shop audit	Contrôle de vente dans les magasins de détail	Einzelhandelsbestandsprüfung
*Significance	Signification	Bedeutsamkeit
Single stratification	Stratification simple	Einfache Schichtung
*Socio-economic group	Groupe socio-économique	Soziologische Gruppe
Split ballot	Questionnaire à 2 formes	Gegabelte Befragung
*Stability	Stabilité	Stabilität
*Standard	Standard, norme	Norm
*Standard deviation	Écart type	Standardabweichung
*Standard error	Erreur type	Standardfehler
*Statistical reliability	Validité statistique	Statische Zuverlässigkeit
*Stratification with variable sampling fraction	Stratification à fraction sondée variable	Schichtung mit verschiedenen Stichprobengruppen
*Stratified sample	Échantillon stratifié	Beschichtete Auswahl
Stratum	Strate	Schicht

Italian	*Spanish*	*Portuguese*
Revisione, verifica delle risposte	Comprobación de las respuestas	Verificação das respostas
Scelta delle unita di campione	Selección de las unidades muestrarias	Selecção das unidades da amostra
Campione ponderato automaticamente	Muestra ponderada	Amostra ponderada
Serie, seriazone	Serie	Séries
Inventario dei negozi rilievo periodoco delle vendite nei negozi	Inventario de detallistas	Painel de retalhistas
Significatività	Significación	Significância
Stratificazione semplice	Estratificación simple	Estratificação simples
Gruppo socio-economico, categoria economico-sociale	Grupo socio-económico	Grupo socio-económico
Questionario a due versioni	Cuestionario en dos versiónes	Questionário em duas versões
Stabilità	Estabilidad	Estabilidade
Norma, standard	Norma, nivel	Norma, nível
Scostamento quadratico medio	Desviación tipo	Desvio padrão
Errore quadratico medio	Error tipo	Erro padrão
Attendibilitá statistica	Fiabilidad estadística	Validade estatistica
Stratificazione con frazione di campionamento variabile	Estratificación con fracciones de muestreo variable	Estrafação de fracções variáveis da amostra
Campione stratificato	Muestra estratificada	Amostra estratificada
Strato	Estrato	Estrato

(Continued)

English	*French*	*German*
*Subsample	Sous-groupe d'échantillon	Zufallsunterauswahl
*Substitution	Substitution	Ersatz, Substitution
Supervision of investigators	Contrôle des enquêteurs	Befragerüberwachung
*Survey	Enquête	Erhebung
*Tabulation	Tri	Auswertung
*Tally	Concordance	Strichlistenauszählung
*Test interviewing	Interview pilote	Probebefragung
*Test market	Marché choisi pour effectuer un test	Testmarkt
*Universe	Univers	Gesamtheit
*Validity of sample	Validité de l'échantillon	Stichhaltigkeit der Befragtenauswahl
*Variance	Variance, divergence	Streuung
*Weighted average	Moyenne pondérée	Gewogener Durchschnitt
*Weighted sample	Échantillon pondéré	Gewogene Stichprobe
*Weighting	Pondération	Wägung

Italian	*Spanish*	*Portuguese*
Sub-campione	Sub-muestra	Sub-amostra
Sostituzione	Substitución	Substituição
Controllo degli inter-vistatori	Control de entrevistadores	Controle dos entre-vistadores
Indagine, inchiesta	Encuesta, investigación	Inquérito
Tabulazione	Tabulación	Tabulação
Concordanza	Concordancia	Concordância
Intervista di prova	Entrevista de prueba	Inquérito piloto
Mercato di prova	Mercado de prueba	Mercado de prova
Universo, popolazione	Universo, población	Universo
Validitá del campione	Validez de la muestra	Validade da amostra
Varianza	Varianza	Variância
Media ponderata	Media ponderada	Média ponderada
Campione ponderato	Muestra ponderada	Amostra ponderada
Ponderazione	Ponderación	Ponderação

APPENDIX D

INDICATORS OF MARKET SIZE OF COUNTRIES
HAVING LESS THAN
$700 PER CAPITA INCOME ANNUALLY

	Population			National Income		
Country	1968 Total *(millions)*	5-Year Increase *(per cent)*	1975 Forecast *(millions)*	1968 Total *(billion dollars)*	5-Year Increase, Current Prices *(per cent)*	1968 Per Capita *(dollars)*
WESTERN EUROPE						
Cyprus	0.6	5.6	0.7	0.35	33.1	580
Greece	8.8	3.8	9.2	5.68	45.9	651
Malta	0.3	−2.8	0.4	0.14	28.4	463
Portugal	9.4	4.7	10.6	4.34	61.4	456
Spain	32.4	4.3	33.4	21.67	79.9	668
Turkey	33.5	13.1	38.0	10.63	60.1	317
FAR EAST						
Afghanistan	16.1	10.8	19.6	0.75	−15.5	85
Burma	26.4	11.1	31.0	1.53	21.4	59
Cambodia	6.5	11.5	8.5	0.76	32.5	120
Ceylon	11.9	12.4	15.6	1.56	24.0	133
Fiji	0.5	16.3	0.8	0.14	5.2	535
Hong Kong	3.9	12.0	5.0	−	−	620
India	523.9	13.7	601.4	37.20	87.2	73
Indonesia	112.8	12.8	133.5	10.48	456.6	95
Korea, South	30.5	13.4	38.1	4.86	209.3	159
Laos	2.8	12.6	4.0	−	−	70
Malaysia	10.3	15.7	12.7	2.12	28.6	211
Pakistan	109.5	10.9	157.0	12.29	62.3	112
Philippines	35.9	18.6	42.0	8.08	51.7	233
Ryukyus	1.0	5.8	1.3	−	−	580
Singapore	2.0	12.0	2.8	1.29	−	651
Taiwan	13.5	15.1	15.4	3.32	88.5	246
Thailand	33.7	16.5	39.0	4.16	52.0	127
Vietnam, South	17.4	13.7	18.0	1.79	191.0	108
MIDDLE EAST						
Iran	27.0	15.8	32.3	6.81	60.2	252
Iraq	8.6	12.7	10.0	1.77	44.6	216
Jordon	2.1	17.2	2.8	0.49	57.4	242
Lebanon	2.6	12.9	3.7	1.02	76.3	426
Saudi Arabia	4.5	12.5	6.0	1.98	−	444
South Yemen	1.2	11.4	1.7	0.16	−	200
Syria	5.7	15.5	7.7	1.13	39.6	203
UAR	31.7	13.3	38.5	5.00	45.5	170
Yemen	5.0	0.0	5.4	−	−	110

LESS THAN $700 PER CAPITA INCOME ANNUALLY

GNP		Passenger Cars in Use		Telephones in Use	Broadcast Media Sets in Use		Electricity Production	
1968 Total (billion dollars)	5-Year Increase, Constant Prices (per cent)	January 1, 1969 (thousands)	5-Year Increase Constant Prices (per cent)	January 1, 1968 (thousands)	1968 Radios (thousands)	1968 TV's (thousands)	1968 Total (billion kwhs)	5-Year Increase (per cent)
0.40	40.1	43	47	34	148	30	0.45	33
7.03	43.5	129	84	660	1,135	60	6.95	117
0.16	26.6	24	26	28	66	53	0.21	114
5.02	35.1	353	81	616	1,348	280	6.20	44
25.26	38.0	1,600	201	3,379	5,000	3,345	45.18	74
11.54	72.2	93	64	428	2,913	10	6.89	73
1.34	–	9	40	10	75	–	0.36	126
1.80	14.7	30	20	21	370	–	0.41	14
0.92	40.2	64	14	6	400	25	0.11	25
1.78	24.7	85	2	56	430	–	0.58	54
0.17	7.3	9	21	13	40	–	0.12	71
2.37	–	75	60	354	715	110	3.46	68
43.24	–	480	42	994	6,490	7	43.82	63
11.45	9.3	166	13	169	2,500	70	1.68	16
5.71	56.7	26	100	421	1,450	114	6.00	172
0.19	–	64	14	1	45	–	0.25	162
3.34	24.4	200	-14	145	450	100	2.92	80
13.07	34.4	146	116	163	1,150	40	3.90	115
9.64	–	204	85	208	1,230	350	5.20	53
–	–	–	–	50	245	160	1.10	99
1.36	40.0	127	16	106	188	108	1.64	99
4.15	68.3	24	100	230	1,400	240	9.80	95
5.09	47.1	132	123	98	2,766	220	2.49	210
2.09	25.3	64	14	27	400	–	0.72	80
7.44	50.9	180	70	220	1,710	200	4.50	84
2.24	2.6	61	16	78	184	250	1.43	44
0.56	15.7	17	98	33	135	15	0.16	51
1.70	10.0	124	61	130	550	175	1.04	66
2.00	–	76	17	29	78	50	0.38	41
0.23	–	18	41	9	1,250	20	0.24	45
1.12	20.2	30	82	91	977	93	0.75	43
5.69	5.2	112	32	335	4,275	500	5.90	32
0.55	–	–	–	2	–	–	–	–

(Continued)

Country	Population			National Income		
	1968 Total (millions)	5-Year Increase (per cent)	1975 Forecast (millions)	1968 Total (billion dollars)	5-Year Increase, Current Prices (per cent)	1968 Per Capita (dollars)
LATIN AMERICA						
Argentina	23.6	8.0	26.3	14.70	267.5	632
Bolivia	4.7	13.6	6.0	0.69	62.4	151
Brazil	88.2	15.8	108.0	15.86	1,202.0	191
Chile	9.3	12.7	11.0	4.98	455.0	545
Colombia	19.8	17.2	23.8	5.33	143.7	273
Ecuador	5.7	18.3	6.8	1.25	54.5	220
Mexico	47.3	18.5	60.6	24.18	73.8	512
Paraguay	2.2	16.8	2.8	0.42	35.0	193
Peru	12.8	16.6	15.2	4.35	126.0	351
Uruguay	2.8	6.4	3.0	1.29	264.0	464
CENTRAL AMERICA						
Costa Rica	1.6	18.0	2.0	0.63	42.5	384
El Salvador	3.3	20.0	3.9	0.80	34.4	245
Guatemala	4.9	16.4	5.9	1.25	29.8	265
Honduras	2.4	18.3	3.1	0.51	39.0	208
Nicaragua	1.8	19.5	2.4	0.62	64.0	337
CARIBBEAN & OTHERS						
Bahamas	0.2	14.7	0.2	–	–	–
Barbados	0.3	6.8	0.4	0.11	36.1	442
Cuba	8.1	11.2	9.1	4.04	34.0	518
Dominican Republic	4.0	16.4	5.1	0.89	50.0	228
Guadeloupe	0.3	7.1	0.4	0.19	–	594
Guiana	0.7	16.0	0.9	0.19	30.0	279
Haiti	4.7	10.5	6.0	0.34	–	75
Jamaica	1.9	12.7	2.0	0.78	38.0	429
Martinique	0.3	7.3	0.4	0.22	–	667
Panama	1.4	17.6	1.8	0.63	57.5	474
Surinam	0.4	18.7	0.5	0.11	53.0	335
Trinidad & Tobago	1.0	10.5	1.3	0.64	46.0	634
Virgin Islands	0.4	8.5	0.5	–	–	–
AFRICA						
Algeria	12.9	15.5	16.8	2.32	5.6	207
Angola	5.4	6.9	5.8	0.32	23.0	64
Burundi	3.4	10.4	3.8	0.12	15.8	38
Cameroon	5.6	11.1	6.0	0.62	21.7	116
Central African Republic	1.5	13.9	2.0	0.13	32.7	102

GNP		Passenger Cars in Use		Telephones in Use	Broadcast Media Sets in Use		Electricity Production	
1968 Total (billion dollars)	5-Year Increase, Constant Prices (per cent)	January 1, 1969 (thousands)	5-Year Increase (per cent)	January 1, 1968 (thousands)	1968 Radios (thousands)	1968 TV's (thousands)	1968 Total (billion kwhs)	5-Year Increase (per cent)
15.42	15.3	1,207	66	1,553	6,000	1,950	15.9	28
0.80	32.5	28	4	30	400	–	0.6	12
22.11	14.3	1,606	85	1,473	5,550	5,510	35.6	28
6.31	22.9	111	69	295	1,375	150	6.8	21
5.50	24.3	139	16	515	2,210	450	6.1	16
1.46	27.6	23	44	45	205	66	0.7	41
26.77	41.6	976	58	1,044	4,825	2,200	22.8	67
0.52	21.8	13	20	16	164	25	0.2	64
4.05	28.6	215	105	152	1,815	310	4.7	38
1.30	4.2	126	13	195	1,075	215	1.8	17
0.75	44.6	28	39	27	105	75	0.8	46
0.91	34.5	27	26	38	398	50	0.5	58
1.56	27.5	39	39	35	215	71	0.5	44
0.63	44.6	14	118	10	140	21	0.2	77
0.70	50.0	21	94	13	105	35	0.3	34
–	–	23	123	32	50	–	0.2	59
0.09	26.0	12	40	22	60	15	0.1	79
4.04	8.0	86	–	238	1,325	575	3.7	21
1.07	12.0	36	115	34	155	85	0.7	56
–	–	20	103	8	18	10	0.1	83
0.23	27.0	15	23	12	140	–	0.2	68
0.37	9.0	7	–6	4	80	10	0.1	5
0.95	26.3	63	37	57	425	50	0.9	33
–	–	17	66	13	29	5	0.1	97
0.79	46.4	42	68	58	225	100	0.5	49
0.95	54.9	10	60	10	88	–	0.8	608
0.76	39.0	71	57	46	169	43	1.2	89
–	–	12	97	13	32	15	0.2	185
3.00	–	104	–48	145	500	83	1.31	20
0.36	26.1	31	–10	20	90	–	0.46	108
0.17	–	3	23	3	55	–	–	–
0.77	21.9	22	69	5	210	–	0.98	–8
0.19	–	6	29	4	44	–	0.03	102

(Continued)

	Population			National Income		
Country	1968 Total (millions)	5-Year Increase (per cent)	1975 Forecast (millions)	1968 Total (billion dollars)	5-Year Increase, Current Prices (per cent)	1968 Per Capita (dollars)
AFRICA (continued)						
Chad	3.5	7.8	3.8	0.19	31.5	60
Congo, Brazzaville	0.9	7.1	1.2	0.14	28.3	167
Congo, Kinshasa	16.7	11.5	18.9	1.40	−3.0	87
Dahomey	2.6	15.3	3.0	0.17	17.1	69
Ethiopia	23.9	9.1	26.3	1.35	36.4	59
Gabon	0.5	5.2	0.6	0.14	49.5	287
Ghana	8.4	14.1	10.5	1.80	70.6	215
Guinea	3.8	12.9	4.3	0.31	29.5	93
Ivory Coast	4.1	11.9	5.0	0.85	47.5	217
Kenya	10.2	15.4	12.0	0.99	28.1	100
Liberia	1.1	9.7	1.2	0.17	12.0	154
Malagasy Republic	6.5	4.8	7.0	0.62	19.2	97
Malawi	4.3	14.2	5.3	0.19	32.9	46
Mali	4.8	10.0	5.6	0.28	26.3	64
Mauritania	1.1	10.3	1.3	0.14	48.4	128
Mauritius	0.8	12.3	1.0	0.16	−8.5	211
Morocco	14.6	15.1	18.9	2.70	29.8	185
Mozambique	7.3	7.1	8.3	0.43	21.6	64
Niger	3.8	14.2	4.0	0.23	33.9	73
Nigeria	62.6	13.3	78.5	4.06	10.4	68
Réunion	0.4	14.8	0.6	0.10	42.7	261
Rhodesia	4.7	16.5	6.0	0.98	27.7	217
Rwanda	3.4	16.2	4.0	0.11	23.3	38
Senegal	3.7	10.8	4.2	0.63	13.2	173
Sierra Leone	2.5	7.7	3.3	0.31	23.1	131
Somalia	2.7	17.8	3.7	0.14	50.0	62
South Africa	19.2	12.5	23.4	11.78	53.5	614
Sudan	14.8	15.1	16.6	1.17	30.3	91
Tanzania	12.6	13.3	14.0	0.73	33.1	59
Togo	1.8	13.2	2.0	0.18	58.4	107
Tunisia	4.7	11.8	5.8	0.85	31.8	182
Uganda	8.1	13.1	9.0	0.65	41.2	82
Upper Volta	5.2	10.8	5.6	0.21	1.5	42
Zambia	4.1	16.6	4.9	0.91	92.4	231

GNP		Passenger Cars in Use		Telephones in Use	Broadcast Media Sets in Use		Electricity Production	
1968 Total (billion dollars)	5-Year Increase, Constant Prices (per cent)	January 1, 1969 (thousands)	5-Year Increase (per cent)	January 1, 1968 (thousands)	1968 Radios (thousands)	1968 TV's (thousands)	1968 Total (billion kwhs)	5-Year Increase (per cent)
0.27	–	3	11	4	50	–	0.03	115
0.15	–	7	17	9	62	1	0.05	29
1.33	–	46	9	20	60	7	2.93	22
0.19	15.3	10	30	5	50	–	0.02	31
1.48	25.6	32	131	32	500	6	0.32	80
0.24	43.4	5	12	4	50	1	0.06	74
1.73	9.4	4	–	37	700	10	2.59	451
0.31	–	14	76	7	85	–	0.20	28
1.09	58.5	44	100	21	67	6	0.37	140
1.28	32.4	89	21	61	500	14	0.38	45
0.24	–	11	76	4	151	4	0.34	86
0.75	11.3	43	43	23	308	1	0.14	51
0.19	17.6	11	37	9	120	–	0.09	117
0.33	–	6	93	7	50	–	0.03	64
0.16	–	2	13	1	45	–	0.04	1,064
0.20	22.7	14	9	15	76	12	0.13	46
3.04	29.5	188	26	145	826	85	1.54	25
0.48	23.9	43	42	21	85	–	0.17	−22
0.32	–	3	26	3	75	–	0.03	97
4.49	26.0	90	77	74	1,260	53	1.11	24
0.12	59.7	16	61	11	54	14	0.05	129
1.07	12.8	107	−3	112	135	46	5.58	66
0.13	–	2	44	1	15	–	0.05	345
0.79	–	34	24	26	265	1	0.25	40
0.37	10.6	19	42	6	177	3	0.12	72
0.13	–	8	50	5	40	–	0.01	52
14.08	39.9	1,513	45	1,322	1,589	–	40.94	52
1.36	3.4	27	47	43	180	20	0.32	95
0.80	24.6	31	−13	29	135	–	0.32	60
0.21	54.7	–	–	3	35	–	0.05	117
1.05	13.6	65	30	65	385	37	0.62	69
0.70	30.9	35	34	23	175	9	0.73	47
0.24	36.6	5	11	3	85	1	0.02	40
1.17	51.8	50	27	43	80	17	0.65	−13

Source: Reprinted from *Indicators of Market Size for 140 Countries* appearing in the December 5, 12, 19, and 26, 1969, issues of *Business International,* with the permission of the publisher, Business International Corporation (New York). The original table gives statistics for most countries of the world, additional columns of market-size indicators, and a number of footnotes, indicating, mostly, that data were from an earlier year than indicated or that 5-year growth was reduced to three or four years. To the author's knowledge, the table is the most up-to-date compilation of such statistics.

APPENDIX E

MARKETING RESEARCH FIRMS
IN DEVELOPING COUNTRIES

This list of marketing research firms in developing countries was derived from various directories, such as the *Directory of Marketing Research Houses and Their Services*, published by the American Marketing Association, 230 North Michigan Avenue, Chicago, Illinois; *The International Directory of Market Research Organisations*, published by The Market Research Society, 39 Hartford Street, London; *Handbook of Marketing Research in Europe*, published by the European Society for Opinion and Marketing Research (ESOMAR), Raadhuisstraat 15, Amsterdam, The Netherlands; and *Bradford's Directory*, published by Marketing Research Agencies & Management Consultants in the United States and the World, Fairfax, Virginia.

AFGHANISTAN   Afghan Advertising Bureau
Mohamed Jan Khan Wat
Kabul

ARGENTINA   A & C Investigación
Jose E. Uriburu 1590
Buenos Aires

G & G Consultores
Cordobe 1512, Piso 1°
Mar del Plata

Industrial Marketing Research (IMR)
Azcuenaga 1583
Buenos Aires

Institute IPSA
Bartolome Mitre 688
Buenos Aires

Latinoconsult Argentina S.A.
Belgrano 353
Buenos Aires

Marplan—Market Planning Services
San Martin 3290, Piso 1°
Capital Federal

Organization Argentina de Encuestas
1400 Avenida de Mayo, Piso 1°
Buenos Aires

BARBADOS   Corbin—Compton (Barbados) Ltd.
Bridgetown

BOLIVIA   Development Corporation
Avenida Comacho
La Paz

BRAZIL   Instituto Brasileiro de Opinão
Publica e Estatistica (IBOPE)
Avenida Henrique Valadares, 41—s/loja
Rio de Janeiro

Instituto de Estudos Sociais e Economicos
31 Rua Mexico
São Paulo

Instituto de Estudos Sociais e
Economicos Ltd. (INESE)
Rua Quintino Bocaiuva, 161-7° Andar
São Paulo

Instituto de Pesquisas de Opinão e Mercado (IPOM)
35, Avenida Franklin Roosevelt
Rio de Janeiro

Marplan
Rua 24 de Maio, 53-50 Andares, P.O. Box 30003
São Paulo

BURMA

Myana Corporation
Sule Pagoda Road
Rangoon

CEYLON

The Market Research Co. of Ceylon Ltd.
44a Alfred House Gardens
Colombo 3

CHILE

Instituto Chileno de Opinion Publica
Pedro de Villagra, 2535 (Vitacura)
Santiago

J. Walter Thompson Chilena S.A.C.
Matias Cousino 64—5° Piso
Santiago

Marplan
Catedral 1165, Pisos 4° y 5°
Santiago

COLOMBIA

Consultores Association
A.P. Aerio 15656
Bogotá

Instituto Colombiano de Opinion Publica (ICOP)
Air Mail Box 5052
Bogotá

McCann, Erickson Corporation
Carrera 13-24
Bogotá

CYPRUS

George Vassilious
Middle East Marketing Research Bureau
Nicosia

EGYPT

A.R.A.K., El Ahrem
Ramses Street
Cairo

Institute for Marketing Research
University of Cairo
Guiza, Cairo

ETHIOPIA

Central Statistical Office, I.E.G.
P.O. Box 1143
Addis Ababa

GHANA

Research Bureau Ltd.
P.O. Box 5753, Accra North Post Office
Accra

GREECE

DATA
Amerikis Street
Athens 134

ICAP Hellas Ltd.
54a Queen Sophia Avenue
Athens 612

Institute for Research Communication
8 Demosthenes Soutsou
Athens 602

HONG KONG

Ling-McCann-Erickson Ltd.
Research Department
902-916 Central Building
3 Pedder Street
Hong Kong

Survey Research Hong Kong
Wing House
23 Connaught Road
Central Hong Kong

INDIA   Bureau of Commercial Intelligence & Statistics
                          Central Bank Building
                          Bombay 1

                          Clarion McCann Ltd.
                          5 Council House Street
                          Calcutta 1

                          Indian Market Research Service
                          5th Floor, Steelcrete House
                          Dinshawacha Road
                          Bombay 1-BR

                          Operations Research Group
                          Karamchand Premchand (P.V.T.) Ltd.
                          The Retreat, Shalibaug
                          Ahmedabad-4

IRAN   N.I.P. Marketing and Public Opinion
                              Research Center
                          P.O. Box 741
                          Tehran

IRELAND   Irish Marketing Surveys Ltd.
                          19 Upper Pembroke Street
                          Dublin 2

                          Market Research Bureau of Ireland Ltd.
                          11 South Frederick Street
                          Dublin 2

ISRAEL   Israel Institute of Applied Social Research
                          19 George Washington Street
                          P.O. Box 7150
                          Jerusalem

JAMAICA   Caribbean Research Ltd.
                          P.O. Box 7137
                          Kingston

JAPAN

A. C. Nielsen Co.
5 Higashi Toriizaka, Azahu
Minato-ku, Tokyo

Cambridge Research Institute
11-45 1-chome, Akasaka
Minato-ku, Tokyo

The Central Research Services, Inc.
c/o, Shisei-Kaikan, 2 Hibiya-Koen
Chiyoda-ku, Tokyo

INRA, Far East Co-ordination Centre
7-12, Rokubancho
Chiyoda-ku, Tokyo

J. Walter Thompson Co. Japan
5 Sanban-cho
Chiyoda-ku, Tokyo

Man-Nen-Sha, Inc.
35, 5-chome Koraibashi
Higashi-ku, Osaka

Marketing Center Co. Ltd.
90 1-chome, Onden
Shibuya-ku, Tokyo

Marplan Japan
7th Floor, Shokakukan Building
2-1 Kanda Hitotsubashi
Chiyoda-ku, Tokyo

Shakai Chosa Kenkyusho Ltd.
2-1 Hongo, 7-chome
Bunkyo, Tokyo

Video Research Ltd.
2-13 Ginza Higashi
Chuoku, Tokyo

KENYA
Marco Surveys Ltd.
P.O. Box 5832
Nairobi

LEBANON
Arab Marketing and Finance, Inc.
Tabbara Building, Manara, 26 Bliss Street
P.O. Box 3299
Beirut

Associated Business Consultants
P.O. Box 5736
Beirut

Middle East Marketing Research Institute
P.O. Box 4904
Beirut

Research & Management Centre
Abdul Asis Street
P.O. Box 5612
Beirut

MALAYSIA
Far East Research Organisation Ltd.
4th Floor, Hardware House
400 Jalan Tuanku Abdul Rahman
Kuala Lumpur

McCann-Erickson (Malaysia) Ltd.
Marketing Division
Chartered Bank Building
Kuala Lumpur

Marketing Research Services SDH. Berhad
Straits Trading Building
Leboh Pasar Besar
Kuala Lumpur

Research Bureau Ltd.
P.O. Box 136
Petaling Jaya
West Malaysia

Survey Research Malaysia
SRM House, 143 Jalan Terap
P.O. Box 2231
Kuala Lumpur

MALTA

Mediterranean Research Bureau Ltd.
249/254 Kingsway
Valletta

MEXICO

Datos de Mexico S.A.
Niza No. 67-204-208
Mexico 6 D.F.

International Research Associates S.A. DE C.V.
Paseo de la Reforma No. 330
Mexico D.F.

Vega Y Asociados, AP
Apartado Postal No. 2414
Monterrey, N.L. Mexico

NIGERIA

Management Services (Nigeria) Ltd.
P.O. Box 2369, 82-86 Broad Street
Lagos

Research Bureau Ltd.
P.O. Box 1360, 4 Tinubu Street
Lagos

PANAMA

First Research Corporation
Apartado 4297
Panama City

PAKISTAN

Nasir-Ud-Deen & Associates
Management and Marketing Consultants
Park Court, Victoria Road
Karachi

PERU

Oisem
866 Azangaro
Lima

PHILIPPINES   Index, Inc.
P.O. Box 650
Manila

International Research Associates (Far East)
1105 Florida Street at United Nations Avenue
Manila

Marplan Philippines
Insular Life Building, Ayala Avenue
Makati, Rizal

Psychological & Research Services, Inc.
Suites 302-303
Abad Santos Building
1810 Taft Avenue
Manila

Robot-Gallup Research Group
El Hogar Filipino Building
Juan Luna, Manila

PORTUGAL   Instituto de Estudos de Mercado (IEM)
Largo Monterroio de Mascarenhas,
No. 2-6°, Apartado 2012
Lisbon

J. de Souza Monteiro IPOP
46 Rua T.A. de Aguiar
Lisbon

McCann-Erickson de Portugal S.A.R.L.
Research Department
Rua de Santa Barbara, 46-4°
Lisbon 1

PUERTO RICO   Business Research Institute
San Juan

RHODESIA   Market Research Africa (Rhodesia) Ltd.
P.O. Box 8320, Causeway
Salisbury

SIERRA LEONE   Auger & Turner (Sierra Leone) Ltd.
                  P.O. Box 1005
                  Freetown

SINGAPORE   Far East Research Organisation Ltd.
                  Chinese Chamber of Commerce Building
                  Singapore

                  Market Research Ltd.
                  6, Balmoral Road
                  Singapore 10

SOUTH AFRICA   Franklin Research (PTY) Ltd.
                  42 James Crescent, Halfway House
                  Johannesburg, Transvaal

                  International Consumer Research (PTY) Ltd.
                  Mobil House, 87 Rissik Street
                  P.O. Box 11260
                  Johannesburg, Transvaal

                  Market Research Africa (PTY) Ltd.
                  P.O. Box 10483, Belray Building
                  178 Fox Street
                  Johannesburg, Transvaal

                  South African Market Research Association
                  P.O. Box 392
                  Pretoria

SPAIN   Bernard Krief Consultants for Europe
                  Conde de Aranda 5
                  Madrid 1

                  Eco, Centro de Investigaciones del Mercado, S.A.
                  Alcala 96
                  Madrid 9

                  Instituto Español de Marketing, S.A.
                  Avenida Generalissimo Franco 520
                  Barcelona

Investigación Y Asesoramiento en
    Distribución de Mercados Y Ventas, S.A.
Calle Tuset 26 8°
Barcelona 6

Metra/Seis
Paseo de la Castellana 86
Madrid 6

Sem Iberica, S.A.
Estudios del Mercado
Clara del Rey 27
Madrid 2

SYRIA   Centre D'Études et de Documentation
                   Économique Financières et Sociales
               Rue Abi el Fadl el Moradi
               Imm Kalii, B.P. 2306
               Damascus

TANZANIA   Market Research (Tanganyika) Ltd.
               P.O. Box 1914
               Dar es Salaam

THAILAND   Business Research Ltd.
               Radjdamri
               66, Radjdamri Road
               Bangkok

               Lever Bros. (Thailand) Ltd.
               Market Research Department
               Tanon Tok, Bangkholaem
               Bangkok, Yanawa, P.O. Box 50

               Ling-McCann-Erickson Ltd.
               Amarin Annex, Ploenchit Court
               P.O. Box 2555
               Bangkok

TRINIDAD &   Economic and Business Research-Information
TOBAGO   and Advisory Service
                    P.O. Box 780
                    Port of Spain, Trinidad

TUNISIA   Service Économique Africain
                    29 Avenue Habib Bourguiba
                    Tunis

TURKEY   Peva
                    Beyoglu Imam Adnan Sokak, No. 5
                    Istanbul

UGANDA   Market Research (Uganda) Ltd.
                    P.O. Box 4112
                    Kampala

URUGUAY   Cenci
                    Misiones 1261, Esc. 14
                    Montevideo

VENEZUELA   Datos, C.A.
                    Apartado 9257, La Candelaria
                    Caracas

                    International Research Associates
                    Apartado 9257, La Candelaria
                    Caracas

VIETNAM   Center for Vietnamese Studies
                    123 Hien Vuong Street
                    Saigon

BIBLIOGRAPHY

Alderson, Wroe, and Shapiro, J. Stanley. *Marketing and the Computer.* Englewood Cliffs, N.J.: Prentice-Hall, 1963.

Theroretical discussions of possible applications are combined with detailed individual case studies of the computer at work as a tool of marketing executives; attempts to show the relevance and benefits of computer techniques.

Applebaum, William and Abers. *Guide to Store Location Research.* Reading, Mass.: Addison-Wesley Co., 1968.

Aquilar, Francis J. *Scanning the Business Environment.* New York: The Macmillan Co., 1967.

Chapter III, "Where Do Managers Obtain External Information?," is of interest to marketing research directors.

Borden, Neil H., and Marshall, Martin V. *Advertising Management.* Homewood, Ill.: Richard D. Irwin, 1959.

Many detailed cases provide ideas and procedures that can be put to work by the reader.

317

Carpenter, Robert N. *Guidelist for Marketing Research and Economic Forecasting.* "Research Study," No. 73. New York: American Management Association, 1966.

Gives a broad outline of available publications and other sources that help marketing researchers and forecasters.

Corey, E. Raymond. *Industrial Marketing: Cases and Concepts.* Englewood Cliffs, N.J.: Prentice-Hall, 1962.

Several cases briefly discuss field testing of industrial products.

Crisp, Richard D. *Sales Planning and Control.* New York: McGraw-Hill Book Co., 1961.

Stresses methods of developing a system for measuring and comparing performance of sales territories and individual salesmen.

Deming, W. Edwards. *Sample Design in Business Research.* New York: John Wiley & Sons, 1960.

Outlines the theory of sampling, discusses the standards of statistical practice, and presents methods of sampling.

Dichter, Ernest. *Strategy of Desire.* New York: Doubleday & Company, 1960.

Treats the motivational research approach to advertising. Although some professionals debate the author's qualitative approach, only a few deny his strong influence on advertising.

Estey, James Arthur. *Business Cycles—Their Nature, Cause and Control.* Englewood Cliffs, N.J.: Prentice-Hall, 1960.

Federalism and the Economic Growth in the Under-Developed Countries, A Symposium. London: George Allen & Unwin Ltd., 1961.

Ferber, Robert, *et al. Marketing Research.* New York: The Ronald Press Company, 1964.

An introduction to marketing research, its planning, techniques utilization, evaluation, and application by management in the solution of marketing problems.

Frank, Nathalie D. *Market Analysis: A Handbook of Current Data Sources.* New York: The Scarecrow Press, 1964.

Gould, Douglas P. *Marketing for Profit.* New York: Reinhold Publishing Company, 1961. (Out of Print.)

Devoted to analysis of individual product lines in terms of over-all profitability and incremental profit contribution. Easy-to-read introduction to managerial accounting for the nonfinancial executive.

Hanan, Mack. *Concept Advertising.* "Management Bulletin," No. 37. New York: American Management Association, 1963.

Describes concept advertising and its role in new-product research and development as a market identifier and as a marketing research tool.

Krulis-Randa, J. S. "Marketing Research in U.S.A. and in Europe," *Neue Züricher Zeitung* (Zurich), January 14, 1969.

Lucas, Darell Blaine, and Henderson, Britt Stuart. *Measuring Advertising Effectiveness.* New York: McGraw-Hill Book Co., 1963.

Drawing on experience in advertising, teaching, consulting, and psychology, the authors bring together the methods and the measurement of advertising messages and media. They provide facts about creative research as utilized in advertising industry and an analysis of the principal methods in use.

Luck, David J.; Wales, Hugh G.; and Taylor, Donald A. *Marketing Research.* Englewood Cliffs, N.J.: Prentice-Hall, 1961.

Lutz, R. R. *Graphic Presentation Simplified.* New York: Funk and Wagnalls Co., 1960.

Marting, Elizabeth, ed. *New Products/New Profits.* New York: American Management Association, 1964.

A summary of experiences of twenty-four companies that have been outstandingly successful in new-product planning and development.

Miller, Myron M. *Using Direct Costing for Profit and Product Improvement.* Englewood Cliffs, N.J.: Prentice-Hall, 1967.

Mountjoy, Alan B. *Industrialisation and Under-Developed Countries.* London: Hutchinson University Library, 1966.

Myint, Hla. *The Economics of the Developing Countries.* New York: Frederick A. Praeger, 1965.

Myrdal, Gunnar. *Economic Theory and Under-Developed Regions.* London: University Paperbacks, 1965.

Newman, Joseph W. *Motivation Research and Marketing Management.* Cambridge, Mass.: Graduate School of Business Administration, Harvard University, 1957.

Detailed case histories still of interest in terms of the principles and practices contained.

Pincus, John. *Trade, Aid Development: The Rich and Poor Nations.* New York: McGraw-Hill Book Co., 1967.

Pricing: Policies and Practices. "Studies in Business Economics," No. 71. New York: National Industrial Conference Board, 1961.

This study covers in detail the pricing techniques of companies in many industries.

Prochnow, Herbert von. *Determining the Business Outlook.* New York: Harper & Bros., 1959.

Rostow, Walt Whitman. *Stages of Economic Growth.* London: Cambridge University Press, 1957.

Schreier, Fred T. *Modern Marketing Research.* Belmont, Calif.: Wadsworth Publishing Company, 1963.

Discusses the fundamentals of marketing research; contains a presentation of the phases of a study; and examines the specific problems, ideas, concepts, and methods of each of the five functions of marketing research—description, explanation, prediction, evaluation, and contributions to decision-making.

Sevin, Charles H. *Marketing Productivity Analysis.* New York: McGraw-Hill Book Co., 1965.

Helpful in orienting the finance manager to the range of marketing activities that lend themselves to financial measurement. Discusses such problems as unprofitable sales territories and realistic effects of advertising media.

Shannon, Lyle W. *Underdeveloped Areas.* New York: Harper and Row, 1957.

Smykay, Edward W., *et al. Physical Distribution Management.* New York: The Macmillan Co., 1961.

A guidebook for helping management analyze and improve its distribution systems through the use of mathematics, economics, and statistics.

Starch, Daniel. *Measuring Advertising Readership and Results.* New York: McGraw-Hill Book Co., 1966.

Contains basic approaches to the subject.

Stephan, Frederick F., and McCarthy, Philip J. *Sampling Opinions—An Analysis of Survey Procedure.* New York: John Wiley & Sons; London: Chapman & Hall Ltd., 1958.

Despite the date, still a practical guide in sampling. Indicates fields open to research.

Suchman, Abe, and Berg, Thomas L. *Product Strategy and Management.* New York: Holt, Rinehart and Winston, 1963.

Selected readings on new-product planning. Includes many key papers from periodicals and other sources. Broad coverage of subject.

Theobald, Robert. *Profit Potential in the Developing Countries.* New York: American Management Association, 1962.

Tucker, Spencer A. *The Break-Even System: A Tool for Profit Planning.* Englewood Cliffs, N.J.: Prentice-Hall, 1960.

Wasson, Chester R. *Research Analysis for Marketing Decision.* New York: Appleton-Century-Crofts, 1965.

An introduction to the principles of marketing research, geared to management. The steps involved in formulating problems and collecting, interpreting, and presenting data are summarized.

ABOUT THE AUTHOR

John Z. Kracmar is Manager of Marketing Research for the European Division of the Singer Sewing Machine Company. He has been involved in the fields of international trade and marketing for over twenty years and is the author of numerous articles on economics and European integration.

Dr. Kracmar has also been guest lecturer at New York University, the American Management Association, and other institutions. He has traveled extensively and has visited every continent.

After receiving his doctorate in law and economics from Masaryk University in Czechoslovakia, he did postgraduate work at the College of Europe in Bruges, Belgium.